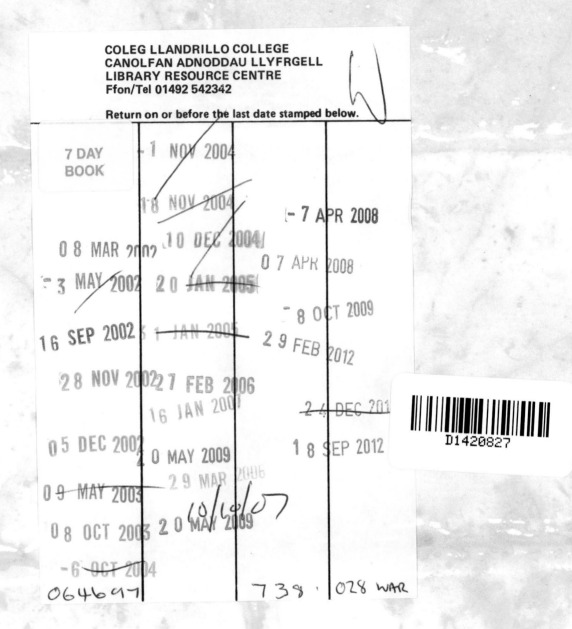

# THE COMPLETE PRACTICAL
# POTTER

# THE COMPLETE PRACTICAL

# POTTER

## Josie Warshaw

With throwing chapter by Richard Phethean

Photography by Stephen Brayne

LORENZ BOOKS

To Ronald and Sylvia,
Peter and Clem, with thanks and love.

This edition published by Lorenz Books
an imprint of Anness Publishing Limited
Hermes House, 88-89 Blackfriars Road, London SE1 8HA

Published in the USA by Lorenz Books
Anness Publishing Inc., 27 West 20th Street, New York,
NY 10011; (800) 354-9657

A CIP catalogue record for this book is available
from the British Library

ISBN 0 7548 0195 0

Publisher: Joanna Lorenz
Project editor: Emma Clegg
Consultant advisor: John Forde
US advisor: Nancy Selvage
Copy editor: Samantha Ward Dutton
Projects copy editor: Gail Dixon-Smith
Reader: Joy Wotton
Designer: Celia Clay
Photographer: Stephen Brayne
Stylist: Diana Civil
Picture researcher: Pernilla Pearce
Illustrator: Robert Highton
Production: Wendy Lawson

Picture credits: Janet Williams (page 1), Lisa Hammond (page 2), Ewen Henderson (page 3),
Josie Warshaw (page 6) and Kate Schuricht and Sue Paraskeva (page 7)

Printed and bound in Singapore

© Anness Publishing Limited 1999
Updated © 2000
1 3 5 7 9 10 8 6 4 2

## DISCLAIMER

Learning a new craft can be tremendous fun, filling many
rewarding hours, but certain materials and equipment may need
to be handled with great care. The author and publishers have
made every effort to ensure that all the instructions in this book
are accurate and safe, and therefore cannot accept liability for
any resultant injury, damage or loss to persons or
property, however it may arise.

Designed for an international readership, terms are occasionally
bracketed to clarify the different specialist and general terms.
To avoid confusion, note that the first firing stage in the UK is
'biscuit firing', whereas the US refer to "bisque firing". Also
that the UK use an additional term "bisque" to mean a
particular firing that has a higher temperature than the
glaze firing that follows.

Captions for photographs of final work give the measurements
of the piece by height, unless otherwise specified.

# CONTENTS

# INTRODUCTION

Like many of my generation I came to clay initially through the influence of the Leach tradition. Bernard Leach's philosophy combined Eastern and Western ideas and was highly influential in shaping and building the studio pottery movement. He set a code of pottery practice that related both to the use of materials and to an appropriate pottery aesthetic. During formative years my attraction to clay was associated with the conventional ideas of the time about the material.

Working with clay seemed then to be accompanied by a resistance to the modern world of the synthetic or the mass produced. For myself, as an impressionable adolescent, my first clay mentor had an aura of oriental mysticism and accompanying spirituality. There was the seduction of the feel of the clay and the fascination of the processes – watching shapes take form on the wheel and seeing how the firing process transformed the colour and glaze. I found wood, oil, raku and gas firing particularly exciting, and could hardly wait for the tantalizing moment when the door of the kiln opened. To this day I still become excited when the temperature creeps low enough to ease open the door and take a peek inside. In time, this fascination turned to an understanding of the technical processes, but the challenge to explore, to invent and to express myself in my ceramic work continues.

LEARNING TO WALK BY J WARSHAW, 1996.

Many of you may just be starting to work with ceramics and will be bringing with you fresh thinking and original creative approaches. This ensures that design and techniques are continually being injected with new ideas, unhindered by the often restricting oriental approach of Leach. The history of ceramics shows that the main processes and techniques have not changed, but that creative design has moved on. With hindsight we can see that it is the ideas of a particular period or culture that makes each historical development distinctive and recognizable, and that current thinking is central to how ceramics is valued and appreciated. In today's climate the choices are open and the contemporary potter is relatively free to interpret and explore ideas of aesthetics, subject, culture and materials in a personal way.

In recognition of this freedom I have tried to accommodate a wide range of techniques and technical possibilities to give methods of working with clay both for the beginner and for the more experienced potter, using clay as a medium for functional craftwork or for other purposes, such as sculptural to architectural work. I have avoided references to "pots" or "pottery" and instead have used the broader word "ceramics"

Words such as "top edge", "additions of clay" and "base" can be interpreted in "pottery" terms as "rim", "handle" and "foot", but they also allow for the fact that working with clay does not only involve making pots. I have also tried to treat each area fairly, avoiding preferences towards individual methods or treatments, rather than implying that a certain form or surface is more important than another.

There were a number of areas that I felt important to include in addition to the basic techniques of handbuilding, making and using moulds, decorating and firing. In the design section I have outlined the range of inspiration and personal expression used by contemporary potters, and included practical tips on how to draw or transfer designs onto clay. In the clay section I have included advice on making and using fibre clay, revived and advanced through the research work of Rosette Gault. Recently revived commercial print techniques that are now also used for sensitive and creative expression are also included. Often dismissed or unrecognized, the use of single firing is also mentioned – this allows a more spontaneous movement from making through to final glaze firing. All these techniques can be developed, researched and redefined to suit your own purposes.

I hope that this book will serve as a practical manual for beginners and provide inspiration for more advanced potters, as well as providing a comprehensive update of the ceramic practice of today.

# CERAMICS: A BRIEF HISTORY

Pottery shards from archeological sites or clay objects preserved in museums speak clearly of humankind.

They give a fascinating insight into past societies – reflecting and documenting their historical

development, from cultural values and social expression to international exchanges in trade and ideas.

### The first pots

Clay has always been shaped and formed. Representations of animals modelled into a clay bank in a cave in France and others found on a site in Eastern Europe can be dated as far back as the Ice Age, from 37,000–12,000 BC. An understanding of the process of firing clay first developed in cultures in

HIPPOPOTAMUS IN BLUE GLAZED
FAIENCE C.2000–1900 BC, MIDDLE
KINGDOM EUROPE (ANCIENT EGYPT).

isolated areas in the Far East, but it was not until 6000–4000 BC that this knowledge became widespread. The production of fired ceramic ware revolutionized people's lives, allowing villagers to make vermin-proof grain storage jars in which to store surpluses to guard against crop failures. Nomads and gatherers were then encouraged to settle and cultivate foodstuffs; trade developed and, with it, the exchange of ideas.

The invention of the potter's wheel was another technological breakthrough. The Egyptians thought it such an important advance that its legendary invention by the god Khum was annotated in stone carvings. Exactly when or where this evolution from a simple turntable happened is uncertain, but the probable earliest date for the first known use of the kick wheel is around 2300 BC in Sumer.

### Early decoration

The first glazes were developed around 4000 BC in Egypt or Mesopotamia. Faience, often also called Egyptian paste, which was used to make blue or green beads, was obtained from the naturally occurring rock, natron. This had soluble sodium in it and when the objects dried, it formed a thin deposit of sodium/silica that created the glazed surface.

Around 1600 BC, glaze was further developed to decorate vessels, figurines and tiles. Techniques were developed through generations to separate several colours on one tile with raised lines of slip, and to produce elegant oxide-painted effects on lead- and tin-glazed plates and bowls. Later, lustrous glaze effects were used in imitation of metals.

Strictures laid down by the religious text of the Koran, to exclude the portrayal of human figures in the mosques, brought about the characteristic floral, geometric and stylized calligraphic designs on ceramic tiles. The rich, arabesque-style ornamentation decorated mosques and palaces throughout the Islamic world. When the Moors invaded Spain, they brought their developed knowledge of glazes and lustres to enrich the European continent.

### The Chinese influence

Through more sophisticated kiln technology the Chinese were able to develop glazes that fired at higher temperatures, enabling the use of a different and greater range of natural materials. Chinese potters of the Han dynasty (206 BC–AD 220) in the kingdom of Yeu experimented with high-fire glazes producing the first feldspathic glazes on stoneware. These greenish glazes were close to the famous celadon glazes of the later Sung dynasty (AD 960–1270), made in an attempt to mimic the colour and surface

BARBARIAN TRADER FROM
CENTRAL ASIA WITH HORN OF
PLENTY, PAINTED TERRACOTTA
FIGURE, TANG DYNASTY, CHINA
7–8TH CENTURY.

STONEWARE BOTTLE, TZ'U CHOU TYPE, PROBABLY NORTHERN CHINA, SUNG AD 960–1127.

of sacred jade. There were many types of celadons produced in various pottery centres, some of which had as many as 200 kilns. High temperature glazes were developed alongside the advanced wood-fired kiln technology of the time.

Controlled, oxidized kiln atmospheres produced the earthenware figures of the Tang dynasty (AD 617–907), which reflected cosmopolitan trade and a tolerant society. The caravans of the silk trade were depicted in clay figurines with fluid blue, yellow, green and brown glazes applied over white slip. Ware from the Yeu kilns of the Tang dynasty was further refined, producing the first true porcelain. Chinese connoisseurs and poets, who called it white snow or silver, revered its translucent quality.

Sometimes as long as 50 m (164 ft), and often built on hills, the kilns of the Sung dynasty were described as 'great spitting dragons'. To prevent wood ash contaminating the celadon-glazed porcelain produced in these climbing kilns, each piece was fired in a fire-resistant container, or saggar, as many as 20,000 at one time.

Towards the end of the Sung dynasty potters became increasingly interested in colourful, high-fire glazes and surface decoration with underglaze used to create pictorial decoration. Blue underglazes were developed using expensive imported Persian cobalt. This Chinese blue and white ware became popular all over Asia and designs were adapted to cater for this

increased demand, extending its market to Persia and, at the turn of the 17th century, to Europe.

Despite the success of the large porcelain factories, the many localized ceramic centres continued to produce a variety of stone-ware. One such centre at Yi-hsing in Kiangsu produced unglazed, red and brown stoneware including original and curious-shaped teapots, which were exported along with tea in the 17th century and went on to inspire many different styles of European work.

China sewed the central thread in the history of ceramics, and its influence greatly affected the work of other Far Eastern countries, for example the graceful, thin-walled porcelain forms of the Korean Koryo and the Yi dynasty from the 10th century onwards. Such forms passed through the Far East and into Europe. By the 17th century there was an established fashion in Europe for collecting Chinese porcelain, which was prominently displayed in many stately homes within "porcelain rooms".

## Japanese individuality and raku

In Japan there were a few ceramic styles that were not subject to the dominating influence of Chinese pottery. One such example is the handbuilt, cord-patterned, unglazed pot style of the Jomon period (10,000–400 BC). The same is true of the sculpted figures, known as haniwa (clay circles), belonging to the Old Tomb period.

After his study of ceramic technique in China, the Buddhist priest Toshiro Kato Shirozaemon returned home to Japan in 1227. His research led to the long tunnel, snake-like "anagama" kilns built on hillsides to make pottery in imi-

tation of the glazes of the Sung period. The Chinese religion, Chan Buddhism, was also being incorporated into society, emerging as Zen Buddhism around 1200.

A highly ritualized tea ceremony developed in tea houses as part of the Zen search for enlightenment. This was accompanied by a demand and an appreciation for chatto or tea ceramics, tea caddies, bowls, jars, flowerpots and tea bowls, which expressed the character of the maker and were made with a variety of surfaces.

CORD PATTERN JAR FROM NAGANO-KEN, JOMON CULTURE MIDDLE PERIOD, JAPAN C.3000–2000 BC, PROBABLY USED FOR STORING FOOD.

ABOVE: CARVED
LOW-RELIEF INCENSE
BURNER, MAYA,
MEXICO
(C.700–1100 AD).

ceramic whistles and whistling figurines are still made in South America today.

Other regional cultures produced a diverse range of ware, such as the Mayan ceramics of Central America, including pots with carved low relief decoration as well as terracotta figurines to bury with the dead. Mimbres potters in New Mexico (around AD 700–1100) made bowls that were used to cover the heads of the dead buried under the floors of their houses. It is thought that a small hole was broken through the bottom of the bowls to release the owner's spirit.

## Ancient Europe

Greek mythology again reminds us of the importance of clay. Helen of Troy moulded the first ceramic wine cup over her breast, and the goddess Athena, patroness of Greek potters, created the earthenware pot. All around the Mediterranean, cultures set a classical style that formed part of Western heritage and set references for domestic forms and sculpted clay.

The potters of ancient Crete made elegant utensils with decoration inspired by nature in imaginative spatial arrangements. Coloured pigments, applied after the ware had been fired,

One pottery family of the 16th century, Chorijiro, which met this demand through successive generations, was the first to use a technique in 1598 that involved removing chatto from a small, red-hot kiln to create cracks and pits on its surface. The Japanese word 'raku', which translates as enjoyment, given to this technique originates from the inscription of a private seal of the then ruler of Japan, Hideyoshi. This was presented to Chorijiro and subsequently stamped on the bases of all chatto made by his family.

## Africa and South America

Many other cultures, such as those in Africa and the Americas, worked in isolation from the technological advances of the Far and Middle East. African women modelled animals and humans and made pots and musical

instruments of diverse tribal forms and styles. Their pots were hand built, first by pulling and stroking up a solid lump of clay, then by squeezing up applied coils, beating forms into shape, and scraping and smoothing surfaces with basic tools. Sticks, shells, wooden roulettes and smooth pebbles were used to make decoration marks and to burnish surfaces, which were sometimes applied with graphite and slips.

The domestic need to carry and store water suited the porosity of the low-fired clay, which allowed the water to evaporate and cool.

Low-fired and unglazed earthenware is also found throughout the entire pre-Columbian age of the Americas. South American pottery traditions from 100 BC–AD 1450 included many regional variations of stirrup handled whistling vessels. The ingeniously constructed internal chambers were often sought to make the sound of the figures depicted on the vessel as they poured. Made primarily for ceremonial purposes, the vessels were formed by hand modelling, building with coils and by press moulding. They were commonly decorated with slips, which were then burnished. Simpler

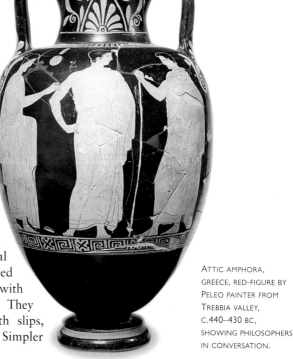

ATTIC AMPHORA,
GREECE, RED-FIGURE BY
PELEO PAINTER FROM
TREBBIA VALLEY,
C.440–430 BC,
SHOWING PHILOSOPHERS
IN CONVERSATION.

depicted subjects such as palm trees, octopuses, dolphins and shells. Early Cretan nobility lived luxurious lives in large palaces with cool subterranean rooms. Grain and oil were stored in large jars, or pithoi, such as those found at Knossos dating from around 1450 BC. These pithoi were, and still are, built up in six wide bands of applied coils, part hand built by pressing together to strengthen the joins, part thrown while rotated on wooden turntables.

Greek potters also created urns decorated with stylized geometric patterns. These initial urn forms were refined to the classical, graceful shapes collected by wealthy Greeks and Italians, such as oil flasks, or amphorae, flaring bowls for drinking wine, known as kylix, and jugs for pouring wine and water, oinochoe. Narrative figures and mythological scenes were painted with red iron oxide slip, which turned glossy black in reduction firing. The slip was scratched through with fine lines using a pointed instrument (sgraffito). The Athenian potters of 525 BC supplanted this style by painting around the figures in a form of decoration known as "reserve ware".

RIGHT: CLAY FIGURINE OF APHRODITE PLAYING WITH EROS, GREEK, FROM TANAGRA, LATE 4TH CENTURY BC.

BELOW: ARRETINE WARE BOWL FROM CAPUA, ITALY WITH RELIEFS OF THE SEASONS PRESSED FROM A NEGATIVE MOULD.

TURKISH WALL PANEL OF EARTHENWARE TILES (ISNIK) 2ND HALF OF 16TH CENTURY, PAINTED IN RED, BLUE AND GREEN.

Greek potters also produced many terracotta figures. Those from Tanagra were formed using piece press moulds, comprising sometimes as many as 14 pieces. The moulds were made by stamping a fired original into soft clay and firing the negative.

Roman pottery, a term that describes ware made in areas under Roman rule, evolved from the earlier work of the classical world and is epitomized by the characteristic, restrained, domestic red earthenware that was decorated in relief on domestic items such as lamps and bowls. The raised decoration was pressed from stamped or carved negative moulds revolved on the potter's wheel. It was coated with a fine, particled slip, known as terra sigilata, which fired black in reduction and rich red in oxidation. Its glossy finish resulted from the fine clay particles and the mica-like material in the clay used to make the slip.

In the second century AD the Romans introduced an unglazed, trailed slip-decorated ware, termed "castor ware", to Britain. Thick lines were trailed above or below a covering layer of slip to create relief scenes depicting heroic themes such as hunting or gladiatorial combat. This technique later re-emerged with the development of post-medieval slip-ware in Britain.

Development of the Islamic techniques of lead and tin glazes and lustre decoration, imported by the Moors in 700 BC, reached a peak of excellence in Spain around the beginning of the 13th century. Combined with Christian influences and new colour possibilities brought about by the importation of cobalt, an evolution and fusion of Spanish style then developed that characterizes the Hispano-Moresque ware of this period. These generous forms, that were energetically, often densely, decorated, included apothecary jars, bowls, jugs,

basins, vases and tureens, which were highly valued and much in demand throughout Europe in the 15th century. The Italian nobility were particularly fond of this highly decorated ware and imitation by Italian potters turned to rivalry as growing consumer demand was fuelled by the renaissance of classical cultural ideals and taste. By the 16th century, Italian potters had captured the whole of the Euopean market.

## Developing techniques

The term "maiolica" was first used in Italy to describe the lustre-ware imported from Spain. It is now used as the generic term for all tin-glazed earthenware including Dutch delft, French faience, English gall-eyware, and work from other areas, such as Scandinavia, Germany and central Europe. The process came to be regarded as a branch of painting, many decorators considering themselves to be artists as opposed to artisans. Influences came from French faience Renaissance painters such as Durer, Raphael and Michaelangelo and prints and designs were made specifically for use in the maiolica workshops.

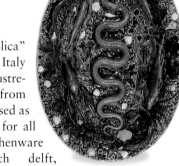

DISH WITH RUSTIC FIGULINES OR SERPENT PLATE BY BERNARD PALISSY, FRANCE C.1510–90.

Despite the popularity of maiolica, other glaze techniques flourished and developed in many parts of Europe during the Renaissance. Inspired by the decorative, ornate metalwork of the time, much work was made in bas-relief by stamping clay pads in moulds and joining the pieces, known as sprigs, to the leatherhard work. In 1564 Catherine de Medici commissioned Bernard Palissy in France to make a 'rustic grotto', a then fashionable garden feature in Italy, for the Tuilleries gardens in Paris. Palissy's moulds of ornate relief work were used long after his death in 1590 and countless imitations were made of his work up until the 19th century.

Renaissance German stoneware, which also used mould technology, was

from the kiln in great white, acid clouds causing enormous pollution problems. After salting, the kiln was sealed with clay to produce a 'reduction' atmosphere that gave the typical grey body of "Westerwald" stoneware.

Pottery imported from France, contemporary styles of ornament and metal vessels influenced the forms and styles of slip-decorated ware made in 12th- and 13th-century England. Elaborate, often figurative, aquamaniles or water containers for washing hands at the table, were enhanced by the use of glossy copper green or yellow lead glazes sprinkled in powder form, dipped or brushed over the surface. Strong continental influence from Germany, Holland and France, coupled with an

### Growing competition and commercialism

Trading activities of the East India Company, the major importer of tea, coffee and Chinese blue and white porcelain, gave impetus to the fashion for porcelain, which spread across Europe and damaged Italy's export market in maiolica. Early Italian and French experiments imitating the delicate translucency of porcelain resulted in the production of soft-paste porcelain from the late 17th century. German potters searched for a way of creating this elusive material. In 1710, alchemist Johann Friedrich Bottger carried out tests on earths and minerals in the hope of producing semi-precious stones, but instead discovered the principle of

characterized by the application of relief ornament often decorated with cobalt blue, developed alongside the early 16th-century introduction of woodblock printing technology. Single sheet designs and book illustration inspired the figurative or botanical friezes of oak leaf and rose motifs and portrait roundels.

By the 16th century, advances in kiln technology enabled fusion of a stoneware body from 1150–1200°C (2102–2192°F). Salt-glaze firing, an important German contribution to ceramic technology, took from 40 to 45 hours, after which time salt was introduced into the kiln's atmosphere through the side and roof openings. The vaporized salt reacted with the surface of the stoneware to form a glassy salt glaze along with noxious gases, which escaped

increased demand from a new emerging mercantile and artisan class, continued to influence the decoration of post medieval slipware. The craft reached its peak in the 17th century with examples such as yellow glazed sgraffito ware of incised, floral motif decoration, revealing the red clay beneath the white slip, which was exported to the American colonies in great quantities.

Also exemplary of this period were the generous, slip-trailed dishes of Thomas Toft. Controlled lines of slip were applied using a cow horn, the end of which was fitted with a quill or reed, and the applied slip was dextrously piped on, like icing on a cake. Multiple colours of wet slip were also combed together to produce feathering, or tilted and coaxed into a marbled effect.

FROM LEFT TO RIGHT:
EARLY MAIOLICA DISH FROM FAENZA, ITALY 1497 SHOWING THE ARRIVAL OF AENAS AT DELOS.

MEISSEN HARLEQUIN DANCING BY J. J. KAENDLER 1750.

JAR WITH PAINTED DECORATION AGAINST TENMOKU-TYPE GLAZE BY BERNARD LEACH, C.1920–25.

TILES DESIGNED BY WILLIAM DE MORGAN ON MORRIS DIAGONAL TRAIL FABRIC.

GROTESQUE FACE JUG BY MARTIN BROTHERS, BROWN STONEWARE C.1895.

HANS COPER, A STONEWARE THISTLE FORM VESSEL C.1972.

hard-paste porcelain. The first discoveries, called jasperware, were made in red clay, but the substitution of a fire-resistant white clay from Meissen heralded Europe's ability to reproduce the quality of Chinese porcelain. The Meissen factory, still in production today, became the envy of an astonished Europe. In England, the Chelsea and Bow factories made their first porcelain in 1745 and, with the discovery of kaolin deposits in France in 1769, the French Sevres and Limoges factories also began production of hard-paste porcelain.

The combination of low-cost printing with slipcasting, jigger and jolley techniques and other methods provided the foundation of the pottery manufacturing industry, firstly in Europe and then

## "Artist Pottery"

Although there were attempts after the Industrial Revolution to combine technical excellence with beauty, particularly in Scandinavia, the two approaches remained separate. In a backlash to the extreme subdivision of labour, handmade "Artist Pottery" developed. The first artist or studio potter was the Frenchman, Theodore Deck, who embarked on making porcelain with reduced flambé glazes.

By 1900 there was an increasing trend towards Artist Pottery throughout Europe and the United States, and by the end of the century, the Arts and Crafts Movement had begun. The aims of the founder, William Morris, were t

although interrupted by World War II, re-emerged in the 1950s.

In Britain, this first period of studio ceramics lasted from about 1920 to the mid 1950s. Within this period a tussle of ceramic thinking ensued between two camps: those who followed William Staite Murray, who recognised clay as a fine-art material, and those who followed Bernard Howell Leach, who introduced a philosophy of 'beauty with usefulness', based on 'pure' Chinese Sung pottery combined with that of pre-industrial English slipware. Leach's traditionalist thinking prevailed through the pre-war Depression, endowing the

  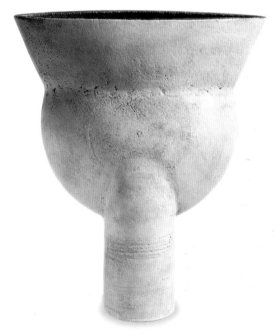

throughout the world. England's Worcester factory was the first to incorporate a wide-scale transfer printing technique by taking a paper pull from an 'inked' copper plate. This was key to the expansion of the English ceramics industry during the Industrial Revolution, which became dominant in the Staffordshire potteries in the 19th century. Mechanical appliances, division and rationalization of labour and the standardization of raw materials were used to produce salt-glazed ware and lead-glazed pottery. The Wedgwood factory produced a range of ware, most notably a cream coloured, lead-glazed earthenware. This was printed and produced at low cost, flooding the European market and forcing European competitors to produce it themselves.

revitalize the industrial arts through design. Earthenware and salt-glazed stoneware became the main preoccupations and artists, such as the Martin brothers, created wonderful salt-glazed work with loose, Japanese mannered, floral or animal motifs and, later, famous grotesque-looking bird figures. William de Morgen painted blue and green Persian colours on to earthenware and decorated with lustre. The art styles of Europe were followed in the United States and work was often shown internationally, exhibitors returning with new ideas. William Grueby made matt-glazed natural forms and Adelaide Alsop Robineau high-fired crystalline glazes and carved pieces. Many others followed this Art Pottery movement giving rise to an enriched ceramic culture, which

ceramic world with an aesthetic philosophy of how to look at pots and stifling the Murray camp enthusiasm for form, colour and abstract expression.

By the mid-1950s abstract expression gained fresh impetus, and aesthetic leadership in the work of three war refugees from Europe – Lucie Rie, Hans Coper and Ruth Duckworth. Lucie Rie's work was influenced by Roman pottery and progressive architecture. Hans Coper was influenced by primitive art and the sculptural work of Jean Arp, Constantin Brancusi and Alberto Giacometti. Ruth Duckworth, by contrast, was influenced by organic form.

These three potters laid the foundation for studio ceramics to develop in the diverse and original forms that we can see today.

# CLAY: THE FUNDAMENTAL INGREDIENT
An abundant natural material, clay forms primarily around large granite outcrops, but is found all around us, in gardens, fields, and along riverbanks or roadsides. It contains alumina and silica, as well as small quantities of other minerals, and originates from feldspathic or granite rock, originally molten when the earth was formed, and transformed over millions of years by decomposition and weathering. Different proportions of the main and subsidiary minerals give each clay its individual qualities.

### Primary and secondary clays

There are two geological categories of clay: primary and secondary clays. Primary clays, which are found where they originally formed, include china clay or kaolin, a very pure clay used to give strength and whiteness to porcelain. Another is bentonite, which can be added to other clay to improve the plasticity of clay bodies. Secondary clays were deposited in sedimentary layers during their formation. Examples are ball clays, often blue or black in their unfired state, which also add plasticity and become white or buff after firing, and red clays that contain iron oxide, which acts as a flux that lowers the clay's firing temperature. This clay is used to make earthenware bricks, floor tiles and flowerpots.

### Altering a clay body

Materials can be added to a clay body to change and strengthen it. Altering a clay body in this way reduces the shrinkage rate and lessens the degree of stress during drying and firing.

You can mix clays at the dry or plastic stage to bring them to a required state of workability or openness and modify the colour and texture at the same time. Grog is a common material that is used to 'open' clay. It is a pre-fired clay that has been ground and prepared to different graded particle sizes ranging from dust to grit. You can add grogs to any clay to make it suitable for raku firing (see Kilns and Firing, raku firing), enabling the clay to withstand the thermal shock of dramatic temperature change. Grog will also bleed through a glaze at high temperatures to give a speckled effect. Ovenware clay bodies are designed with the addition of clay 'openers' such as lithium feldspar or talc in a silica-free body.

Other materials used to change a clay body include molochite, quartz, sand or fibrous material such as paper (see fibrous and paper clay techniques).

### Obtaining clay

Clay can be dug from the ground and prepared by slaking (see reclaiming clay), sieving and returning it to its plastic state. It is marginally easier to buy clay in dry, powdered individual materials which can then be mixed together. Both methods are labour-intensive and, in the case of preparing clay from dry materials, you will need to have access to specialist equipment.

Alternatively, it is possible to buy ready-made clay in a plastic state, packaged in sealed polythene bags, from a ceramic supplier. As you will also need to pay for the cost of delivery, then the more clay you buy the cheaper it will be per unit of weight. You can also buy or prepare different clays in a liquid state, called casting slip, for slip casting (see Making and Using Moulds, slip casting).

### Choosing a clay

Each clay has its own distinct make-up, resulting in a different handling quality, colour, temperature range and plasticity, or workability. These qualities are specified by ceramic suppliers and many will be willing to send small sample bags of clay through the post for you to test. The choice of clays is wide and you can also combine them, which will increase the possibilities further. Ready-prepared clays can be combined by weighing out the selected proportions of each clay and wedging and kneading them until thoroughly mixed (see preparing clay).

There are many things that you should find out about a clay that you are considering using. First of all, test its plasticity (see plasticity test). You should also establish whether a clay is suited to oxidized or reduced firing, if it is appropriate for your planned working methods, and what is its texture and fired colour, as well as its price. Most clays are suitable for any making technique, but there are some that are specifically designed for certain ones. A very plastic clay body designed and developed specifically for throwing purposes, for example, might not be suitable for the task of modelling fine detail where a smooth fine-particle clay will be more effective. If the correct clay is not selected, then you might find the forming clay stage to be a struggle, or encounter problems with the drying and firing processes.

Remember that changes can be made to the colour or texture of clay, as well as to its actual physical properties – namely its plasticity, workability and shrinkage rate. Alternatively, changes might be made to the clay body by either raising or lowering the degree of heat necessary in the kiln to achieve the required fired density.

The list of available clays is wide depending on the ceramic supplier you use and the range they have on offer (see suppliers and services).

### Throwing clays

These are dense, plastic and responsive. To increase the plasticity of a clay for throwing, up to 30 per cent ball clay is added (more than this will cause shrinkage and drying problems and also make the clay sticky). To give throwing clay extra staying power when standing on the wheel after being intensively worked, add up to 10 per cent grog or coarse clay at a particle size that will pass through a 30–60 mesh.

### Handbuilding and modelling clays

These tend to be open clays to enable limited shrinkage and safe drying and firing, combined with adequate plasticity. A coarse or fine grog, or silver-sand addition can be introduced into a smooth clay body – depending on the texture that you require, add up to 20–30 per cent to prepare a clay in this way.

T-material is a handbuilding clay (only available in the UK) with a plastic coarse texture that fires to a white or off-white colour. Its specially developed formula means that it is plastic to work with and has a low shrinkage rate, so does not warp or distort.

### Fibrous or paper clay

This is any clay to which fibres have been introduced. The raw clay is very strong (see fibrous and paper clay techniques), giving extra stability to fragile constructions. It is also easy to dry and to mend if broken or cracked.

### Casting clays

These clays must deflocculate, or break up into fine particles, to create casting slips. Clays that contain a large amount of iron or free alkali do not deflocculate and are not suitable for casting. The purer clays such as kaolin and ball clay, many buff burning stoneware clays and fire clay deflocculate and therefore cast well. A body that casts well is usually not plastic enough for throwing.

### Jigger and jolley clays

These clays are designed for use with the jigger and jolley technique (see Making and Using moulds, jigger and jolley). They need to have moderate plasticity and should dry with a minimum of shrinkage and warpage. Trial and error is the best way of determining how a particular clay will perform with this making process.

### Plasticity test

If you need to add grog or sand into plastic clay to reduce its shrinkage rate, you can calculate how much to add by weight or volume. To test how much grog can be kneaded into clay without losing its plasticity roll out a coil of clay to a width of about 2 cm (¾ in) and bend it to form a ring. If the clay cracks, it is 'short' and will be difficult to work. You can also measure plasticity by noting the amount of water you need to add to a measured amount of dry clay to take it to a suitable consistency. A finer clay requires more water than an open clay. If a clay contains more water, it will subsequently shrink more.

### The clay temperature range

Clay can be subdivided into five various temperature range groups:

- Earthenware has a maturing range of 1000–1180°C (1832–2156°F).

- Stoneware has a maturing range of 1200–1300°C (2192–2372°F).

- Porcelain has a maturing range of 1240–1350°C (2264–2462°F).

- Bone china has a maturing range of 1240–1250°C (2264–2282°F).

- Coloured clay has a maturing range of 1040–1220°C (1904–2228°F).

### Earthenware

Fired earthenware has a much lighter feel to higher fired clays, which have a more compact, dense quality. The colour of earthenware ranges from grey or white, to red, orange, buff, yellow and brown. Earthenware clay is abundant and available in nearly every part of the world. Red clay is a secondary clay found near the surface of the ground, which contains iron oxide, accounting for its relatively low firing temperature. Red clay is usually plastic and therefore suitable for modelling, building, throwing or pressing. Light or white earthenware bodies are made by blending light burning clays, such as ball clay and china clay, or a stoneware clay with fluxes, such as talc frit or nepheline syenite, to give sufficient plasticity.

### Stoneware

The name "stoneware" comes from the dense, hard character of the clay body. The colour range for stoneware includes off-white, tan, grey and brown. Fired stoneware clay that is fully matured or vitrified has a water absorption rate of 3 per cent or less. The higher firing temperature of this clay means that adding a flux is less necessary. However this high temperature also means that feldspar can be used as a flux (as a 10–20 per cent addition) whenever necessary in order to lower the maturing temperature.

### Porcelain

The word "porcelain" is said to have evolved from "porcellno", a descriptive word given by Marco Polo in the 13th century to a translucent cowrie shell that looked like a little pig. This white-firing vitreous clay is translucent if worked to a thin wall and is fired to temperatures of 1240°C (2264°F) and above. It is made by combining white burning clays with feldspars and flint. The high firing temperature causes the particles to become dense and impervious and gives fired porcelain similar qualities to glass.

EGYPTIAN DIARY
(32 x 7.5 CM/12½ x 3 IN)
CLAY COLLAGE WALL PIECE, THIN PIECES OF COLOURED
CLAY ARE LAID ON TOP OF THE BASE SLAB
(SABINA TEUTEBERG).

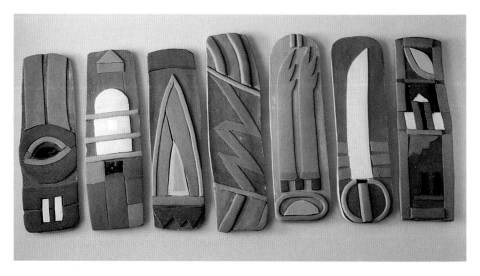

CLOCKWISE FROM TOP LEFT: PLASTIC CLAY FOR BONE CHINA, COLOURED CLAY, PORCELAIN, STONEWARE AND EARTHENWARE.

The ball clays, china clays or kaolin used in porcelain must be iron free and as plastic as possible. It is difficult to develop a porcelain for throwing, as the majority of white clays are characteristically non-plastic.

## Bone china

This porcelain clay is made from calcined ox bones, and is produced mainly in England and Japan. It was developed in the 18th century to meet the demand for a white translucent ware to compete with imported oriental porcelain. The clay body is difficult to work, being very short when plastic and fragile when dry. It is most suitable for slip casting, but with the addition of up to 6 per cent bentonite can also be press moulded. Glaze firing is at a low temperature of 1080–1100°C (1976–2072°F).

## Coloured clay

Any clay can be coloured with oxide or stain additions, although a light or white coloured clay will give the best colour response. Adding colour will often lower a clay's firing temperature, so tests should be carried out.

## Maturing temperatures

Clay is often referred to as "maturing" or "vitrifying" at a certain temperature. This is the point at which a body reaches its maximum fired strength and compactness, resulting from its progressive fusion during firing. Below this temperature the body is underfired, and will be weak and porous. Conversely, if a clay body is fired beyond its maturing temperature range then faults can occur, such as warping, bloating, collapsing or eventual transformation to a molten state. In the case of porcelain and bone china a state of near complete fusion is obtained resulting in their translucent qualities.

Research and consider carefully before selecting a clay – it should not only be suitable for your working method, but also have a temperature range to suit the glaze and the firing. Consider this when you are designing the format, scale, finished surface and the overall "feel" of the piece.

## Clay shrinkage

One aspect of clay not always detailed in a supplier's catalogue is its shrinkage rate. Clays shrink at an approximate rate of 10–13 per cent from their raw to fired state, the highest shrinkage rate taking place from the leatherhard to the bone dry state. A higher shrinkage rate is very difficult to work with, so a fine-particle, dense clay can be "opened up" by adding materials, such as sand or grog (see preparing clay, kneading in additions) to reduce shrinkage. However, the grain structure of a clay is closely related to its plasticity or workability – the more open a clay, the less plastic it will become – so take care not to add too much grog.

Clays that are very dense can pose problems when attaching clay to clay, as in the case of slab building or joining handles. The high shrinkage rate increases the chances of cracks forming at joints during drying and firing. Surfaces you wish to remain flat can also warp or curl at the edges when dried and/or fired. Slow drying by wrapping the work in plastic and slow firing can get around some of the problems, but if this does not work, you will need to rethink your design or experiment with the composition of the clay body.

### Shrinkage test

Any clay body with or without added grog or other openers can be tested for shrinkage using the following method:

**1** Roll out a sheet of plastic clay approximately 1 x 2 cm (½ x ¾ in) thick and cut it into three strips about 14 x 4 cm (5½ x 1½ in).

**2** Accurately mark a line 10 cm (4 in) long with a sharp knife point and leave the strips to dry.

**3** Turn them frequently to avoid warping.

**4** Measure the length of the lines when the clay strips are bone dry.

**5** Fire the test pieces to their intended maturing temperature and measure the length of the lines of shrinkage again. If the final shrinkage rate from plastic to fired exceeds 10–13 per cent, i.e. if the line ends up at 9 cm (3½ in) or less, the clay body will be difficult to use and you will need to add grog (see Preparing Clay, kneading in additions).

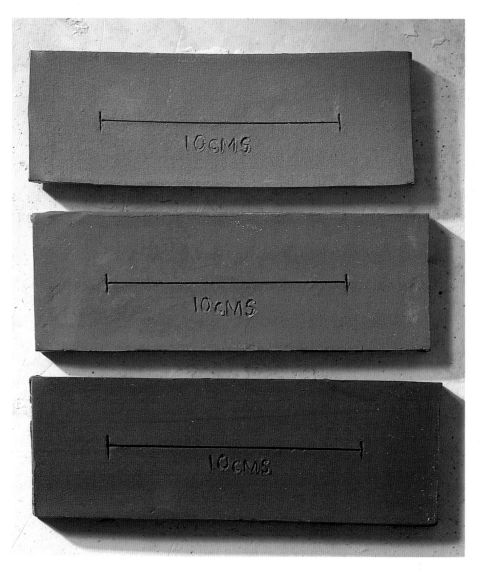

THE PHOTOGRAPH ABOVE SHOWS THE SHRINKAGE TEST RESULTS FOR FIRED EARTHENWARE (TOP), DRY EARTHENWARE (MIDDLE) AND PLASTIC EARTHENWARE (BOTTOM). THE LINES MARKED ON THE PLASTIC CLAY ARE 10 CM (4 IN) LONG AND ARE MEASURED AFTER FIRING TO RECORD SHRINKAGE RATES.

### CALCULATING PERCENTAGE LINEAR SHRINKAGE

The following equations give the method of calculating shrinkage rates from plastic to dry, dry to fired and plastic to fired clay.

$$\% \text{ DRY SHRINKAGE (plastic to dry)} = \frac{\text{Plastic length} - \text{dry length}}{\text{Plastic length}} \times 100$$

$$\% \text{ FIRED SHRINKAGE (dry to fired)} = \frac{\text{Dry length} - \text{fired length}}{\text{Dry length}} \times 100$$

$$\% \text{ TOTAL SHRINKAGE (plastic to fired)} = \frac{\text{Plastic length} - \text{fired length}}{\text{Plastic length}} \times 100$$

## Fired maturity test

In some instances, such as if you are planning a piece of work that must resist taking in water to prevent frost damage, you will need to establish whether a clay has reached its fired maturity or full vitrification. To test the degree of water absorption on fired clay, weigh and mark for indentification three clay bars, which have been fired at the required temperatures to be tested. Boil them in water for two hours and weigh them again. Compare their weights – if there is no change, no water has been absorbed and the fired clay will be fully vitrified.

## Consistency

The consistency of a clay will affect the limits of the work to be made. A firmer clay will stand longer working time on the wheel or allow a higher wall to be built from joined coils. If additional elements are made from softer clay, this will allow a coil or handle to be attached with less pressure to a supporting form or a turned lid.

Clay should be soft enough to move but firm enough so that it does not stick to hands and surfaces. It does not take long to acquire a feel for the correct "give" and to assess the best consistency for using clay for the particular job in hand. If it is a struggle in either direction, wedge either softer or firmer clay, depending on which way the clay needs to go, into the mass.

Clay that is too wet can be kneaded on dry plaster slabs (see techniques, preparing clay) until enough moisture has been extracted and the clay is in a usable plastic state. If your clay is too firm and you have no spare soft clay, the only option is to leave the clay to go dry for reclaiming. You can save clay that is verging on being too firm to use by making holes in its mass, pouring in water, letting it soak in and then wedging the clay. Alternatively, you can leave the clay to soak and soften in a container of water.

## Clay storage

Clay can be stored for long periods of time in airtight plastic bags. If the bags get torn, seal them with strong plastic tape to prevent air reaching the clay. Clay can also be stored in airtight containers. For shorter storage periods wrap clay in sheets of plastic to prevent it from drying out. You can also use this system to store and retain work at the leatherhard stage.

## Using clay within the projects

The type of clay used in each of the projects is always specified and suitable alternatives are given. Weights of clay are given for some of the projects, although the exact quantity needed will depend on the scale and volume of work you are making. Remember that unused clay will keep for long periods as long as it is stored in airtight polythene or plastic.

DARK POT WITH SLATE BLUE RIM (15.5 CM/6 IN) T-MATERIAL COLOURED WITH OXIDES, PINCHED, COILED AND OXIDIZED (JENNIFER LEE).

WHITE GARDEN (14 CM/5½ IN) PORCELAIN, WHEEL THROWN, PAINTED WITH ACRYLIC RESIST AND SUCCESSIVE LAYERS SPONGED AWAY, FIRED UNGLAZED IN A REDUCING ATMOSPHERE (PETER LANE).

# EQUIPMENT
# PREPARING CLAY

Bought clay needs to go through the initial preparation processes of wedging and kneading, or alternatively pugging, before being ready to work with. In addition to this, and because about one third of plastic clay is water and clay delivery is paid for by weight, many makers who work with large quantities find it economical to make their own clay using dry materials or by refining local clay.

**For large quantities**

**A large clay blunger** is used in combination with a filter press for preparing large amounts of plastic clay. It contains a rotating vertical shaft with mounted paddles or blades. The dry materials are weighed then mixed with water in the blunger and passed through a vibrating sieve into a filter or clay press. This squeezes the water out of the liquid clay using pressure. The slabs of freshly made plastic clay are then peeled away from the cloths in the press to be stored or pugged ready for use.

**An electric clay mixer** is also used for preparing large quantities of clay, blending 500–750 kg (1000–1500 lbs) of dry materials into a clay body at a time. The materials are measured and added to the water in the mixer. This rotates and blends them to a plastic workable consistency.

**A small blunger** (shown above) is used for mixing clay with water to prepare liquid casting slips (see Making and Using Moulds, slip casting).

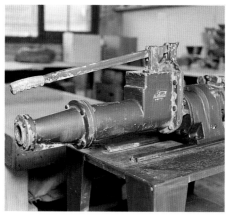

**A pugmill** is a metal barrel or cylinder, tapered at one end to a die. Clay is forced through the die by a rotating screw that consolidates and homogenizes the clay as it passes through. Clay that has been pugged can be used without wedging and kneading, as long as it is used immediately.

**For small quantities**

If you are preparing smaller quantities of clay, then you will need the following equipment:

1   A fixed bench from a heavy material, such as a concrete paving stone or slate. Ensure it is at a comfortable height for wedging – roughly as high as the top of your thigh.

2   A dry plaster slab (bat) for reconstituting wet clay can be simply made with potter's casting plaster (see Making and Using Moulds, preparing to pour plaster). Damage to plaster slabs should be avoided as plaster contaminates clay.

3   Scales and weights are also needed to weigh prepared clay into equal-sized balls.

4   A flat-headed paint scraper to clear any surplus clay on the bench (not shown).

5   Cutting wire for cutting the clay.

6   Plastic for storing prepared clay.

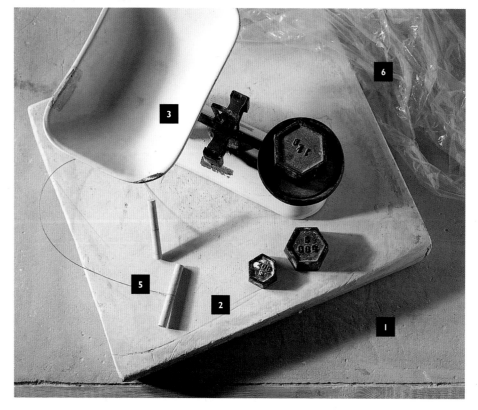

# TECHNIQUES
## PREPARING CLAY
Whether you use a handbuilding or wheel-based technique, you first need to ensure an even consistency throughout the clay's mass. This involves physically coaxing the clay into a homogenous state by wedging and kneading. A pugmill can be used for this process, dispensing with the need to wedge and knead the clay by hand, but many still prefer to wedge and knead after pugging to ensure that the clay particles are evenly aligned. A clay mass with an uneven consistency that has not been prepared well will be almost impossible to throw on the wheel or to roll into an even slab or coil.

### Wedging clay

**1** To prepare the clay for kneading, the clay is first wedged by cutting the mass into pieces with a cutting wire. The pieces are cut so that they can be rearranged to break up the distribution of the firmer and softer clay.

**2** Lift one piece of clay at a time to shoulder height and slam it down onto the piece below. Reassemble and turn the faces into a new order to realign the firm and soft areas of clay within the mass. The new distribution of clay will now be easier to move during kneading.

### Kneading clay

Do not attempt to prepare too much clay at one time. While it is valuable to have thinking time in which to finalise ideas and get ready for the 'hands on' work, kneading is a rhythmical physical exercise and should not be made overly strenuous. There are two types of kneading: spiral kneading and oxhead kneading. The names relate to the shape that the clay forms. Both methods are equally successful – choose the one that suits you.

For either method, stand with your feet astride and with one foot slightly in front of the other and use your body weight to rock into the clay.

**1A** Spiral kneading: turn the clay with one hand and, keeping your arm straight, use the heel of your other hand to apply a downward pressure by rocking your body. Rock the clay backwards and forwards, turning the mass by a hand's width and repeat the downward pressure completing an entire rotation of the mass.

**1B** Oxhead kneading: fold the clay in on itself, using the heel of both hands to exert a downward pressure. Rock the clay up with your fingers towards your body and then down again with the heels of your hands away from your body.

**2** Then cut the clay with a wire to check for lumps, air pockets and foreign bodies and if still uneven continue to knead, turning the clay by 45° before resuming.

This shows the spiral kneading technique with porcelain clay.

## Kneading in additions

Coloured clays for using in inlay, agate and millefiori work are prepared at the kneading stage by adding powdered stains and oxides (see Glazes and Decoration, colouring oxides). When making colour additions to clay at the kneading stage, you should decide what colour to use and at what strength you want to use it. Whether you are using colouring oxides or commercial stains, the colours are always added to a light- or white-coloured base clay body to obtain a good colour response.

Before kneading in stains and oxides, calculate the dry weight of both your colour addition and the clay to achieve a controlled colour. As 30 per cent of wet clay is water, 150 g (5 oz) of wet clay is equal to 100 g (3¾ oz) dry weight. Once the dry weight of your clay is calculated weigh the stain or oxide to give the desired percentage of colour shading. Moisten the stain before kneading to help distribute it evenly.

Cut through the clay and check that the additions are distributed evenly or unevenly as desired.

If you are using commercial stains for colouring clay, then remember that each stain will vary in its colour strength. Generally a darker colour will need a lower percentage of colour to give it a strong colour stain.

Experiment with colour additions of anything from 1–10 per cent (see Glaze and Decoration, sources of glaze colour). Note that blue oxides need only up to 2 per cent to give a strong blue.

You might also choose to carry out a number of fired test pieces to see the colour strength of the fired clay for different percentages of added colour.

As well as colour additions, materials such as sand, grog or mica can be added to plastic clay to create clay which, when fired, will be ovenproof. These materials can also be kneaded into the clay to reduce the shrinkage rate (see clay shrinkage) or to add texture or colour.

## Reclaiming clay

If clay has not been fired it can be reclaimed to be used again in its plastic state. To prepare clay for reconstitution you must first leave it to become bone dry – break or cut it into small pieces to allow maximum air contact.

**1** Once the clay is bone dry, 'slake' it by covering it with water in a large, plastic bowl. Leave it to soak overnight until it becomes a thick slop.

**2** Any excess water that has not been absorbed should be removed the next day by carefully pouring it out or scooping it off.

**Note:** The length of time needed to reclaim clay will depend on how dry the plaster is, the room temperature and the consistency and amount of clay being reclaimed. You can cover the clay in plastic overnight to prevent it from drying out too much. When the clay has reached a manageable state, remove it from the plaster.

**3** Spread the slop in a 5–15 cm (2–6 in) thick layer on to dry plaster bats. It can then be turned to bring more surface area in contact with the plaster, which then absorbs moisture from the clay.

**4** If necessary, leave the clay slop on the plaster bats overnight to bring the clay consistency back to a firmness that is suitable for pugging or for wedging and kneading. Great care should be taken to ensure that pieces of plaster are not scraped or chipped off the plaster slab and therefore allowed to get into the clay, as this will contaminate it.

# TECHNIQUES
# FIBROUS AND PAPER CLAY The origins of this technique go back thousands

of years. As a mixture of rice husks, fresh cows' dung and clay, fibrous clay is still used in Asia as a versatile building material for plastering walls and building large rice storage containers or for making decorative shelving and alcoves.

■ Mixing clay with other fibrous materials, such as straw, fabric, hair or polyester fibre, extends its creative possibilities. Fibre clay greenware, or unfired clay, is very strong and this makes it easier to transport large or awkward pieces into the kiln. It is possible to attach wet or plastic fibre clay to dry and even biscuit (bisque) fired clay. As the fibres in the clay create a strong bond there is no need to worry about cracks or breakages, and you can make large or otherwise difficult forms with carefree success!

Fibre clay is extremely versatile, warp free and light after firing. It can be thrown on the wheel, rolled to a paper thinness, printed, impregnated with additives to give texture, or embedded with fired objects, such as mosaic or glass. String, leaves, wire and fabric, scrim or bandage can be soaked in fibre clay and used to build up forms by applying more layers with a paintbrush. The slop can be used for building up surfaces on to dry or leatherhard clay, giving increased strength to the structure.

## Making fibrous or paper clay

Fibre or paper pulp can be added to any clay to achieve fibrous clay. Shiny paper is not suitable as it will not break down sufficiently due to its waterproof latex resin content. Newspaper or cardboard egg cartons or fruit trays are most suitable. The print dye in newspaper will release into the pulp slop, but it can be washed off hands with soap and water and will burn out of finished work in the firing.

Preparing paper pulp is labour intensive. As a short cut, you can buy shredded paper pulp and cellulose fibre from ceramic suppliers. The cellulose fibre can be kneaded directly into plastic clay, or alternatively added to the slop if combined with other pulp or fibres.

**To make paper clay** you will need 7 or 8 half-dozen, cardboard egg cartons for each 25 kg (55 lb) plastic clay. Ensure that the amount of fibre or paper pulp never exceeds 50 per cent of the mixture.

**1** Tear the egg cartons into small pieces. Soak them in hot water until they have softened, ideally overnight.

**2** Beat the soaked paper using a paint mixer attachment fixed to an electric drill. It is important to break down the paper fibres until they become a smooth even slop of roughly the same consistency as the clay slop you are going to add it to.

**3** Put the clay slop in a straight-sided bucket, level it off and stand a ruler in to measure its height. Work out how much paper slop can be added (a maximum of 50 per cent) and add the right amount of paper slop.

Continued ....

**4** Use your hands to mix the clay and paper slop thoroughly. Pour the mixed paper and clay slop on to plaster slabs in order to reclaim it into a plastic state. Once the slop has become firm, treat it in the same way as reclaimed clay.

## Storing fibrous or paper clay

Airtight bags or containers should be used for storing paper clay. The organic matter can become mouldy after a while and you can either reconstitute it or use it in this state. Apart from creating a smell during the making process, the mould will not affect the work itself.

## Firing fibrous or paper clay

Paper fibres burn in the kiln at approximately 300°C (572°F). The kiln must be fired slowly and will need good ventilation, as smoke will appear as the fibres ignite in the kiln. This is not a problem in an open-flued gas, wood or oil kiln, but an electric kiln will need to be well ventilated.

FROM THE SERIES ZIG ZAG
(40 CM/16 IN)
CLAYS, PAPER AND WIRE
SANDWICHED IN BLOTTING PAPER
AND PRINTED WITH CERAMIC
STAINS, OXIDIZED STONEWARE
(EWEN HENDERSON).

# HEALTH AND SAFETY

Many of the materials used in ceramics, particularly those for glazing, are toxic and should be handled with great care. Wearing and using the right equipment will protect you from any hazardous substances. Take precautions, especially when preparing dry materials, to prevent the inhalation of dust particles.

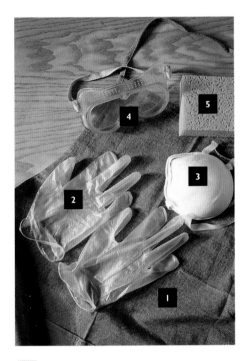

1  Apron.

2  Protective gloves.

3  Face mask that meets the appropriate particle size safety standards, BS6016 type 2 (dual cartridge respirator with a dust capturing prefilter).

4  Safety goggles.

5  Sponge for cleaning surfaces (avoiding dust creation).

## Take particular care with the following materials:

HIGHLY TOXIC
- Antimony
- Barium

USE WITH EXTREME CARE
- Lithium oxide sources – spodumene, lepidolite
- Boron sources – borax, boric acid
- Silica sources – quartz, flint, frits, feldspars, clays
- All of the colouring oxides and stains and underglazes

USE WITH CARE
- Aluminium oxide sources – feldspar, clay, calcined alumina, alumina hydrate
- Sodium oxide sources – soda feldspar, pearl ash, nitre
- Calcium oxide sources – whiting, dolomite
- Magnesium oxide sources – magnetite, dolomite, talc
- Zinc
- Strontium

## LEAD

Lead is a hazardous substance. Many makers use lead in their glazes, while others prefer to avoid it. Some low-fired lead glazes are hazardous and should not be used in combination with copper or chromium oxide. These combinations are not suitable for the internal areas of domestic ware. In addition, all glaze wash water from work with lead glaze must be contained, collected, recycled or treated as toxic waste. Fritted leads should be used at all times (see Glaze and Decoration, frits). If you are unsure of the composition of a particular lead glaze you wish to use, you can take your work to a specialist laboratory for them to carry out a standard test for lead release on commercial ware. Lead should not be used when there are children around.

The book includes information and advice on using lead and some recipes with lead glazes. Ensure that you seek advice before using lead in your ceramic work and protect yourself with a face mask (respirator) and gloves that meet appropriate safety standards.

When beginning to use glazes, use only commercially prepared lead-safe glazes and never add copper to them. Use lead only if you have a safe way of collecting all waste water and having it collected as toxic waste.

## Safety tips

1 Never inhale or ingest powders.

2 Wear a safety mask (face respirator) and protective gloves when preparing glaze by mixing soluble materials. Wear gloves when using wet glaze. This prevents toxins being absorbed through the skin.

3 Wear a safety mask (face respirator) when spraying glaze and colour, or if incising, rubbing or manipulating dry glaze before firing. Use proper extraction equipment when using a spray gun or airbrush.

4 Avoid making dust at all times when preparing work or when cleaning up.

5 Keep working areas clean and free from glaze. Vacuum floors (wet or dry) or wash them down with water to a drain. Use an absolute filter that collects very fine clay and chemical particles if vacuuming a dry floor. Avoid sweeping, and any activity that will create dust.

6 Wear protective clothing and wash it regularly.

7 Store materials in carefully labelled, fireproof lidded containers and always check the instructions on raw materials carefully.

8 Do not store containers near kilns.

9 Keep all ceramic materials away from children and pets.

10 Never eat in your work area.

# WORKSHOP LAYOUT

The type, volume and scale of work that you make will be the dominant factor in deciding the layout, size and location of your studio or workshop space. It is not always possible to site a workshop on a ground floor, but there are obvious advantages to this when bringing in heavy materials or moving out large pieces of work. When starting from scratch, it may be necessary to compromise on your ideal workshop by acquiring expensive equipment in stages, prioritising which pieces are most important and therefore those that should be purchased first.

## The kiln

No matter how your work is made, there can be no finished ceramic work without the initial, and largest, financial outlay of a kiln (unless you use a communal one). It is possible to buy a second-hand electric kiln for considerably less than a new one, but check the model and number first and make sure you can still order replacement parts.

When purchasing a kiln for installation make sure there is adequate access through doorways, corridors or stairways to bring it to the intended site. All electric fired kilns, apart from the smallest, require an isolation switch and wiring in from the mains supply. Large electric kilns may require a three-phase electricity supply, which if not already present will add to the installation cost.

All kilns must be installed in a place that is ventilated near a window or extraction fan. Also consider whether its position will be practical for the type and quantity of work to be loaded into it. Fuel burning kilns require a flue or, unless located under an open-sided covering, a hood to collect fumes. Gas and oil kilns require a convenient source and access for fuel, as well as a safe storage place that is away from the direct heat of the kiln. Gas kilns can be adapted to portable gas where on-site delivery is not possible.

## Floor

Be practical – flooring should be hard wearing and smooth to allow for repeated and effective washing down. The ideal floor for heavy-duty or large-volume production is one that slopes down towards a drain. A heavy-duty vacuum cleaner with an adequate filter and the capacity to take up water is a good alternative.

## Water

Your main working space should ideally have a running water supply. Hot water can also make a difference when deciding whether to commence throwing on the wheel or not in the winter months. The sink should be large enough to wash out a bucket comfortably and its draining water should run into a settling or sediment tank (sink trap). This should be installed to take out heavy clay and glaze residue, preventing blockages to the drainage system and toxic materials entering the water system.

## Heating and ventilation

In cool conditions clay can be uninvitingly cold to work, glazes will freeze in their buckets and cold fingers are unable to carry out any task. This means that heating becomes essential to include for the worker as well as the work itself. However, overly heated studios during firings, in hot summer months, or those in the Southern Hemisphere can create adverse conditions of their own. In these conditions it becomes a race against time to apply handles or slip, as the work will move from leatherhard to dry in the brief moments taken to go to the fridge for a cool drink. In hot climates, organize some sort of ventilation, create areas that avoid direct sunlight and plan an open-sided, working space to keep conditions as comfortable as possible.

## Shelving

The type of shelving and storage you use will depend on the type of work you make. Makers of production ware will tend to choose an adjustable rack system. This means that long, narrow boards full of freshly made work can be easily transferred from the working area directly onto the drying rack. These boards or shelves can then be conveniently taken on and off the rack to turn the work for even drying. Large workshops in cold or wet climates will locate some form of heating near or under their drying racks to speed the drying process or prevent the wet work being frost damaged.

## Storage, surfaces and power

As well as storage for ongoing work, you will need a space for the finished work, to store clay and glaze materials and large containers. Other large pieces of equipment, such as slab rollers, extruders, pugmills and blungers should also be taken into consideration when planning space or electrical installation with isolation switches. If you need a spray booth, it must be located next to an outside wall to allow for extraction.

You will require one or more sturdy tables or work benches in the main clay area and an additional area or wedging bench for preparing clay. And do not forget to plan your lighting – you may wish to place the main working table or wheel next to a window.

## Organization

Plaster should always be kept separate from the main area used for working with clay to avoid contamination of the clay used for finished work. When trapped in the fired clay of a finished piece of work, plaster acts as a contaminant by absorbing and expanding. Any plaster that finds its way into a finished piece of work will irritatingly emerge from the fired clay or glazed surface months, sometimes years, later, leaving behind it an unwelcome scar. For this reason, ensure that all buckets and equipment used for plaster work are kept solely for plaster activities.

## Planning

Whatever size of workshop you are planning, whether you make buttons or large sculptural pieces, take time to visit the studios and workshop spaces of other makers. Look at their layout solutions and ask about their kilns and equipment before you decide on a final plan.

You could also consider renting or sharing a well-equipped studio. Such workspaces can often be found in the classified section of specialist magazines or on noticeboards in specialist shops and organizations. It is sometimes possible to hire the use of a kiln and, for short-term projects or small quantities of work, this may be adequate. Some craft associations offer grants for setting up a workshop and purchasing equipment.

## Studio layout

The photograph shows the working studio layout of a maker specializing in wheel-thrown work. The kiln and the sink with settling tank (sink trap) are sited on the other side of the studio.

1 Electric wheel.

2 Pugmill.

3 Scales.

4 Light for use when working at wheel.

5 Wooden bats for use on the wheel.

6 Banding wheel.

7 Paint stripper gun.

8 Heater.

9 Preparing clay area and worksurface.

10 General worksurface.

11 Storage area with adjustable shelving for finished work and work in progress.

12 Underbench storage area for clay and other large-scale materials, such as plaster or mixed glazes.

13 Work in progress wrapped in plastic.

14 Practical flooring.

# DESIGN

**CLAY IS A VERSATILE MEDIUM THAT CAN BE WORKED TO SIMULATE** JUST ABOUT ANY OTHER MATERIAL. ANY DESIRED COLOUR OR EFFECT – SMOOTH, DRY, SHINY OR TEXTURED – CAN BE APPLIED TO ITS SURFACE TO GIVE THE VISUAL QUALITY OF WOOD, FABRIC, PAPER OR METAL. HOWEVER, THE SURFACE EFFECT IS NOT THE ONLY CONSIDERATION WHEN PLANNING A NEW PIECE OF WORK. THE MALLEABILITY OF CLAY ALLOWS ENDLESS DESIGN POSSIBILITIES, AND IN THE END THE DECISION-MAKING PROCESS HAS TO BE NARROWED DOWN BY A PROCESS OF ELIMINATION. IT IS OFTEN BEST TO STICK WITH ONE AREA OF INTEREST OR SUBJECT MATTER, AND TO BUILD UP A KNOWLEDGE OF PARTICULAR MAKING, DECORATING AND FIRING TECHNIQUES. THE POSSIBILITIES AND VARIATIONS WILL BE ENOUGH TO FILL A LIFETIME OF CREATIVE DISCOVERY.

# PLANNING

Once you have developed an understanding of the physical making process, and some knowledge of applied surfaces, you are then in a position to think about design. Whether you are making functional ware, sculptural work or something that is a mixture of both, you should always start from an initial design. This means choosing the surface, thinking about the scale, the type and form of firing, and selecting a suitable clay to meet the requirements of what you want to make. Some design decisions will rest on a vision of the finished piece, while others will emerge through the evolving progression of work, or they will come through experimentation with ideas, forms and new materials.

■ Domestic ware designs will always be influenced by practical considerations unless they are to be deliberately disregarded in favour of an aesthetic. Is the shape of the handle suitable for grasping comfortably? Does the spout pour adequately? Does a lid stay on a teapot when it is poured? Will the glaze craze excessively and be unsuitable for domestic use? Once the practicalities are solved the form can be evolved and reassessed to tie in with your chosen methods. Design will involve meeting the practical considerations and working them out while keeping true to the desired visual appeal of a finished piece.

With sculptural or decorative work there is a wider freedom in the choice of design, but the constraints of the making process, materials and firing may sometimes impose limitations. Being ideas-led and overcoming the restraints of a material will often require experimentation and exploration until you can achieve the desired result. If a clay does not suit the limitations imposed by a chosen form you may need to rethink the material and change, for example, to a sandy or fibrous clay. If a surface does not match what you had planned, you will need to find a new decorating medium, glaze recipe or colour addition.

Drawings are not always sufficient when making a three-dimensional design that needs to be considered from all angles. It is a good idea to build a small-scale version, called a maquette, in clay or another material, such as cardboard, before embarking on a large piece of work. A maquette is used as an accurate, physical reference for scale and points of change of direction and as a reference to the overall feel or mood of a piece. This allows you to view and plan the work from all possible angles and enables you to explore alternatives without wasting working time on a large piece.

With the current use of technology to aid the design process, a new generation of computer-literate designers is emerging. Computer design can be valuable when it is appropriately applied, but should not be used to supplant the "soul" of contact and knowledge of clay as a material.

MAQUETTES AND DRAWINGS ARE IMPORTANT METHODS OF EXPLORING AND DEVELOPING IDEAS.

Forms can be transformed or accentuated with decoration that can give the work individual characteristics or act as a vehicle for self expression. Whatever your chosen idea, observation and thought are essential ingredients in order to make the idea work in practice. Many potters will make a prolonged study of a certain area before starting to make an actual piece of work. Images, ideas and objects can be collected or recorded by any process of drawing, painting, writing, collage, photography, video or documentation.

Designing on a three-dimensional surface opens up interesting possibilities for ways of arranging surface application. Inner and outer walls can be played against each other, changes in direction can be used as a transition point of the design, and the circuits of a design can be divided or made continuous.

THESE ORGANIC SURFACE SHAPES WERE CHOSEN TO BE IN KEEPING WITH THE ASYMMETRICAL FORM OF THE DISH AND WERE CAREFULLY PLACED UNTIL THEIR SPATIAL ARRANGEMENT LOOKED AND FELT RIGHT.

## Transferring designs to clay

The simplest and most immediate way to mark out a design on the surface of any biscuit (bisque) fired, dry or powdered glaze surfaces is to draw a pencil line freehand. Pencil marks will disappear in any type of firing. Add a little gum arabic or gum tragacanth in liquid form to an applied glaze as a binder or adhesive to toughen the powdered glaze surface for handling and application of a pencil line. The following techniques are suitable alternatives to freehand drawing.

Repeat designs or intricate designs can be indented into leatherhard clay using a pencil to follow traced or photocopied lines. Depending on the firmness of the clay this method can be used to leave a pleasingly rounded line as deep as the pressure applied to draw it. The indented line creates an inverted cloisonné look to the work when filled with colour.

To transfer a repeated design or one that is overly intricate and difficult to draw, use carbon copy paper to mark it out onto dry or biscuit (bisque) fired clay.

Pouncing is a useful and quick technique for transferring repeat designs to flat surfaces, such as tiles, to make a guideline for decorating with colour. This method can be used on a basic clay surface or on top of a powder glaze surface in preparation for onglaze decoration. The technique involves pushing lead graphite powder through holes in a stencil using a stiff brush or stencil brush.

# INSPIRATION

There are many ways of making use of forms and organizing surface design, whether using a restrained, classic approach or a dramatic, thought-provoking one. There are also a number of ways in which you can accumulate ideas for your ceramic work.

Looking around at different objects, images and forms of design heightens artistic judgement. As well as looking at ceramic work in museums and galleries, there is an endless list of everyday things that surround us – such as natural objects, buildings, people, machines or domestic items – which can be observed and reinterpreted as images or ideas. The creative challenge is to interpret a subject in a way that has aesthetic appeal.

You may, for instance, start with the idea that you would like to make a functional bowl using natural textures, or produce a figurative sculpture that conveys a particular mood. Whatever your starting point, it is inevitable that your idea will involve making a number of choices: which particular clay to use, whether to use handbuilding, to make and use your own moulds or a throwing technique, and which methods and types of decoration, glazing and firing to use to finish the work. This may seem far too much to think about at first and all at the same time, but the amazing selection available gives unlimited opportunities to develop ceramic work that is personal, original and exciting.

When starting out, establishing and developing a personal vocabulary around a particular choice of materials or ideas can take a considerable amount of time and wide experimentation. Finding the avenues that might be productive and interesting is exactly how many established makers have developed the work shown on the following pages, and throughout the book. This contemporary work reflects a variety of inspirational starting points, ranging from functional production work to one-off sculptural forms, and from classic simplicity to work with a complex dynamic. These individual methods, styles and routes of exploration can be referred to for inspiration or as illustrations of how to combine ceramic techniques.

## Echoing ideas or beliefs

Many ceramic artists react in a sensory way to the world around them, or indeed to strongly held beliefs and ideas. This category could include work motivated by philosophy, music, literature or politically held views. Such motivation could be an individual reaction to a contemporary idea, or reflect or reinterpret a movement or belief within our history.

FISH FOUNTAIN (81 CM/32 IN)
IN CHINESE MYTHOLOGY FISH SYMBOLIZE PLENTY AND WATER IS A UNIVERSAL SYMBOL OF LIFE, THEREFORE THIS PIECE REPRESENTS LONG LIFE (PAMELA MEI YEE LEUNG).

ART – FASHION SAME THING (55 CM/21½ IN) COILED EARTHENWARE WITH STENCILLED SLIP AND SGRAFFITO. THE FAMILIARITY OF THE CLASSICAL VASE SHAPE DRAWS THE VIEWER IN. THE FASHION MODELS ARE CHOSEN FOR THEIR AWKWARD POSES AND BLANK EXPRESSIONS – "DOOMED TO BE DECORATIVE IN THEIR ART PRINT DRESSES" (GRAYSON PERRY).

## Observing patterns and structures

We are surrounded by patterns and structures in our everyday lives, whether organic forms such as trees or plants or man-made ones such as scaffolding and buildings. Interpretations of such patterns could be symmetrical or asymmetrical, repeated or irregular and they could be applied to both the construction of a ceramic form or to the surface texture and colour.

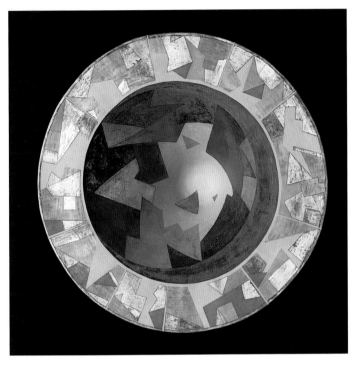

BARCELONA MOON (46 CM/19 IN DIAMETER)
COILED AND LUSTRED BOWL INSPIRED BY EGYPTIAN AND GEOMETRIC DESIGNS THAT ARE EVOLVED INTO ASYMMETRICAL ARRANGEMENTS (JUDY TRIM).

BLOCK VESSEL (25 CM/10 IN) WAX RESIST AND MULTIPLE LAYERS OF GLAZE. THIS DESIGN IS INFLUENCED BY THE LANDSCAPE WITH PARTICULAR REFERENCE TO ANCIENT AND CONTEMPORARY EGYPT (PETER BEARD).

ANGULAR FORMS (15 CM/6 IN)
BOTH THE SURFACE AND FORM SUGGEST AN ANGULAR INTERPRETATION OF A HONEYCOMB PATTERN. THE TRANSPARENCY OF THE THIN, CAST PORCELAIN WITH APPLIED TRANSFERS MAKES THE OUTSIDE AND INSIDE DECORATION INTERACT WITH THE LIGHT (BODIL MANZ).

PORCELAIN BUTTONS
LIMOGES PORCELAIN IS HAND PAINTED WITH CERAMIC COLOUR USING STYLIZED INTERPRETATIONS OF STEM, LEAF AND FLOWER SHAPES. THE SLAB OF CLAY IS PIERCED WHEN WET TO CREATE THE HOLES, AND THEN LOW-FIRED AND SANDED (HELEN SMYTHE).

## Making an abstract interpretation

An abstract interpretation will set an idea or technique free from an familiar visual pattern of recognition. As with all these categories, abstraction can relate both to the form of a piece or its decorative effects. Rather than relating literally to what is around us, shapes and applied surfaces are explored, often alongside less tangible ideas and thoughts. Abstract work can powerfully evoke a particular mood or movement, it can focus on the interrelation of shapes or immerse itself in a particular making process.

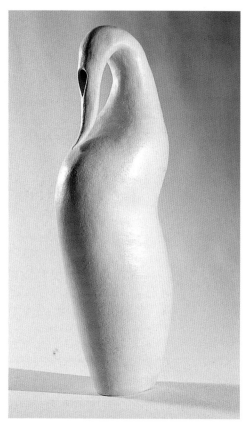

SHYNESS (45 CM/18 IN)
COILED WHITE STONEWARE CLAY, SANDED AND WAXED TO PRODUCE A SENSUAL, HAPTIC SURFACE AND A FORM THAT SUGGESTS THE TITLE "SHYNESS" (KAY SUCKLING).

HIGH SPOUTED POT (37 CM/15 IN)
THIS SLAB-BUILT FORM EXPLORES BOTH THE PHYSICAL PROCESS OF MAKING A POT AND THE BOUNDARIES SUGGESTED BY THE APPLIED DECORATIVE MARKS (ALISON BRITTON). PHOTOGRAPH BY DAVID CRIPPS.

DARK SCROLL WITH WIRE SNIPPERS (33 CM/13 IN WIDE, 15 CM/6 IN DEEP)
STRIPS OF FIBREGLASS MATTING DIPPED IN COPPER PORCELAIN SLIP ARE WOUND ROUND AND ANCHORED AT THE BASE BY EGYPTIAN PASTE COILS, CRAWLING GLAZE AND OXIDIZED FIRING. THIS ABSTRACT ASSEMBLAGE COMBINES CERAMIC MATERIALS WITH FOUND OBJECTS (GILLIAN LOWNDES).

PACKAGED HEAD (35 CM/14 IN)
CLAYS, PAPER AND WIRE, OXIDIZED STONEWARE, CREATING AN ABSTRACT AND EVOCATIVE FORM (EWEN HENDERSON).

BOWL (8.5 CM/3¼ IN) AND BOTTLE (18.5 CM/7¼ IN)
THROWN AND ALTERED PORCELAIN, HIGH FIRED TO A SOFT, LUMINOUS, TRANSLUCENT
QUALITY. A SEARCH FOR SIMPLICITY AND QUIETNESS MOTIVATES THIS WORK ALONG WITH
AN INTEREST IN OBJECTS TO BE HELD AND USED (PRUE VENABLES).
PHOTOGRAPH BY TERENCE BOGUE.

TALL POT WITH LUGS (50 CM/20 IN)
SOFTLY THROWN CLAY USING A THICK SLIP AND A SLOW TURNING KICK WHEEL, OXIDIZED
FIRING. THE FIRED POT IS PAINTED WITH COBALT OXIDE. THIS ABSTRACT WORK EXPRESSES
SENSUALITY, VITALITY, ASYMMETRY AND MOVEMENT (SANDY BROWN).
PHOTOGRAPH BY JOHN ANDOW.

## Capturing or evoking a memory or an experience

In the same way that we might take a photograph of a sunset, sketch a village scene or write a love poem, such moving experiences can also be translated sensitively into clay. As well as taking the form of a direct or stylized visual record, this area of inspiration can also respond to a particular emotion associated with an individual memory or experience.

LEAVING BRISTOL, MATTHEW TILE PAINTINGS (24 X 34 CM/9½ X 13½ IN) ONGLAZE ENAMELS ON EARTHENWARE TILES. INSPIRED BY MEDIEVAL ILLUMINATED MANUSCRIPTS. ONE OF A COLLECTION OF TILE PANELS, ECHOES THE RICH COLOURS OF THE PERIOD. THE TILES COMMEMORATE THE 500 YEARS SINCE JOHN CABOT SAILED FROM BRISTOL TO DISCOVER NEWFOUNDLAND IN HIS TINY BOAT THE MATTHEW (ROSIE SMITH). PHOTOGRAPH BY MAGGIE JENKINS.

BITING (70 CM/28 IN) CERAMIC, GOLD LEAF AND EPOXY. FROM A SERIES
OF SEVEN WORKS INVESIGATING GESTURES AND SENSES (ANDREW LORD).
PHOTOGRAPH BY PETER WHITE.

## Capturing what is seen and translating it into a personal representation

This inspirational technique uses the familiar visual forms that surround us, but adapts them to a specific personal view. This could involve exaggerating or simplifying observed physical attributes, stylizing a subject to make it decorative, or translating a subject into a more subjective perspective. Although reinterpreting an observed subject, the individual style and personality of the potter is strongly represented in the finished work. This approach is structured entirely from the perspective of the creator rather than by what is observed.

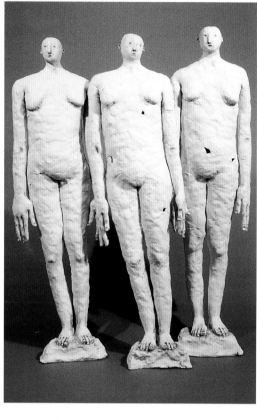

FIGURES
(60 CM/24 IN)
HANDBUILT
PORCELAIN WITH
STAIN WASHES
ON HANDS,
HEAD AND FEET.
THE FIGURES ARE
INTERPRETED
WITH
EXAGGERATED
BODY
PROPORTIONS
(CLAIRE
CURNEEN).

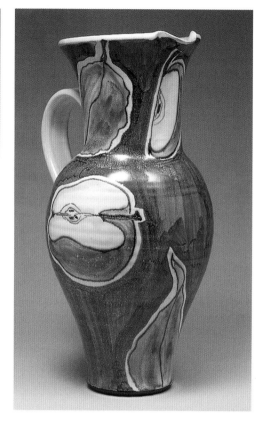

TALL JUG
(38 CM/15 IN)
INFLUENCED BY THE
PEASANT POTTERY OF
SPAIN, ITALY AND
FRANCE, THESE
SIMPLIFIED NATURAL
FORMS ARE PAINTED
WITH OXIDES USING
A MAIOLICA AND
TIN-GLAZE
TECHNIQUE
(DAPHNE CARNEGY).

BOWL WITH FLYING BIRDS (40 × 48 × 15 CM/15½ × 19 × 6 IN)
COILED, SCRAPED AND FETTLED, WITH BIRDS MODELLED AND APPLIED AT LEATHERHARD
STAGE. THIS INTERPRETATION OF BIRDS HAS AN ILLUSTRATIVE QUALITY, ENHANCED WITH
SOFT UNDERGLAZE PAINT COLOURS ON MATT BLACK GLAZE INLAY (ANNA LAMBERT).

OX (50 CM/20 IN)
HANDBUILT FORM WITH PAPER CLAY, SHOWING A FINELY OBSERVED YET UNIQUELY
PERSONAL VIEW OF THIS ANIMAL (BRENDAN HESMONDHALGH).

## Investigating the material used or a making process

Some makers working with ceramics choose to focus their work particularly on the actual materials used and the physical process of making instead of the making process being incidental or secondary to an overall purpose. This way of working can result in an intensity and compatibility with the materials that produces a dynamic, fresh perspective.

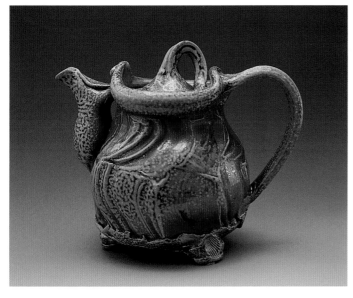

TEAPOT (18 CM/7 IN)
THROWN AND MANIPULATED STONEWARE, SHOWING THE TECHNIQUE OF FLUTING USED IN A FLOWING, RHYTHMICAL WAY. A SODA VAPOUR GLAZING AFTER AN INITIAL FIRING ACCENTUATES THIS METHOD (RUTHANNE TUDBALL).

GEO-VECTOR (33 CM/13 IN)
SLAB-BUILT PORCELAIN WITH MOLOCHITE INSPIRED BY GEOLOGICAL FORMATIONS, TEXTURED WITH RIVER MUD, COLOURED WITH SLIPS, BEACH AND VOLCANIC SANDS, DECOMPOSED GRANITE AND OTHER FOUND MATERIALS, OXIDIZED FIRING (JENNY BEAVAN).

## Using personal or symbolic imagery to make the form or decoration

Symbolism is always a powerful tool within creative work. Many motifs and objects, such as a mother and baby, a monkey or a crown, have strong connotations of emotion, of character and of status.

Beyond these familiar symbols, further ones are continually developing that relate particularly to a maker's own perspective, experience and interest.

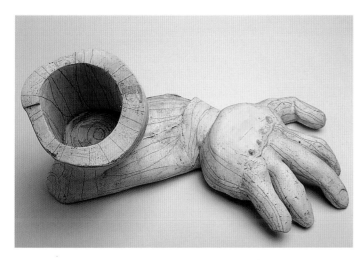

FINGERS AND THUMB (20 × 43 × 25 CM/8 × 17 × 10 IN)
SLAB BUILT FROM C-MATERIAL AND WHITE EARTHENWARE. THIS PERSONAL SYMBOL WAS DEVELOPED TO CELEBRATE THE GROWTH AND DEVELOPMENT OF THE AUTHOR'S SON, AND ALSO LINKS TO HER DOMESTIC, NURTURING AND EMOTIONAL ROLE AS MOTHER (JOSIE WARSHAW).
PHOTOGRAPH BY PETER NORMAN.

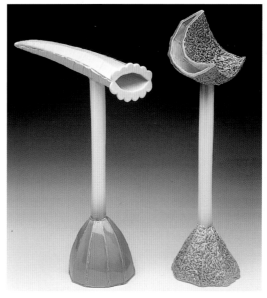

COMET AND MOON (47 AND 54 CM /18½ AND 22 IN)
HANDBUILT, GLAZED EARTHENWARE. SLEE'S INDIVIDUAL WORKS FORM COLLECTIONS, SOMETIMES AROUND A THEME. SOURCES ARE ECLECTIC, BUT OFTEN REFLECT CONTEMPORARY SOCIETY (RICHARD SLEE).
PHOTOGRAPH BY ZUL MUKHIDA.

# HANDBUILDING

**THERE ARE MANY PROCESSES INVOLVED IN POTTERY,** BUT THE ACTUAL PHYSICAL MANIPULATION OF CLAY IS CRUCIAL. THIS CHAPTER EXPLORES THE DIFFERENT HANDBUILDING TECHNIQUES: PINCHING, COILING, SLAB BUILDING AND EXTRUSION, AS WELL AS METHODS OF DECORATING INTO CLAY, SUCH AS SPRIGGING, PIERCING AND BURNISHING. THE FINAL SECTION INTRODUCES A RANGE OF IDEAS FOR PROJECTS THAT USE AND BUILD ON THE TECHNIQUES COVERED HERE.

# EQUIPMENT
# HANDBUILDING
Working efficiently and accomplishing a good finish to your work in clay is much easier when you have access to the correct tools. As well as those shown here, you will need a well lit, flat, level working area (see Workshop Layout).

**1** A cloth for rolling out slabs.

**2** A rolling pin for rolling out slabs.

**3** Rolling slats or guides.

**4** Thin polythene (plastic) for wrapping work and maintaining leatherhard clay.

**5** Wooden boards for supporting work or larger boards for rolling out slabs.

**6** Rubber kidneys for smoothing, in different sizes and degrees of flexibility.

**7** An assortment of metal kidney shapes for paring, scraping and smoothing.

**8** A surgical scalpel is the sharpest knife available. Stocked in good art shops, they come with interchangeable blades.

**9** A potter's knife with a pointed tip that will not drag on clay.

**10** Hooped wire (trimming) tools for carving, modelling and hollowing out.

**11** Hardwood tools for modelling.

**12** Hole cutters make clean cuts to leatherhard clay.

**13** Plastic cards make ideal kidneys and can be cut to shape and filed to a profile.

**14** A paddle for tapping or beating soft clay.

**15** A forged steel tool for modelling and carving.

**16** A needle to pierce enclosed shapes.

**17** A harp (wire) for slicing slabs.

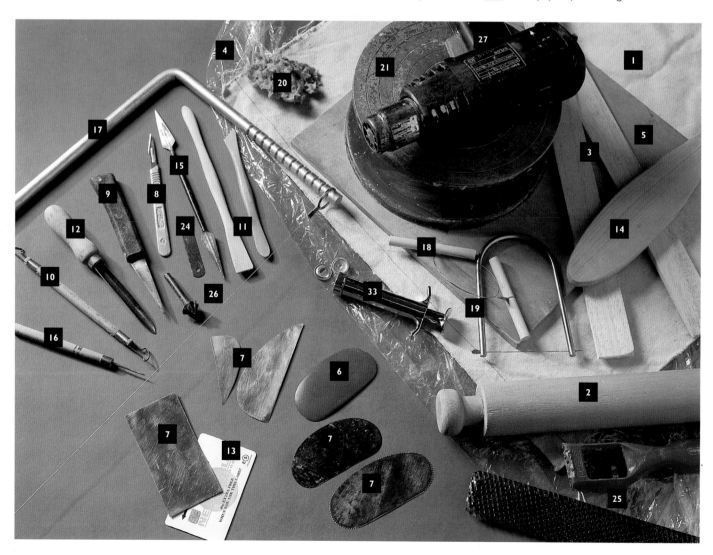

**18** A cutting wire for preparing clay or for cutting work free from a board.

**19** A trimmer enables the cutting of soft clay with one hand.

**20** A soft, natural sponge makes fewer ridges when wiping back any uneven clay.

**21** Banding wheels for turning work vary in weight and size – heavier ones give greater stability and momentum.

**22** Large pieces of foam are useful to support and protect awkward work (not shown).

**23** A slab roller makes rolling a large number of sheets of clay much easier (not shown).

The equipment above is available through standard pottery suppliers. The four items below are available from building suppliers.

**24** Fine-toothed hacksaw blades for paring and modelling.

**25** Curved and straight surform blades shave away clay and make straight edges.

**26** A countersink can be used with clay to countersink holes, as for woodworking.

**27** A paint stripper gun to speed-dry clay (a powerful hairdryer can be as effective).

**Extruding tools**

**28** A wad box or extruder creates extruded shapes by forcing plastic clay through a die. The height of the box will dictate the maximum length.

**29** Various shaped dies are available to modify the shape of the extrusions.

**30** To extrude hollow shapes a metal plate is fixed to the centre of the die.

**31** An extrusion from a square shaped hollow die.

**32** A selection of handle extrusions.

**33** A clay gun for decorative extrusions.

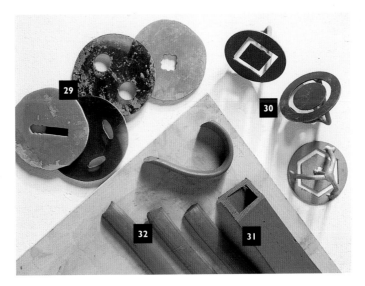

# T E C H N I Q U E S
# P I N C H I N G
The technique of pinching is one of the simplest ways of manipulating clay and as a result is often underestimated in its potential to create different surfaces or tensions. At the start pinched clay has a flaccid quality with a surface similar to overly ripe, dimpled fruit, but it can be transformed to a taut or precise form, full of vigour and life.

## Pinching

Always pinch out the bottom area of clay first, leaving the rim until last, to avoid cracks forming. If cracks do appear at the rim, smooth them down with a finger, smooth in a piece of soft clay, or cut the cracks away with the tip of a potter's knife.

**1** To start a pinched shape using prepared plastic clay (see preparing clay), take a ball that fits comfortably in your hand. Press your thumb down into its centre to within 5 mm (¼ in) of the ball's opposite wall.

**2** Starting at the deepest point, pinch the clay between your finger and thumb. Rotate the ball as you continue to pinch, moving up to the top edge while supporting the opened ball in your other hand. Turn and pinch with even pressure to reach the required wall thickness.

## Changing and manipulating a shape

**1** You can make an elongated shape in a similar way, but you roll the initial ball into a cone shape and pull the sides of the wall up over your thumb. Any ridges that form can be pinched out or removed once the shape is leatherhard.

**2** To shape a form outwards, stroke the inside with your finger tips while supporting the clay in the other hand. Check the profile of the shape all the way round as you do this. If the clay has been shaped beyond what you require, you can bring it back in while it is still soft.

**3** To shape a form inwards, gather or fold the wall and squeeze it together. V-shaped cuts can also be made to a rim, or leaf-shaped cuts to a bellied wall where unwanted bulges occur. The cut shapes are removed before pushing and smoothing the wall back together again.

**4** Top edges and walls can be pinched to a paper thinness to give a pinched shape a feeling of tension. It is often easier to wait until the shape has firmed before you finish the rim of a pinched shape. To level a rim, wait for the shape to become leatherhard and then cut the edge with a knife tip or grate it down with a surform blade. When it is level, pare the section of the rim with a hacksaw blade so it is even. Pinch the parts that need further thinning. Final paring to round, flatten or taper the rim can be done with a hacksaw blade or a metal kidney and then wiped with a damp sponge. Alternatively, you can leave shapes with a fat rim and add coils or slabs to give the shape a chunkier feel.

CLOSED BOWL WITH
CONVOLUTED MOUTH
(14 CM/5½ IN)
PORCELAIN, THROWN
AND PINCHED
(DEIRDRE BURNETT).

## Making a hollow enclosed shape

Made from two pinched cups, hollow, enclosed shapes can be manipulated while still soft. This joining technique can start a figuratively based piece of work or make a main or additional component of a piece.

**1** To join two pinched cups together leave a level, fat edge on each cup so there is enough excess clay to pull one edge over the other. The second cup should be slightly larger than the first to allow the rim edges to sit together and to allow for an overhang of clay on the second cup, which can be pulled over the edge of the first. Smear or pull the clay around the circumference of the seam line.

The trapped air inside the shape will keep it inflated while you continue to work. If it is not completely sealed the shape will buckle inwards or deflate, so seal a hole or weak point straight away with very soft clay.

**2** When it is completely sealed the enclosed hollow shape can be tapped, rolled or beaten with a paddle to finalize its form. Again, if the shape is punctured or feels weak at a particular point, ensure it is repaired before manipulating it further. Once leatherhard, the shape can be pared and smoothed.

**3** Before allowing the shape to become too dry, make a small hole with a needle to allow some of the air to escape. This will prevent the shape from cracking as it shrinks and dries.

## Using a pinched shape as a starting point

Pinched open and enclosed forms can be used as starting points to make components or to begin a piece of work.

A fat edge left on a pinched, open shape that is intended as a beginning for a coiled or soft slab piece, gives a good fixing surface from which to proceed. It can be thinned down once the join has been made.

Walls, joins and pinch marks can be pared and thinned on plastic clay using a hacksaw blade and a metal kidney. Support the wall with your non-working hand when applying pressure with tools. You may find it more comfortable to rest the shape in your lap to give it extra support. The clay can be worked while it is still plastic, but any last-stage finishing should be left until the clay is leatherhard.

**Note:** Remember to finish off the inside areas of a tall, narrow piece before it gets too high, as this may prevent you reaching inside. Pare the inside of a curved shape with a curved edge of a metal kidney and the outside with the flat edge. This will prevent flat ridges and scars from marring a final surface that is meant to be smooth.

### Leatherhard clay

In a cheese-like state of leatherhardness, recognised by its cold feel and firmness, the once soft clay can support the weight of further additions of applied clay without buckling or distorting. Leatherhard clay can still make a strong bond with any additional plastic clay applied using the score and slurry technique (see using slurry for joining slabs). It is also suitable for paring and smoothing work with tools and can support the weight and stress of applied coils, slabs, handles, footrings (feet) or other components.

### Pinching fibre clay

Pinched forms made from fibre clay can receive additions beyond the leatherhard stage until bone dry. Soak any dry surfaces with water first before applying further clay using the slurry and scoring technique (see using slurry for joining slabs).

RIDGED POT (25 CM/10 IN)
PINCHED FORM IN PORCELAIN AND STONEWARE WITH
POWDERED MOLOCHITE MIX AND INLAID T-MATERIAL STARS.
STAINED BODY CLAY WITH BLACK IRON OXIDE, MANGANESE
OXIDE. RAKU FIRED AND REDUCED (JANE WALLER).
PHOTOGRAPH BY CRISPIN THOMAS.

# TECHNIQUES
## COILING
This fast, practical and versatile method can be used to construct complicated or simple forms. It permits a freedom to create large, imaginative, unrestricted forms that are built up in a series of stages and can be used in conjuction with any other techniques of forming clay. It is important to have a clear idea of the finished shape before you start to coil so that the size and shape of the base or beginning fits the scale and direction of the planned piece.

Everyone has their own particular style of making and attaching coils. Alternative methods for making coils to the one shown are extrusion (see extrusion) or cutting flattened strips or irregular shapes of flat clay from a rolled slab (see slab building). Some makers prefer to show the workings of the technique and not to pare away the pinch marks or join seams.

The wall can be made to look taut or flabby, chunky or thin, smooth or dimpled. There are no set rules, except that the coils or flattened pieces should be consistent along their entire length and that the coils are soft enough to join without having to apply unnecessary pressure, which could distort a soft supporting wall.

### Making coils

**1** Start by squeezing out a length of prepared plastic clay.

**2** Give yourself plenty of room on the working surface so the coil can be fully rolled while using your fingers to apply pressure where the coil is thick. You can make coils in bulk and store them in polythene (plastic) or roll them out as you progress with the work.

ADDING COILS TO THE FULL-BELLIED COILED POT (SEE PROJECT).

FULL-BELLIED COILED POT IN PROGRESS. COILS ARE PINCHED AS THEY ARE BUILT UP PRODUCING A DELICATE POT WALL (SARAH SCAMPTON).

## Building a wall

A coiled wall can start from a point or from the top edge of a flat or curved base, and it can be joined to an existing piece of leatherhard work made by an alternative method (see using slurry for joining slabs). The important thing to remember is that what you are coiling onto must be able to support the weight and pressure required to join the next coil. If the wall is soft and unable to support the applied weight, allow it to firm to leatherhard before carrying on. A little patience here will pay off as this will prevent the form from sagging, cracking or collapsing. Making changes of direction includes allowing the piece to firm at particular points before continuing to work.

If a wall is straight and vertical, you should place and join coils directly on top of each other. To direct a wall outwards, place and join the coils to the outer edge of the coil below. Conversely, to direct a wall inwards, place and join coils to the inner edge of the coil below.

When joining circuits of coils to build up a wall, it is helpful to turn the work on a banding wheel (see handbuilding equipment). Slurrying and scoring is unnecessary when joining soft plastic coils, unless you are joining the first coil to a base or continuing to coil a piece that has become leatherhard.

**1** When attaching the first coil, either to a flat or curved base made of plastic or leatherhard clay, you must first apply slurry and score the area using a pointed tool, such as a knife tip. This roughens the surface so that the applied coil will make a firm bond with the clay below. It is a good idea to slurry and score along the attaching edge of the first coil as well. Roughening both surfaces will knot the coil and clay surface together.

**2** Give the coil a slight wiggle and apply pressure as you lay it into place before tearing or cutting it to the correct length to encircle the shape.

**3** To join coils, smear down clay from the upper coil onto the base or coil below it, covering the seam line completely. Do this around the entire circumference both along the inner and the outer face of the wall. If you want the seams to show on the outer face of the wall, join from the inside wall only. As the coil is smeared onto the clay below, support the wall with your other hand so the pressure does not move the wall out of alignment. As long as the rhythmical joining strokes are consistent and evenly pressured the wall will remain under control as it begins to grow. Join the coils thoroughly: if the joins are weak the work is likely to crack on drying and firing.

**4** To even and reinforce a join while the clay is still plastic, use the curved edge of a serrated kidney on the inside of a curve.

**5** On all other areas use the toothed edge of a hacksaw blade. Alter the direction and angle of the tool to come into or over a curve of a wall without leaving flat ridges. Use sweeping motions with the tools to strengthen the coil joins and thin the wall, crossing the previous strokes diagonally.

## Heightening the wall

Pinch or pull up the wall evenly along its length to thin it out and add height. To make a paper-thin wall it is easier and quicker to add as thick a coil as you can and to continue to pinch it as far as the clay will allow. Individual makers develop their own methods of doing this.

## Making a wall smooth and even

After the piece has been left to to become leatherhard, pare and smooth down the walls again with greater pressure on the tools. When working on an enclosed form that is narrower than the width of your hand, smooth and finalize the internal walls after each coil circumference so you can avoid going back to the inside of a narrow shape. Inside such a shape it would be awkward, and sometimes impossible, to manoeuvre tools.

## Checking the shape

Every time you add a coil, check the shape and direction of the work. Closely inspect the entire "side-on" profile of the piece while turning it on a banding wheel, making sure it is exactly as required. Next, get a bird's eye view of the the top profile and check this as well. If the shape has gone askew, you can recover it by the following.

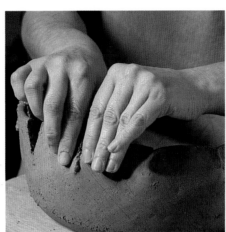

You can alter a bulge or an uneven profile by making cuts or tucks. The cuts can be slurried and scored on both meeting edges to join them back together or, if the clay is still soft and thick enough, the cuts can be smeared back together. An additional small piece of soft clay, slurried and scored over the join, will give added reinforcement and can be pared down once the join has firmed.

To bring the shape out on an edge, pinch the coil to lengthen it. A wall shape or slight depression that is still plastic can be eased out by stroking with your fingertips.

BAD ART BAD POTTERY
(60 CM/24 IN)
COILED EARTHENWARE, MARBLED
AND STENCILLED SLIP WITH INLAID
TEXT, SGRAFFITO DRAWING AND
PHOTO SILK SCREEN ENAMEL
TRANSFERS AND GOLD LUSTRE
(GRAYSON PERRY).

### Finishing rims and edges

Once you have finished building up the shape of the form, then attention can be given to finishing off the edges of the piece cleanly and neatly.

TWISTING POT (30 CM/12 IN)
HANDBUILT STONEWARE, PINCHED FLATTENED COILS ADDED TO
A PINCHED BASE, WITH NO SURFACE ALTERATION. THREE LAYERS
OF GLAZES ARE USED – HIGH MAGNESIUM GLAZE, COBALT
CARBONATE AND VANADIUM PENTOXIDE/IRON OXIDE MIXTURE
WITH A TOP COAT OF HIGH BARIUM AND SILICON CARBIDE
(JULIAN KING-SALTER).

Use a surform blade on leatherhard work to level a rim or a top edge. You can also use a surform blade or knife tip to maintain a level working edge as the work progresses. Make sure your eyes are level with the edge to be cut. You may find it easier to measure and score a line first.

To create an even rim or top edge, pare down the top edge until the width is the same along its entire length. Bring the edge to a uniform thickness before shaping the edge or rim with a hacksaw blade. Apply pressure with the blade wherever the section is thickest while looking down onto the edge. Finish the edge or rim by removing any unwanted tool marks with a damp sponge.

### Working in stages

In most cases, it is usual to work on a coiled piece over a number of sittings, interspersed with waiting time while the work becomes firm enough to carry on. A paint stripper gun (see handbuilding equipment) is a useful piece of equipment to speed up the drying. If you decide to use one of these, keep it on the move to prevent any areas of clay becoming too dry. If the clay goes beyond the leatherhard stage and gains the characteristic pale colour of dry clay, the piece is ruined; the coils will not join and the walls will be hard and too brittle to work. To continue a piece over any number of working sessions, wrap it in plastic to keep it airtight and damp.

### Coiling fibre clay

The only time that there is no need to keep a piece in a leatherhard state is when working with fibre clay, which can still be worked when bone dry. Coils of plastic clay can be added to dry clay by first wetting the attachment area then slurrying and scoring in the usual way. Fibre clay can also be carved and cut at the bone-dry stage.

# TECHNIQUES
# SLAB BUILDING

There are two areas of slab building: leatherhard and soft slabbing, although, technically speaking, there will be times when you will need slabs of a certain flaccidity that fall somewhere between the two. Leatherhard slabs are required for work that has straight edges and planes and are worked with a precision and order similar to cutting and joining cardboard or wood. Soft slabbing is a more spontaneous and immediate method of working with slabs, suited to fluid, curved, folded or swollen forms. A slab that falls between the two will stand upright, but can still be curved.

■ Use prepared clay (see preparing clay) that is soft enough to move freely, but is not wet or sticky, when making leatherhard or soft clay slabs. Before rolling out prepared plastic clay work out the size and quantity you need. It is always a good idea to make a few extra slabs just in case.

Finer bodied clays have a tendency to warp when drying and firing so clays that are open (grogged, sandy or fibre clays) are more suitable for large, flat, planed slab work. The reduced shrinkage of an open clay also causes fewer problems with weak joins and lessens the risk of work pulling apart at the seams.

### Rolling fibre clay

Fibrous clay is particularly suitable for slab building as although it still shrinks on drying, any stress cracks can be repaired when the clay is bone dry.

### Rolling large quantities

For rolling out large quantities of slabs, use a slab roller (see handbuilding equipment). This is appropriate for large, architectural work, sculptural work or for preparing slabs for repeat production purposes.

## Rolling slabs

Work on a wooden board, a cloth or a sheet of plastic. If you do use either of the latter two, make sure there are no creases as these will imprint on your finished slab causing weakened fault lines.

Slabs can be rolled with or without the use of slats or guides. Without slats you can feel the distributed weight of a slab by picking it up and checking that its section is even throughout. Resting a rolling pin on slats can restrict the slab size by the length of the rolling pin. If you decide to use slats, choose a pair that are thick enough for the scale and feel of the piece you are making. When you are preparing to work with leatherhard slabs roll them out larger than they need to be. This is because a certain amount of "dry edge" surface will always be wasted because the edges tend to dry before the centre.

**1** Stand up to roll out a piece of clay to get your body weight behind the rolling pin. Press the clay out, pushing with the heel of your hand spreading the clay as far as it will go. Do this evenly over its entire surface.

**2** If you are using slats, rest the rolling pin ends on the slats and roll from the centre outwards. Push harder on the rolling pin where the clay is highest and continue until the clay will not spread any further. Lift the clay at its edges to put a pocket of air under the clay so it will free up and move again. Repeat the process, crossing previous rolls diagonally until you have an evenly rolled slab to the thickness required.

CURVED VASE (28 CM/11 IN)
RED EARTHENWARE CLAY, BUILT WITH
LEATHERHARD SLABS, DECORATED WITH
SLIPS AND SAWDUST FIRED. THE VASE IS
GLAZED INTERNALLY AND IS THEREFORE
NON-POROUS (TESSA WOLFE-MURRAY).

## Harp-cutting slabs

Instead of rolling out slabs, you can slice them out of a solid mass of prepared clay using a harp cutter (U-shaped rod).

## Making fibre-clay slabs

When using fibre clay, you can spread the slop on to make sheets or slabs in preparation for printing, decorating and slab building.

If you are planning to print texture into a slab (with or without fibre clay), do so while the slab is soft and flat on a work surface.

■ Make sure the block of prepared clay is sitting on a flat surface large enough to site the ends of the harp level with the bottom face of the block. Draw the wire of the harp through the block from top to bottom, one slab at a time. After each cut, move the rings of the harp wire down a notch to cut the next slab.

**1** Deposit the clay between the two roller guides and begin to scree the slop with a straight edge.

**2** Continue until the surface of the slop is completely smooth.

**3** When the slab is firm enough to peel away from the plaster, lift it away for immediate use or wrap it in plastic for later use.

The advantage of using fibre clay slabs is that they are particularly strong when working with thin structures. They are also flexible to bend and mend easily if broken or cracked (see fibrous and paper clay).

## Bringing flat slabs to leatherhard

All rolled or harp cut slabs will curl at the edges unless they are dried slowly and weighted with flat boards. Place one or two sheets of newspaper on the top and bottom faces of each slab to prevent them sticking to the board. The newspaper will also absorb moisture from the slabs and help bring them to the required firmness. If you do not have enough boards, interface the slabs with newspaper and stack them two to three high and weight them down. Put any larger slabs under smaller ones so they all remain flat. Slabs and boards can be interspersed in a stack. Check the slabs periodically to make sure they are not getting too dry. As soon as they can stand on their edge like cardboard without buckling, they are ready. Leatherhard slabs should be made at least a day in advance to allow them to firm up sufficiently.

It is vital to keep slabs at this leatherhard stage until your joining work is complete, so remove the boards and cover the entire stack with plastic to keep it airtight and prevent further drying. Weight the stack with a board at the top and leave it overnight so that it evens out to a consistent firmness.

TWO LIPPED VASES
(21 CM/8¼ IN AND 31 CM/12 IN)
WHITE EARTHENWARE LEATHERHARD SLABS ARE ROLLED OUT BY HAND, CUT OUT, SCORED AND JOINED. THE PIECES ARE DECORATED WITH COLOURED SLIPS USING SGRAFFITO AND RESIST TECHNIQUES. FINALLY THE PIECES ARE BURNISHED, BISCUIT (BISQUE) FIRED, GLAZED INSIDE AND FIRED AGAIN (LIZ BECKENHAM).

## Soft slabbing

Unlike leatherhard slabs, soft slabs should be made as you need them. The degree of flaccidity required will depend on the slab's height, its plasticity, extremity of curve and the angle at which it is to be placed. The only way to gauge the correct flaccidity of a soft slab is through trial and error.

To keep soft slab work alive and fresh it is best to approach it with the minimum amount of handling possible. The more you touch the slabs, the more tired their appearance will become. Wait until the work has firmed up and become leatherhard before you do any cleaning or trimming. Likewise, to retain the tautness to a piece, any further alterations should be made when the work is able to support the pressure and weight of more clay. This rule also applies when treating the final stages of the top edge or rim of a piece.

When soft slabs are very wet they can be pressed together with little more than a damp sponge or by pinching or pressing an overlap. The resulting seams can be left untouched to show the workings of the joining process. Edges and planes can be treated in many ways – squeezed and pinched, pushed and eased, manipulated and bellied, cut and pierced, gouged and rolled or dropped from a height to take on the feel of billowing fabric.

'FROM A DREAM', USING LEATHERHARD SLABS (KARI CHRISTENSEN).

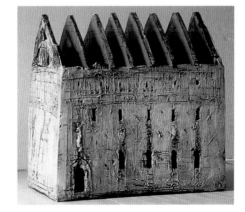

## Using soft slabs

Soft slabs can be wrapped around straight sided formers, such as cardboard tubes or shaped blocks of wood. This is a fast method suitable for making cylinders or other shapes that can be distorted to other shapes, such as ovals or squares, before attaching them to a base or leaving them to become firm. Once leatherhard, you can also use the formed shapes as components and you can make further additions.

**1** Cover the former tightly with a sheet of newspaper and secure it with sticky tape. Wrap the slab around the former. To make a chamfered join, place the edge of the slab to be cut so it overhangs the bench edge. Hold a knife tip at an angle and run it through the overlapping slab. Remove the excess piece before preparing the edges for joining.

**2** Join the wrapped shape to its base while it is still on its former, but remove the former before the clay firms and shrinks onto it. The newspaper around the former will help it slide out of the shape without sticking to the soft clay. Finally, cut away the excess clay of the base and pare and clean the shape. Final cleaning up to the piece can be done at the leatherhard stage.

STANDING FORM (39 CM/15½ IN) USING SLABS BETWEEN SOFT AND LEATHERHARD, THE SLABS STAND ALONE, BUT WILL ALSO CURVE (ALISON BRITTON). PHOTOGRAPH BY DAVID CRIPPS.

## Using slurry for joining slabs

This technique is used for all types of slab building and for any joining process with clay – it is used when joining soft clay to leatherhard, leatherhard to leatherhard, and soft or leatherhard slabs to bone dry fibrous clay. Ensure that you are familiar with this process before embarking on any of the projects or starting any work in clay.

Start the joining process by making the slurry, which must match the clay you are using. Cover small, bone dry pieces of clay with water. Allow the clay to dissolve before stirring to a consistency between single (light) and double (heavy) cream. Make an ample supply of slurry and store it in an airtight container.

Apply the slurry to the faces of each piece to be joined using a stiff brush or toothbrush. Next, thoroughly score the slurried faces using the tip of a pointed knife. Push the two pieces together giving them a slight wiggle as you do so until the scored surfaces knot together.

Remove any excess slurry emerging from the join using a damp sponge, tool or kidney before it dries. No matter how small the pieces are, clay must be joined using this method to make an effective bond that will not pull apart during drying and firing. Let the work become firm before giving the slurried seams a final trim and cleaning them up. This will give a cleaner finish to the work.

### Joining fibre clay

When attaching a slab to bone dry fibrous clay, the fibrous clay face should be soaked with water before slurrying and scoring (see above).

### Cutting out

Trim the slab to size and get rid of any dry edges to ensure the work will join firmly and will not pull apart when drying. Allow extra length for an overlap if butt joining (see above), which can be trimmed and cleaned up later. This gives a cleaner finish to flat work. Before making a final cut to a slab to be joined, check its fit by holding where it is to be placed. Mark where the cuts should be with the tip of a knife.

**1** When making a butted join allow an extra length for an overlap which can be trimmed and cleaned up at the leatherhard stage.

**2** Trim and straighten a butted join or corner once leatherhard by running a metal kidney along a metal ruler, slightly inset to the edge.

**3** When joining slabs end to end follow the same process, apply slurry, score the edge faces and push them to knot together.

**4** Slabs can also be overlapped when joined. When joining slabs to a flat base, stand the walls on the top of the base, rather than on its sides. This will pull the walls in and prevent the work pulling apart at the seams.

- When joining clay slabs or other forms, the internal face can be reinforced by applying a soft coil of clay along the internal corner and smoothing it back with a tool. If the join is thorough, this added labour is not always necessary.

- To trim the base edge of the joined slabs when the piece is leatherhard, drag the work to overhang the surface on which it is sitting to get a clear line of attack with the hacksaw blade, kidney or any other tools.

**5** Making a chamfered cut to a slab will allow it to sit at an angle. The degree of the chamfer will dictate the slant of the wall.

# TECHNIQUES
# EXTRUSION The principle of extruding clay extends from the idea of a wad box (extruder) that is used for making wads, or snakes, of clay for setting saggars. The extruded strips of clay can be varied in profile by using interchangeable dies that fit into the wad box (see handbuilding equipment).

■ Wad boxes or extruders can be used for making strips in various shapes and sizes suitable for coiling. Narrow sheets can be produced for slab building, which combined with an open clay will not warp and can be cut to form tiles or test pieces for glaze tests (see Glaze and Decoration, simple testing and line blending). You can also use it to make handles for repeat pieces or domestic ware (see Throwing, extruding handles). Dies can be cut to suit the scale or design of the piece.

Soft strips can be altered, curved and waved, and then left to firm before fixing into place. The extruded clay lengths can be given a fluid or rigid feel as required. Left to become leatherhard they can be cut cleanly without leaving finger marks. Straight, long extruded strips should be turned frequently while drying as they are prone to curling and warping. Hollow extrusions can be used as components of an assembled piece or to form containers by attachment to a base.

## Joining
Use the usual slurry and score method to join extruded strips of clay or hollow shapes at the leatherhard stage (see using slurry for joining slabs). Joins to cut sections or components can be filled with soft clay once the work has firmed to leatherhard to clean up any gaps. Wipe away marks or excess joining slurry with a damp sponge.

## Preparing clay for extrusion

An extruder or wad box is used to extrude clay strips by forcing them through a die (see examples of dies shown in handbuilding equipment). Make a rolled, flat-ended sausage to fit inside the collar of the extruder. The clay should be soft enough to push through the extruder with ease.

## Extruding shapes

Hollow sections of any shape can be extruded using a die with a fixed inner plate. Their thickness is dependent on the space between the inner and outer plates of the die. Cut into pieces, the extruded shapes can be treated as components to be joined when leatherhard or to make complicated or simple, functional or sculptural structures.

If you don't have access to a wad box, you can use a hooped wire (trimming) tool or shaped hoop of wire. Pull the hooped tool through a prepared, soft block of clay and ease the clay apart to remove the clay strip (see also Throwing, extruding handles).

A clay gun is a useful alternative for making smaller decorative extrusions that can be applied to work as raised relief. Soft extrusions will join to plastic clay with slurry alone and a little pressure applied with a damp sponge. Allow the work to dry slowly to prevent extruded pieces falling away from the surface.

Small coils made with a clay gun can be arranged as a "drawn" line and attached or rolled into a slab of clay while both are soft. Use compatible clays that have a close shrinkage rate.

St Bride's Tower (60 cm/24 in)
Slab built and decorated with extruded coils that are then indented with a modelling tool at regular intervals to create a convoluted edge (Rachel Kneebone).

# TECHNIQUES
# CLAY RELIEF
Small, soft pieces of clay can be built up in stages onto firmed previous applications of clay until the required height or shape is achieved. Modelled clay can be integrated or joined on to clay formed by any of the handbuilding techniques using the score and slurry technique wherever the surface is leatherhard. When joining soft clay to soft, however, a gentle pressure to smear on the clay is usually sufficient. Leave any final carving of the modelled clay until the built-up clay is leatherhard to achieve a crisp finish.

■ Clay bas-relief that is thicker than 2 cm (¾ in) must be hollowed out from the back to reduce the thickness of the wall for drying and firing. This enables water in the clay to escape as the work is heated in the kiln and prevent it from exploding with the pressure of evaporating water or steam. Thick forms should be fired slowly in the initial stages until the kiln has reached red heat or 600°C (1112°F).

## Modelling

All solid, modelled forms should be scooped out from the inside and emptied. Use a hooped wire trimming tool and leave a wall thick enough to support the modelled clay outer structure. Solid figures can be cut with a knife, hollowed and rejoined by slurrying and scoring (see using slurry for joining slabs) while they are still leatherhard. This allows access to a solid area that cannot be reached from a base opening, such as for a head or the upper body sections of a figure.

When hollowing out a thick wall, use a hooped wire (trimming) tool to scoop out a little at a time when the work is firm enough to hold and turn without damage. Rest the overturned work on a pad or sponge to protect the front face.

## Applying bas-relief

Small pieces of clay can be built up following the usual rules of joining to leatherhard clay (see using slurry for joining slabs). Soft clay can be joined to soft with applied pressure using fingers or tools. Modelled surfaces built up in this way can be applied to any angle or area of clay made by any forming method, as long as there is sufficient strength to support the weight of the applied clay and the pressure of the tools.

COCKEREL TUREEN WITH TAIL FEATHER LADLE (35 CM/14 IN) WHITE EARTHENWARE AND C-MATERIAL, COILED, SCRAPED AND MODELLED WITH BASE COILED ONTO A CURVED SLAB. ALL DETAILS HAVE BEEN MODELLED BY BUILDING UP SMALL PIECES OF CLAY (ANNA LAMBERT).

# TECHNIQUES
## DECORATING INTO CLAY

Clay is a wonderful material for picking up texture and can be treated in a number of ways to achieve a range of textural qualities and surfaces. There are many techniques to create raised and applied texture or to decorate into clay. When working into clay, the wall or slab must be thick enough to manage the depth of the imprint or tool. Separately worked pieces of clay can be fixed onto a surface with the slurry and score method (see using slurry for joining slabs).

### Indenting

Indenting techniques involve making a mark into clay with a tool, such as a stamp, roulette or carving tool. These raised clay surfaces look effective with colour washes which pick out the raised textures, glazes that break at high points or coloured transparent glazes that collect in the indented areas making rich tones.

Detailed textures can be picked up on soft clay, which is laid flat, or by impressing stamps into built or thrown walls still soft enough to imprint. You can also attach individual pieces of stamped clay to a wall.

   Stamps can be made by carving plaster (see making moulds or models) or clay, which is fired before use. Roulettes can be carved in plaster, clay and wood or improvised using items such as cogs or bottle tops. Unlike stamps, they make a continuous, patterned circuit, which can be applied quickly to a soft piece of work. Strips of rouletted clay can also be cut and attached to a piece of work.

Clay can be carved in the same way as wood, using any tool that gives the required effect. For a crisp, hard edge carve clay when it is leatherhard. The softer the clay, the softer the finish will be. The tool you use and the state of the clay will dictate the quality of the carved edge. Carve into a thick-walled flat surface or a raised relief area to produce a sharp-edged sculpted feel.

Pieces of foam sheet, card (cardboard) or plastic sheet can be cut and rolled into soft clay to give a variety of edges and depths to the impressed shape. This is a useful technique for impressing letters or numbers into clay. You can also cut out shapes when they are firm and apply them to a formed clay surface.

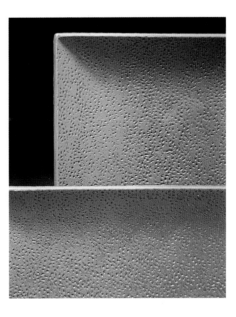

TRAYS
SLAB BUILT WITH IMPRESSED
TEXTURE, HIGH FIRED STONEWARE
WITH THIN SHINO GLAZE (TAVS
JORGENSEN).

## Inlaying

When indented areas or lines of clay are filled with a contrasting coloured clay or thick slip, this is known as inlaying. The inlaid clay or slip is scraped back level with the surrounding clay once it is leatherhard.

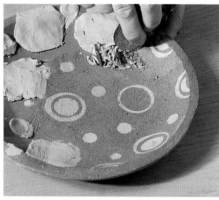

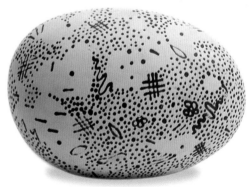

EGG (18 CM/7 IN)
SLIP CAST FORM, INLAID
AND COLOURED (JANE WALLER).

**1** Allow the surface to be inlaid to become leatherhard. Indented areas can be inlaid with a contrasting soft clay or a thick, yogurt consistency slip applied with a brush. Fill the inlay so it is proud of the height of the impressed areas for both methods if you require a final level surface. If using clay slip, build it up in successive layers after each has first become dry to the touch. If using a contrasting coloured clay, select one with a similar shrinkage rate to the main clay.

**2** Ensure the clay is at the dry end of the scale of leatherhard to prevent any contrasting colours in the inlay from blurring. For a clean, level finish scrape back the inlaid clay or slip using the edge of a metal kidney until it is level with its surrounding surface. Allow the work to dry slowly to prevent the inlaid clay from cracking.

## Sprigging

Sprigs are made by pushing soft clay into a plaster mould (see Lady Daisy Jug project), then levelling with a wire harp or plastic card.

**1** The dry, plaster mould absorbs moisture and makes the sprigs shrink so they come out of the mould easily. Remove the sprigs with a needle, by tapping them out or lifting them out with a piece of soft clay.

**2** Slurry the sprig's attaching face while supporting it in your other hand with a piece of clay before joining it to the surface you are decorating. Thicker sprigs should be slurried and scored, as should the attaching surface. Use an appropriate tool to clarify any details and remove excess slurry. Work should be dried slowly, particularly if you have used fine sprigs that could not be scored before attachment.

EARTHENWARE VESSEL (10 CM/4 IN)
SPRIGGED DECORATION, THICK, HIGH SHRINKAGE SLIPS
APPLIED AND IRON AND CHROME GLAZED IN AN
OXIDIZING ATMOSPHERE (ASHLEY HOWARD).

## Fluting and faceting

The technique of fluting involves cutting a series of parallel, concave grooves into clay using a round-ended tool. This traditionally wheel-based technique gives a controlled, carved, gouged pattern to a clay wall. Faceting, on the other hand, involves making regularly spaced and sized flat cuts to a clay wall using a straight-edged tool, such as a cutting harp (U-shaped rod) or knife. This technique results in a carved or chiselled pattern. These methods are particularly dramatic when combined with glazes that break at the high points of the cuts, such as a black tenmoku glaze that breaks to orange or tan. This method can also be used in a less rigid manner to create fluid or assymmetrical forms.

To cut flutes into a clay wall, measure and mark out the point at which the cut starts and ends to ensure the circuit will meet. If you require a clean, hard edge, ensure the clay wall is leatherhard. Fluting appears to be a simple technique, but it requires a trained hand and eye to cut each flute evenly to the right depth and alignment. Flutes can be cut at any angle running parallel or at an angle, as shown here.

Faceting, like fluting, involves marking out where each cut will run from and to, as well as the width of each cut. The fewer cuts made around the piece, the thicker the wall needs to be. For clean, hard-edged cuts, and to avoid a thin wall collapsing, facet the wall when it is leatherhard.

BOTTLES AND LIDDED FORMS(20–35 CM/8–14 IN) KEUPER RED STONEWARE CLAY (OCHRE), AND EARTHENWARE CLAY (PURPLE). BOTTLES ARE THROWN AND FLUTED (EMILY MYERS).

## Piercing

This technique can be used to cut, pierce or prick a formal, complicated or loose pattern of holes into a clay wall. The holes can be made into leatherhard clay for a clean effect; loose, free piercing into soft clay will add movement to a wall.

Plan and mark complicated, lattice style piercing before cutting and wait until the clay is leatherhard for clean cuts.

## Wiping back, scraping and compressing

To alter the finished surface of plastic or leatherhard clay, the top layer can be roughened or smoothed by wiping back, scraping or compressing. These techniques can be used and combined to build up decorative surfaces. They can either be applied to a clay slab before it is formed, or to a form that has already been thrown, moulded, or handbuilt.

**1** Prepare the slab or form your piece.

**2** Place a piece of newspaper or paint wax resist in the shape of your chosen decoration on the surface of the clay. Allow any wax resist to dry.

**3** Sponge clay away from areas around the resist. The resist will leave a raised area of clay with a soft edge.

Scraping with a metal kidney or sponging with a damp sponge on open or sandy clay will drag or reveal sand on the surface giving a rough texture. Conversely, smoothing pressure with the edge of a metal or plastic kidney will compress the clay to give a smooth texture. You can use surface scraping, smoothing and wiping back to make contrasting textures of clay – the result will be affected by the nature of the clay you have used.

## Burnishing

A smooth object, such as the back of a spoon or a smooth pebble, can be used to burnish the surface of leatherhard clay. Most clays are suitable for burnishing, although finer clay gives a smoother surface. A greater shine will be achieved when the clay surface is on the firm side of leatherhard. Clay painted with decorating slips can also be burnished. Terra sigillata, a fine particled, siliceous slip, gives an extremely smooth burnished finish.

Move the burnishing tool in circular or linear strokes. Once dry, fire the burnished piece at 950–1080°C (1742–1976°F) to retain the shine. Finally apply the burnished areas with a clear wax or neutral shoe polish to enhance the colour and seal the surface.

## Combining coloured clays (millefiori)

The random or controlled combining of coloured clays is known as millefiori. The name derives from a Roman glass making technique using brightly coloured discs of glass, fused together to make a sheet.

The white clays here were stained by kneading in colour additions (see preparing clay) and then rolled together in layers. Strips of coloured clay have also been sandwiched in layers that have been sliced while the clay was still plastic.

Place the coloured pieces together in a hollow plaster mould while still soft and cover them with thin plastic. Pound them together using a pestle. Leave the work to become leatherhard, close to dry, and then scrape the surface with a metal kidney to give a smooth finish.

Different coloured clays with closely matched shrinkage rates can also be combined. Such work must be dried slowly by wrapping loosely in plastic to extend the drying time. This prevents the coloured areas separating, appearing as cracks on seams between adjacent colours. Work should be covered with a glaze that will react with or reveal the coloured clays on firing.

## Marbling or agate work

Contrasting clays used for marbled or agate work are loosely combined at the clay preparation stage (see preparing clay). The combined clays should have the same or similar shrinkage rates.

To obtain a dramatic marbled effect the proportion of lighter clay should exceed that of the darker clay. Agate is a stone that displays multicoloured layers when sliced, hence the term agateware.

Combined clays can be used for thrown work or used with any handbuilding technique. Thrown agateware is turned at the leatherhard stage to reveal clean areas of coloured clay; all other methods of forming are scraped back at the firm to dry leatherhard stage. Work made using marbled clays should be covered with a glaze suitable for reacting with the coloured clays on firing, or a transparent glaze to reveal them.

## Using Egyptian paste

This is essentially a clay body that has the glaze ingredients contained within the clay, Egyptian paste lacks plasticity and is difficult to handle. It is therefore best worked by moulding, carving and piercing; the glaze colour will reveal itself when the clay is fired.

It is important to ensure that glaze never comes into contact with kiln furniture as it will stick fast. Because anything made from Egyptian paste cannot be placed directly on a kiln shelf, they need to be suspended. Beads, for example, should be fired on Nichrome wire racks.

### Shiny Egyptian paste recipe

It is not easy to buy Egyptian paste ready made, so you will need to have a reliable recipe to follow. Here is one of the many tried and tested ones. You will also need weighing scales, a face mask (respirator), protective gloves and an old washing-up bowl. Use cone orton 06–04 (see Kilns and Firing, firing times and temperatures).

### Ingredients

BASE
800 g (1 lb 12 oz) Potash feldspar
400 g (14 oz) Flint
500 g (17½ oz) China clay
100 g (3½ oz) Ball clay
120 g (4¼ oz) Sodium bicarbonate
120 g (4¼ oz) Soda ash
100 g (3½ oz) Whiting
160 g (5⅗ oz) Fine white sand

COLOUR ADDITIONS
For a green paste:
  3% chrome
For a turquoise paste:
  3% black copper oxide
For a blue paste:
  1–3% cobalt carbonate
For a black paste:
  3% manganese dioxide
For a brown paste:
  3% red iron oxide

### Method

**1** For the base mixture weigh each dry ingredient and place them in the bowl.

**2** Add a little water at a time until there is enough to make a doughy mixture similar to the consistency of plastic clay.

**3** Remove the base mixture and knead it on a flat surface until all the ingredients are thoroughly combined.

**4** Add the required percentage of colour addition to the dry ingredients in the bowl or knead it into the base.

AZTEC BOWL (12 CM/4½ IN)
WHITE EARTHENWARE CLAY STAINED WITH NATURAL OXIDES AND BLACK BODY STAIN. EACH SHAPE IS BEATEN INTO A SPECIALLY MADE PLANTER MOULD AND THE PIECES ARE PESTLED TOGETHER. THE MILLEFIORI PATTERNING IS SCRAPED CLEAR AFTER THE PIECE HAS DRIED TO LEATHERHARD (JANE WALLER).

**Materials**
White St Thomas clay

**Equipment**
Box of junk
Sketchbook
Pencil and colour pens
Potter's knife
Toothbrush
Sponge
Rolling pin
Wooden tool
Narrow pointed tool
Paintbrushes
Electric kiln
Raku kiln
Gas bottle (propane tank)
Thick leather gloves
Protective goggles
Purpose-made tongs
Metal bucket
Sawdust
Wire wool (for cleaning off
    burnt sawdust)

**Glaze**
Commercially prepared
    brush-on glazes

**Firing**
Biscuit (bisque) fire to 1080°C
    (1976°F)
    60°C (140°F)
    300°C (572°F)
    120°C (248°F)
    1080°C (1976°F)
Glaze fire to 990–1040°C
    (1814–1904°F)

# Raku Bug

In this project Jola Spytkowska has assembled a selection of nails, screws, a hinge and other items from her junk box to make a creature that resembles an insect. Through drawing she has explored and modified the shapes. Once the idea had developed it became clear that pinching and coiling were the ideal techniques to form the piece.

**1** Design your creature. Outline your drawing in black ink and then colour it. The drawing will enable you to decide what you need to make and how to make it. Do this by looking at its separate parts.

**2** Make the body by pinching out two lemon-shaped, shallow forms of equal size. When these have become leatherhard, score up the edges, add slurry (see using slurry for joining) and join firmly. Make small air holes.

**3** Prepare the flange that will go around the edge of the body. Roll out a long coil about 5 mm (¼in) thick and very lightly flatten this coil with a rolling pin.

**4** Cut the flattened coil in two. Join the flanges to the edge of the body with slurry, pressing firmly. Cut the edges where the two flanges meet so that they join without a gap.

**5** Prepare the legs. Roll out a long coil and cut into six sections. Curve them. Roll out six small balls of clay for the feet, flatten them a little and then join them onto the legs with slurry. Leave the legs to become leatherhard.

**6** Roll out another coil for the spine. Join it onto the body. Take the edge of a wooden tool and impress it into the spine at regular intervals to imitate the form of a hinge.

**7** Roll out a short coil for the tail, which is narrow and pointed at one end. Curl round the pointed end. When it is leatherhard join the tail to the main body.

**8** Roll out a small coil for the antennae and curve it into a U-shape. Add small balls of clay to the ends and pierce holes through them.

**9** Join the legs to the body when they have become leatherhard. Score and slurry first then press them down firmly and smooth around the joins. Stand the bug upright and adjust the legs so that they touch the surface of the table. Add eight little balls of clay around the flange. Impress them with a narrow pointed tool to imitate screws.

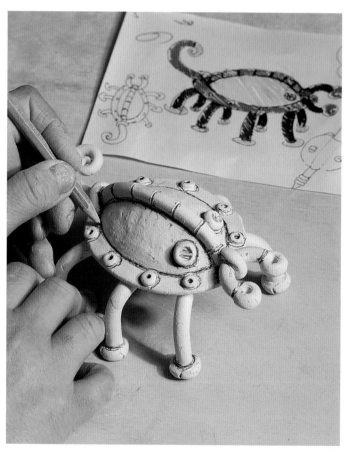

**10** Finish off the bug by adding the eyes. Make two small balls of clay, flatten them slightly, attach to the body and impress them with the head of a screw. Biscuit (bisque) fire to 1080°C (1976°F).

**11** Outline the bug all over with a pencil around the edges. These edges will remain unglazed. The unglazed areas will smoke a charcoal black in the sawdust, to recreate something of the effect of the black ink in your original drawings.

**12** Choose the appropriate colour glazes. Those used in this project fire to a low temperature which makes them suitable for raku. Apply three coats of each colour. When ready, fire the bug in the raku kiln. Remember to wear protective gloves and goggles. When the temperature reaches 1000°C (1832°F) remove the kiln lid and lift out the bug with purpose-made tongs. Place it in a metal bucket full of sawdust and leave it to smoke for about 15 minutes. Remove and cool it before cleaning and scrubbing gently with wire wool.

**Materials**
50% T-material clay (or any grogged white clay)
50% White earthenware (mixed together).

**Equipment**
Paddle
Toothbrush
Sponge
Potter's knife
Wooden modelling tool
Paint stripper gun
Hacksaw blade
Metal kidney
Plastic sheet
Gloves for glazing
Raku kiln
Gas bottle (propane tank)
Thick leather gloves
Protective goggles
Purpose-made tongs
Metal bucket
Sawdust
Wire wool

**Glaze**
WHITE GLAZE
High alkaline frit        95%
SMD ball clay              5%
COLOUR ADDITIONS
Tin oxide                  6%
Bentonite                  1%

**Firing**
Biscuit (bisque) fire to 1000°C (1832°F)
Raku fire to approximately 1000°C (1832°F) or until the glaze looks fluxed

# Balancing Tricks

These figures by Josie Warshaw use pinching, coiling and modelling techniques. Photographs of modelled "balancing tricks" by her young son were used as a reference to develop the forms in clay. You could decide to give a figurative piece a different emphasis by also modelling a head and further body details. The approach used here is particularly effective for capturing the feeling of movement.

**1** Form the lower half of the figure up to waist level by making a pinched cup, using plastic clay. Make tucks in the clay and squeeze them together to narrow the neck of the pinched cup, keeping the edge thick in preparation to take the applied coils at the next stage.

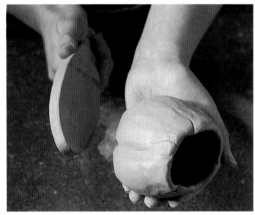

**2** Use a paddle to alter the shape until there is an approximate feel of the contours of the body, which will be refined at the paring stage. Next, tap the base on the flat working surface to tip the cup backwards, giving it a leaning movement. Ease the shape from the inside using your fingertips to belly the shape out. Leave it to become leatherhard.

**3** Remove pieces of V-shaped cuts along the edge to bring in the shape of the body and rejoin with the slurry and score method (see using slurry for joining). Pinch up the top edge to lengthen the shape and to achieve the contour and direction of the body.

**4** Add coils to extend the body and bring the shape in or out where necessary. Because the top working edge is leatherhard, slurry and score it to attach the first coil. Pinch and smear all the subsequent coils into place – use a modelling tool on the internal side of the wall, but use a finger tip to smear down the coils on the external wall.

**5** Join two circles of coils to form the legs, slurrying and scoring them into place. To complete this in one sitting, speed-firm the first coils with a paint stripper gun so that the weight and direction of the subsequent coils are supported.

**6** Apply further coils to extend the legs. Check their shape, angle and proportions as you go along.

**7** Use a small modelling tool with a rounded end to join the internal wall of the leg coils.

**8** Pare the surface of the figure with a hacksaw blade to accentuate the contours and to even the external wall.

**9** Remove the hacksaw blade marks with a metal kidney and further accentuate the contours of the figure.

**10** Build up the feet with small coils and push them together with the small wooden tool. Close in the soles of the feet with a flat piece of clay joined on the external wall. Model the feet with a hacksaw blade and metal kidney. Cover the whole figure in plastic and leave it until it becomes leatherhard. Finally even out the surface and contours with a hacksaw blade and metal kidney, and wipe with a damp sponge. When the work is bone dry biscuit (bisque) fire it to 1000°C (1832°F).

**11** Pour a fairly thick layer of white raku glaze over the biscuit (bisque) fired figure and wipe the resting points clean of any glaze with a damp sponge. Raku fire the figure to around 1000°C (1832°F), or until the glaze looks melted. Remove it from the kiln with tongs while it is still red and reduce it in sawdust where it will smoulder until it is cool. Remove the loose carbon left on the surface from the sawdust reduction with wire wool.

# Full-Bellied Coiled Pot

This pot by Sarah Scampton uses a simple coiling technique, ideal for creating shapes that form themselves with a minimum of interference. With its seamless, continuous rhythm, coiling allows the form to simply emerge and you need to use no tools except for your hands.

## Materials

Clay C-material or T-material
Earthenware (can make up to
    ⅓ of mix)

## Equipment

Round kiln shelf or bat
Banding wheel
Sponge
Paint stripper gun
Potter's knife
Small brush
Clay props
Wooden modelling tool
Paddle
Gloves for glazing
Brushes for glazes
Electric kiln

## Glaze

BASIC SLIP – GORDON BALDWINS
500 g (18 oz) Black ball clay
500 g (18 oz) China clay
200 g (7 oz) Borax frit
Oxides and underglaze
    colours
Multiple layers are painted on
by brush until the required
depth is achieved.

## Firing

Biscuit (bisque) fire to 1000°C
    (1832°F)
Glaze fire to between
    1120–1180°C
    (2048–2156°F)

**1** Place your round kiln shelf or bat on the banding wheel. Wet the area around the outside edge of a round kiln shelf or bat. Apply a thin coil, squeezing it onto the shelf so that it sticks.

**2** Make sure the clay is soft enough to add to the next layer without too much pressure and no water. Continue to add coils on the inside of the edge so that the diameter gets smaller and smaller until you have six or more layers.

**3** Use the edge of your index finger to stroke the inside to keep the shape full while you support the outside with the whole of your other hand. Take a paint stripper gun and gently dry the clay until it is just firm.

**4** Brush the edge of the coil with water then add the next coil. Make sure that the coils are really well joined together as this could become a weak spot in the finished pot.

**5** Think about the emerging shape as you add the coils and decide whether you want to change the inwards angle.

**6** At this point a dome shape appears and the inwards angle becomes much steeper. You should now dry off the clay more often, particularly if it becomes too floppy.

**7** Close off the form to the desired diameter then add more coils to form a rim. Add these almost vertically. Coil the rim higher than you need.

**8** Trim the rim to just below the chosen level, straightening it with a sharp knife, then add the final coil that should fit neatly around in one length. Dry the pot until leatherhard, when it will be ready to turn over.

**9** Turning the pot is a tricky manoeuvre. First slip a knife between the kiln shelf and the first coil, working your way around until the clay is no longer stuck to the shelf. Gently slide the pot towards you, maintaining its shape until one third is beyond the edge of the kiln shelf. Do not let go of the pot! Put one arm inside the pot and spread your fingertips around the inside of the rim. Gently lift the pot off the shelf and turn it over in your arms.

**10** Carefully lower it back onto the kiln shelf on its rim. You may have to use clay props under the rim.

**11** Cut off the first coil of this new uppermost edge. It is usually thicker so when removed, it is easier to join on to the subsequent coils. You are now working inwards towards the base of the pot.

**12** Wet the edge and start coiling. Make sure that the first join between the leatherhard clay and the soft clay is good. Squeeze the clay around the same joint several times.

**13** Continue to work in towards the base, checking the profile of your pot. You can trim off any section at any time and rebuild, but this can put a kink in the natural flow of the developing shape.

**14** As your aperture becomes smaller, it may be necessary to go over the areas again. Continuous pressing between fingers and thumb, pincer-like, creates the texture and strength.

**15** You should have a small hole left in the base. Dry round this area until it is firm, then brush the edge with water.

**16** Make a small pad of clay roughly the size of the hole. Trim it to the shape of the hole and place it over the gap and work in the edges with a wooden tool. You may have to beat the base with a paddle to get it flat.

**17** Dry the base to leatherhard then turn the pot over again, keeping it well supported.

**18** Push some clay props underneath the pot before removing both your hands. Put one hand into the pot and push the inside of the base area against the kiln shelf to make sure it balances. It is often worth biscuit (bisque) firing the pot with the props in place to prevent it slumping. Apply the glazes wearing gloves and glaze fire the pot.

# Coiled Snake

This coiled, inlaid and burnished snake was made by Josie Warshaw in memory of a friend's departure to Australia. The construction technique combines pinching and coiling, starting from a pinched cup and building up the form with coils using the score and slurry method. The snake's shape forms an interesting surface on which to apply a repeat decoration with inlaying and burnishing, giving a finished effect that is reminiscent of an actual snakeskin.

## Materials
Grogged Red Earthenware

## Equipment
Paddle
Potter's knife
Hooped (trimming) tool
Hacksaw blade
Wooden modelling tools
Needle
Toothbrush
Kiln shelf
Small mouse-shaped flexible
    metal kidney
Wooden stick
Paintbrush
Face mask (respirator) and
    gloves
Burnishing tool
Clear wax
Soft cloth
Electric kiln

## Slip
| | |
|---|---|
| SM ball clay | 60% |
| China clay | 40% |
| COLOUR ADDITIONS | |
| Yellow stain | 10% |
| Moss green stain | 10% |
| Black stain | 10% |

## Firing
Biscuit (bisque) fire to 980°C
(1796°F)

**1** Form a pinched cup using plastic clay that is on the firm side of soft to make the head. Narrow the pinched cup considerably at the neck. Paddle the pinched shape while it is still soft to achieve the diamond-shaped head and flattened underside. Leave it to firm enough to handle without distortion, but soft enough to still move the clay. Cut a line to form the open mouth. Carve away the unevenness made by pinching on the internal area of the mouth and carve in contours using a small hooped tool. Leave the head to firm a little more before any further work.

**2** Pare the external surface and shape of the head with a hacksaw blade and then paddle it until it is the shape you require. Use small, soft, flattened coils to form the eyes, one for the eyelid and two for the eye using a wooden modelling tool. Pierce the eyes with a needle to allow excess air to escape as the piece dries. Attach and model the teeth. Use a temporary prop of clay to hold the mouth open while it firms to leatherhard.

**3** Roll plenty of coils before coiling the body so there is not a continual switch between tasks. Attach the first coil of the snake's body to the head by slurrying and scoring. Use your fingers to make the external joins and a small wooden modelling tool to make the interior joins. Make the first part of the coiled body while supporting the piece in your lap. When the body becomes too long and unwieldy, transfer it to a kiln shelf where it can stay until it has been fired. Even, smooth and reinforce all the external coil joins on the external wall with a hacksaw blade as the piece progresses.

**4** Bend the shape upwards while the body is still soft. Prop it with a clay support to create a space under which the curled body will pass. (Leave the prop in place for drying and firing then remove it.) Add coils to extend the outer curve of the acute, sideways and upward bends of the snake.

**5** Pare the body and reinforce the joins on the exterior walls using a hacksaw blade and metal kidney. Bend the body upwards while it is still soft and reinforce the joins on the underbelly of the snake – once it is leatherhard it is not possible to bend the body upwards.

**6** Make the tail end with shorter, tighter coils around a stick. Use joined sections made by the same method. Make the final point of the tail solid and knot it while still soft. Partly shape the surface with a hacksaw blade and metal kidney before joining it to the main body.

**7** Leave the snake to become leatherhard. You can then model and finish off the surface with wooden modelling tools and a small metal kidney. Carve lines into the surface to achieve the texture of snakeskin.

**8** Fill the carved lines with thick, yogurt-consistency, coloured slips in green, black and yellow using a paintbrush. Apply two or three layers. Wait for each layer to become dry to the touch before applying the next.

**9** Allow the inlaid coloured slips to firm then pare them back with the curved edge of the carving tool.

**11** Apply clear wax to the snake once it has been fired, then buff it with a soft cloth to bring it to a shine.

**10** Carefully burnish the top surface of the snake over its entire area. Leave the piece to become bone dry and biscuit (bisque) fire.

## Materials

Camberwell buff
   stoneware clay
Underglaze colours
Cobalt oxide solution

## Equipment

Rolling pin
Canvas
Lace fabric
Newspaper
Plastic sheet
Paintbrush
Sponge
Electric kiln

## Glaze

DORA BILLINGTON SEMI-MATT
Lead sesquisilicate 48%
Whiting 10%
Potash feldspar 26%
China clay 16%

## Firing

Biscuit (bisque) fire to 1140°C
   (2084°F)
Glaze fire to 1080°C (1976°F)

# Crouched Figure

Using handbuilding techniques, Suzanne Lanchbury makes sculptural, figurative pieces. Her work is an unusual combination of fabric textures and clay. She uses rich colours, achieved through the use of underglazes and oxides. The strong surface qualities are inspired by textiles and the freely built, organic form describes the human body.

**1** Roll out the clay with a wooden rolling pin onto dry canvas.

**2** Place the lace fabric on the clay and roll out onto the clay to create a textured surface.

**3** Tear the sheet of clay into pieces and fold them into shapes. Form the clay while it is still quite plastic to make the joining easier.

**4** Join the pieces of clay together by overlapping them and squeezing them together. Smooth the joins on the inside using your fingers. Support the form with scrunched-up newspaper.

**5** Continue to build upwards. Do not build it up too quickly or the piece will collapse. Support the inside with scrunched up newspaper and the outside with clay props.

**6** Wrap the top in plastic to keep it moist, but leave the lower clay to dry out enough to hold the increasing weight as you continue the building process.

**7** When you have finished building, leave it to dry completely before biscuit (bisque) firing to 1140°C (2084°F). Then paint a solution of cobalt oxide over the work.

**8** Make sure that the solution of cobalt oxide stains all the recesses in the texture.

**9** Wipe the oxide solution off the raised areas with a damp sponge.

**10** Paint on the underglaze colours to decorate the piece, especially highlighting the raised areas.

**11** Allow the underglaze colours to dry fully. Then begin to paint the figure with the transparent glaze.

**12** Paint the glaze all over the upper surface of the figure, but leave the underside unglazed. Allow it to dry, then fire it to 1080°C (1976°F).

# MAKING AND USING MOULDS

**MOULDS CAN BE USED IN MANY WAYS** IN CERAMICS – FOR PRODUCING REPEAT FORMS, FOR MAKING COMPONENTS THAT CAN THEN BE ASSEMBLED, FOR CREATING SHAPED BASES OR STARTING POINTS FROM WHICH A PIECE CAN BEGIN, OR FOR APPLYING TEXTURE AND DECORATION. MOULDS RANGE FROM SIMPLE DROP OUT MOULDS TO MORE COMPLEX PIECE MOULDS. READY-MADE MOULDS ARE AVAILABLE TO BUY, BUT THE ADVANTAGE OF MAKING YOUR OWN IS THAT IT IS POSSIBLE TO TAILOR THE MOULD TO YOUR DESIGN, COMBINING AN INDUSTRIAL PROCESS WITH A PERSONAL CHARACTER AND STYLE. AFTER AN INTRODUCTION TO THE MAIN WAYS OF WORKING WITH MOULDS, THERE IS A SELECTION OF PROJECTS FOR MAKING MOULDS AND INTEGRATING THEM WITHIN CERAMIC WORK.

# EQUIPMENT

## MOULDMAKING

Many straightforward plaster moulds, such as one piece press, hump or sprig moulds, can be made with limited and easily obtainable equipment. Mould and model making at a more advanced level, such as making and using block and case piece moulds and turned plaster models, however, require a range of specialist tools and larger pieces of equipment.

■ If you have space, it is advisable to designate a separate area for plaster work as even small pieces of plaster that find their way into a finished piece can cause "blow outs", where plaster makes its way out of the fired clay. Keep moulds separate from clay and ensure that the working moulds are handled with care when in contact with clay, particularly when trimming the edges of pressed shapes.

Plaster working tools are prone to rust and will lose their edge unless they are well cared for. Always clean them with a knife blade or wire brush after use. Frequent applications of oil help prevent rusting.

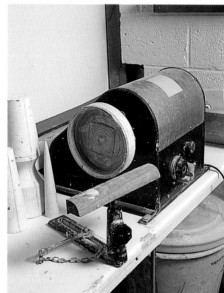

A SEALED LATHE IS USED FOR TURNING PLASTER MODELS TO FIT THE WIDTH RESTRICTION OF THE LATHE.

A BANDSAW IS USED FOR CUTTING PLASTER MODELS AND MOULDS.

A WHIRLER (BANDING WHEEL) IS USED FOR TURNING WET PLASTER MODELS USING A HANDHELD OR BRIDGE FIXED TEMPLATE.

**1** An indelible pencil for marking plaster.

**2** Flexible plastic sheet, plaster sheets or slabs to make up side and base sets for containing plaster when poured for casting.

**3** String for securing side sets (retaining walls).

**4** Inner tube lining cut into strips for holding together assembled mould pieces.

**5** Bench scraper for cleaning off work surfaces and equipment.

**6** Profile former to shape clay or plaster.

**7** A steel hammer (a) and a rubber mallet (b) for releasing plaster models.

**8** Solid steel shock absorber disc to disperse hammer blows to plaster.

**9** Carpenter's saw to cut and scrape or smooth plaster.

**10** Surform blade to pare cast plaster.

**11** Cottle to form the sides of a cast

**12** Bristle brush (a), soft soap (b) and a sponge (c) for separating plaster piece moulds and plaster cast from plaster models.

**13** Plaster turning tools and forged steel serrated modelling tools for turning plaster.

**14** Straight edge and metal scrapers for screeding (spreading) wet plaster.

**15** Small spirit level (a), surface gauge (b), steel square (c) and callipers (d) for levelling, measuring and marking.

**16** Sandpaper for final smoothing of plaster surface (not shown).

**17** Scales and a scoop for weighing plaster (not shown).

**18** Wearing a face mask (respirator) will avoid the inhalation of plaster dust (not shown here – see health and safety).

### Additional equipment

For slip casting, a blunger is needed for preparing casting slip and a tray for collecting excess slip. For jigger and jolley techniques you will require a jigger or jolley arm fixed to the wheel head with a template former for forming soft clay on plaster moulds.

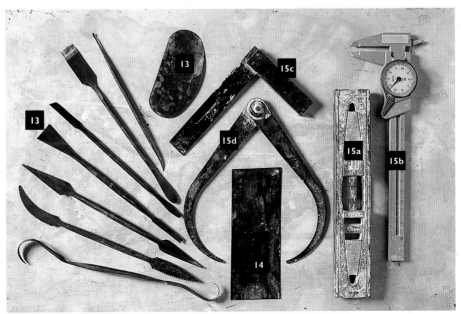

# TECHNIQUES
## PLASTER

A naturally occurring gypsum, plaster was first mined for commercial ceramic purposes in Montmartre, Paris in the 1770s, hence the name "plaster of Paris". It is made by a calcination process of crushing, grinding and heating the gypsum to remove chemically bound water.

Plaster is crucial for the production of commercial ceramics. It is also invaluable for the individual craftsperson producing highly original work.

When plaster is mixed with water to produce a pourable mix, the water lost in the calcination processes is taken up again to form a solid, set mass. Excess water is dried off leaving numerous minute pores that give moulds their essential porous quality.

Abundant, and inexpensive, there are many types of plaster. Among the most widely used are Pottery plaster or Newcast plaster for mouldmaking, and Crystacal R and Keramicast plaster for modelmaking. Avoid buying more plaster than you can use within a few weeks. It is difficult to keep plaster for long periods, unless it is in a completely airtight container.

## Mixing and pouring plaster

For most ceramic purposes, you can achieve a good, average water-to-plaster ratio visually without any weighing. Remember that the higher the water to plaster ratio, the weaker the set plaster will be.

Measuring plaster to water proportions by weight rather than volume is recommended when greater casting precision is required. For example, piece moulds for slip casting require each section of the mould to be consistently porous. This is achieved by accurately weighing and measuring the water-to-plaster ratios. The various Newcast plasters vary in both wear strength and surface finish. All plasters will become hot and expand slightly as they set.

### TYPICAL PLASTER-TO-WATER PROPORTIONS
The best results with plaster are achieved when plaster and water are accurately measured.

|  | POTTERY (moulds) | NEWCAST 71/80 (moulds & fine detail) | NEWCAST 96 (moulds) | KERAMICAST (modelmaking) | CRYSTACAL R (modelmaking) |
|---|---|---|---|---|---|
| PLASTER | 1.4 kg (3¼ lb) | 1.3 kg (3¾ lb) | 1.4 kg (3¼ lb) | 1.5 kg (3¾ lb) | 2.8 kg (7 lb) |
| WATER | 1 litre (1¾ pints) | 1 litre (1¾ pints) | 1 litre (1¾ pints) | 1 litre (1¾ pints) | 1 litre (1¾ pints) |

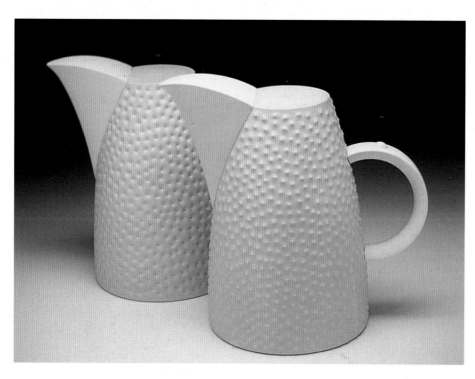

TEXTURED JUGS
(24 CM/9½ IN), MADE WITH
PLASTER MODELS (TAVS
JORGENSEN).

**1** To work out proportions visually, look at the area to be filled and estimate the volume of water it will take. Pour it into a plastic container. Add a little extra water just in case as plaster for a mould or slab should be poured in one batch. Gradually sift or strew in the plaster until it breaks in small peaks through the surface of the water. Always add plaster to water, never the other way round.

Leave the plaster undisturbed to soak up water for 1–2 minutes and then stir. Be careful not to pull in air by breaking the surface. Use one hand to stir, keeping the other plaster-free. Periodically remove air bubble scum from the surface with a rubber kidney. Continue stirring until the plaster begins to feel heavy. It is now ready to pour.

**NB** Never wash large amounts of plaster down the sink because it can block your plumbing. A settling tank (sink trap) will enable you to wash small amounts of plaster down the sink (see workshop layout).

**2** Pour the plaster immediately in a thin continuous stream against the inner side of the cottle (see mouldmaking equipment), again to prevent air being pulled into the cast causing bubbles on the surface of a model or weaknesses in the plaster.

Before the plaster has set, give sharp successive taps to the supporting board under the cast until air bubbles no longer rise to the surface of the poured plaster. While the plaster is still wet, remove any excess using a rubber kidney. Wash any residue off your hand and the container immediately before it sets.

**3** Once the plaster is set and has been released from the model and/or the retaining wall, file away sharp corners of the cast mould using a surform blade then allow it to dry before use.

Plaster casts should be dried to a maximum of 60°C (140°F) and removed from the heat as soon as they are dry. They will deteriorate rapidly if they are dried at too high a temperature.

Store your plaster and made casts in a very dry place. If they absorb moisture the setting time of plaster will shorten and they will lose strength.

LARGE BOWLS (14 CM/5½ IN) WHITE EARTHENWARE CLAY, COLOURED SLIP, TRANSPARENT GLAZE, JIGGER AND JOLLEY PRODUCTION METHOD (JULIE GOODWIN).

# TECHNIQUES
# MOULDMAKING Using one shape of mould can be repetitive and limiting, but if moulds are used for assembling components or as a starting point for work this does not have to be the case. Many makers who concentrate on the decorated finish rather than the making process choose to use moulds as an efficient, commercial option.

## Making moulds and models

Solid models for slip casting, press moulding and sprig moulds are made either using plaster or clay.

Circular shaped models can either be turned from plaster on a lathe, or plaster can be shaped with a profile former or a model thrown in clay as a solid shape on the wheel.

Whether to use plaster or clay depends on the form to be cast and the quality and precision required. Other shapes can be sledged in clay (see hollow and hump moulds) or hand modelled in clay. Producing a model in clay involves fewer steps, though it can also be used in conjunction with the waste mould technique as a starting point for developing a clay model into a plaster one (see Mug with Handle project).

Plaster models have advantages over clay in that they do not distort during casting, their surfaces can be sanded with wet and dry carborundum paper (wet and dry sandpaper) to a smooth surface and any breakages can be repaired with polystyrene (rubber) cement or strong glue. Found objects such as pebbles, shells and screws can be used as models from which to make moulds. Plaster casts can also be taken of such objects.

Indents and scratches on clay models can be filled by smoothing in soft clay. Those on plaster models can be temporarily fixed with clay or, if deep, filled with plaster and smoothed down once the plaster has set.

FIG. 1

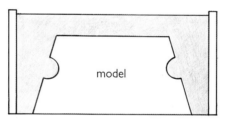

model

Undercuts in plaster moulds are caused by indents, small scratches or changes in direction in a model, particularly one made in plaster. The plaster sets around an undercut shape therefore "locking it" into the plaster (see Fig. 1). In this case it would not be possible to remove this model from the mould without breaking it. This does not necessarily restrict the design of the model from which you are making a mould (the problem in Fig. 1 can be overcome by using the three-piece mould in Fig. 2). However, adapting a design might make the mould-making process a less complex one, so always consider the practical application of your mould as soon as you start designing.

FIG. 2

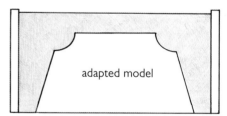

model

A piece mould (a mould made up of pieces) allows you to plan for undercuts and changes in direction (see Fig. 2). The three pieces are dismantled to release the model.

FIG. 3

adapted model

When plaster is cast over a model to produce a mould, the plaster will expand outward away from the surface of the model. When casting a hump mould, for example, plaster is cast into a negative to make a positive shape, the expansion is directed towards the walls of the mould. Therefore each wall of the mould, except the top one, must be tapered, known as 'draft', allowing the positive mould to be withdrawn easily from the negative model (see Fig. 3).

## Using seam, or parting, lines

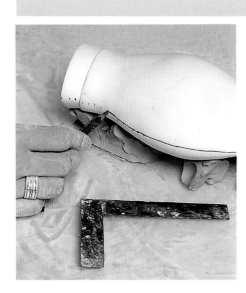

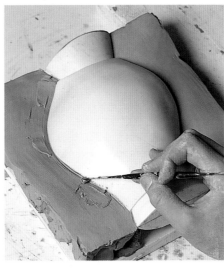

**1** If your model is asymmetrical and, because of undercuts, cannot be split in a straight line to create two halves, you need to set up the point where the mould divides, known as the seam, or parting, line. The line is first marked out on the model with an indelible pencil if the model is made from plaster or by scoring if the model is clay. Rest the model on clay supports and use an end face as a guide to rest the model at 90° to its base.

**2** The clay is then built up around the model, to the marked parting line drawn on the model. Doing this blocks off the areas that will be cast at a later stage. The built up clay is modelled to a smooth surface.

The irregular design of the Open Vase Form project (shown in full at the end of this chaper) involved establishing the seam line before casting the mould in three pieces: one for each side of the vase and the third mould for the base.

GRAIN TEMPLE 11 (23 × 15 × 30 CM/9 × 6 × 12 IN) CERAMIC, TERRA SIGILLATA, STAINS, OXIDES (JANET WILLIAMS).

## Running plaster and facing up

When running (pouring) plaster onto another piece of plaster, you must apply the separating agent "soft soap" in a process that is known as "facing up" ("sizing"). It is essential that any plaster piece to be cast is wet before being faced up (sized), so it needs to be soaked in water for at least 10–15 minutes unless it has been freshly cast, in which case it will still be wet.

Facing up (sizing) must be done thoroughly. The agent (size) should be applied to boards, table surfaces and cottling walls – in fact to any surface that is likely to come in contact with the poured plaster, particularly if it is made of a porous material. The soft soap should be dissolved from its jelly-like state into a liquid consistency using warm water before being applied to any of the surfaces.

Other releasing agents that are sometimes used are petroleum jelly when casting body parts or various oils when soft soap is not available.

Apply liquid soap with a natural sponge and allow it to soak into the plaster for about 15 seconds. Remove any excess suds with a second wet-to-damp natural sponge, rinsing it out with water when necessary. Repeat the two soaping and wiping actions using the different sponges until a gloss appears on the plaster surface. This can take up to 12 applications. No suds or water droplets should remain – use a paint brush to clean any crevices and difficult spots. Any further handling of the soaped (sized) model or mould should be avoided until after the plaster has been poured.

## Preparing to pour plaster

Before mixing or pouring plaster over a model you need to set up a wall or dam of stiff material, called a cottle, framing board or side set to form the sides of the cast. Cast plaster bats or smooth wood can be used for straight side sets; thick, flexible plastic or sheet metal is normally used for curved walls.

For total accuracy, plaster bats are cast on a sheet of glass and scored or sawn to the correct size when they are set. Remember, plaster side sets must be faced up (sized) before they come into contact with poured plaster.

## Fixing a cottle

Fix a cottle with strong tape to reinforce it and prevent the cottle from being forced outwards with the weight of the plaster.

The cottle must also be secured to prevent any leaks. You can use clay coils to help secure the retaining wall. Straight-sided walls can be secured with a builder's strap or tightened string secured around the outside of the retaining wall.

Make a final check by holding the wall or walls and testing them for any play or weakness, particularly for any shapes that require a great volume of plaster. If you are using a clay model, ensure it has not been damaged by the cottle.

Any clay used for cottling, as with any clay contaminated with plaster, should be either thrown away or stored separately from clean clay. This should be reused solely for plaster making purposes.

Take into account the fact that any cottle must be solidly secured in to place about 3–5 cm (1½–2 in) from the edge of the model and ensure that the supporting board or base set allows room for this gap (see below). The base set is the flat, smooth and level board on which the model sits. It should be 1–2 cm (½–¾ in) thick to provide a guide against which to rest the base edge of the cottle wall at 90° to the board. The base set will ultimately provide a neater finish to your cast shape, as well as greater accuracy, which is an essential requirement for making piece moulds.

## Making a plaster bat

When making side sets (retaining walls), plaster bats for intaglio printing (see intaglio printing from plaster) or clay reclaiming bats (see preparing clay), you do not need to spend time planning as there is no model to take into consideration.

In this case plaster can be poured directly on to a smooth flat surface, such as formica, marble or glass, inside a secured cottle wall. Four wooden bats are used to form a square cottle, secured with a brick on each corner.

When making plaster bats for reclaiming clay, they should be of a greater thickness than printing or side set bats. Make a higher cottle wall from wooden boards, securing them with clay or string. This gives added strength for the extra plaster when casting.

# TECHNIQUES
# HOLLOW AND HUMP MOULDS These moulds, also called press moulds, are

used for press-moulding shapes. You can buy ready-made moulds for press moulds but the disadvantage

of this is that you are limited by a set design. The technique that follows explains how to make your own.

**1** To form a clay model for a dish or hollow mould, sledge a profile around a clay body using a profile former made of metal or wood. Pull the notched former along the edge of the base set, which will act as a guide to shape the soft clay.

**2** Position a faced up (sized) (see running plaster and facing up), supported side set (retaining wall) around the base set and model and fix it in place. Carefully pour the plaster inside the supported walls covering the clay model to a depth of approximately 3 cm (1 in). Leave the plaster to set for 15–30 minutes and then remove the side set (retaining wall). Gouge away the clay model with a wooden tool to reveal the plaster mould. Clean up the freshly made hollow mould with a surform blade.

**3** Face up (size) the hollow mould before positioning and securing the side set (retaining wall) around it. Ensure the side set (retaining wall) is positioned to allow for the height of plaster that is to be poured into the hollow mould to make the hump mould.

BLACK BOWL (24 CM/9½ IN)
CRANK CLAY, PRESS MOULDED
AND SLAB BUILT, INLAID
COLOUR AND STAINED BODY
(PHILIP JOLLEY).

**4** When the cast of the hump, or drape, mould is set, hold a metal disc against the plaster cast and apply firm, muted taps with a rubber mallet. Repeat the taps around the sides of the cast to send dispersed shock blows through the plaster parts until you detect movement of the parting line or until the tone of the tap changes. This will indicate that the plaster is going to release. Ease the positive and negative casts apart. Pouring water onto the parting line can also help to release the plaster parts.

# TECHNIQUES
# PRESS MOULDING Press moulding with plaster moulds achieves identical shapes in

large quantities with relative ease. The pressed shapes can be used as a base on which to coil, slab build

or otherwise extend the work. The rims of pressed shapes can be cut or adjoined with handles or

decorative applied relief. Press moulds are used for millefiori and hump moulds and enable inlaid or

textured decoration to be pressed out without interfering with the upper face of the pressing.

## Press-moulding hollow moulds

Symmetrical clay shapes can be made as a pair and joined together while leatherhard to make an enclosed form. Assymetrical shapes such as handles, teapot spouts, figurines and pots can also be press moulded in two halves that are then joined.

**1** Lie a rolled, soft slab of clay over the hollow mould using a cloth to hold onto the clay.

**2** Ease the slab into place using a damp sponge to prevent your fingers indenting the soft clay. Any folds in the clay slab can be smoothed away using the curve of first a serrated and then a smooth metal kidney. Use a flexible rubber kidney to make a final finish.

**3** Trim the edges level with the mould. Do any final shaping, trimming and cleaning when the clay is leatherhard and it can be removed without distorting. Rounded bases can be tapped flat on a surface while the shape is firm, but soft enough to give.

## Draping over a hump mould

Slabs of clay that are printed, inlaid or textured while they lie flat on a work surface, are ideal for using with the draped working method. A coiled or separately moulded footring (rim) can be joined to the shape, often an open dish, while it is resting on the hump mould.

**1** Inlaid or textured slabs can be draped over a hump mould (drape mould) and pressed in place without interfering with the inlaid or textured face. Ease the slab into place using a damp sponge and rubber kidney.

**2** Trim back edges with a cutting harp (wire), either level to the mould's edge or with an overhang as required. Further shaping and cleaning of the edges can be done when the shape has firmed and been removed from the mould.

**3** To prevent the shape cracking as it shrinks onto the mould, remove draped shapes before they become too dry.

# TECHNIQUES
# JIGGER AND JOLLEY
The technique of jigger and jolley involves the use of accurately made and centered plaster moulds placed and held by a cup wheel head, which revolves like a thrower's wheel. Jiggering is an efficient method of producing quantities of bowls and plates – most commercial dinnerware is manufactured in this way.

■ The plaster mould in jiggering forms the inside shape of plates and other flatware, while in jollying it forms the outside shape of open cups and bowls.

A pivoted, counter-balanced arm holding a fixed metal profile is brought down onto the clay. The profile then spreads the clay onto the mould in an even section. Excess clay spread along to the rim of the mould is then trimmed with a knife and the arm is brought down again to contact the clay with the profile giving the clay its final shape.

Many working moulds can be cast from the master models which are usually turned using a lathe or whirler (banding wheel). As with other plaster mould techniques, large numbers of working moulds may be necessary as work cannot be removed from the mould until it is leatherhard.

The picture above shows the jigger and jolley process used with a pre-decorated slip tailored and laid into the mould, finished off with the revolving template.

PLATE (24 CM/9½ IN) WHITE EARTHENWARE CLAY, COLOURED CLAY INLAYS AND TRANSPARENT GLAZE (SABINA TEUTEBERG).

COFFECUP SAUCERS JOLLEYED, HIGH FIRED STONEWARE WITH BARIUM GREEN GLAZE, DESIGNED FOR THE ROYAL CRESCENT HOTEL, BATH, ENGLAND (TAVS JORGENSEN).

# TECHNIQUES
## SLIP CASTING
Suitable for making large volumes of identical work, the slip casting technique also requires the use of plaster moulds. The moulds are one piece for "drop out" shapes and multiple, keyed piece moulds for any other shapes. The moulds are held together with rubber bands or slices of car inner tube (see Kilns and Firing, Slim Raku Vessels project).

■ An extra piece or collar of plaster, called a "spare", is designed to fit onto the mould at the point where the slip is poured into the mould (see mouldmaking projects that follow). This spare acts as a reservoir of extra casting slip above the level of the top of the cast piece. The spare has two purposes. It cuts down the necessity for continual topping up of the slip as it is taken up by the porous mould walls and, because the spare retains this reservoir of slip, a constant pressure is created as the slip level sinks as it dries ensuring an even wall of clay throughout the entire area of the cast piece. A spare is only designed into moulds that are made specifically for slip casting.

Casting slip is available ready made from ceramic suppliers, or you can make up your own from suitable plastic clay or dry clay materials with a slip blunger (see mouldmaking equipment). Casting slip differs from a decorating slip as it contains a deflocculating agent, such as sodium silicate or carbonate. These enable a great quantity of clay to be held in a small amount of water by altering its composition while still allowing the clay to flow freely. The particles then remain in suspension when the slip is poured.

Making up casting slip is part science, part trial and error. It has three main qualities – density, fluidity and thixotropy. Casting slip that has been left for any length of time seems to thicken while undisturbed, however when stirred it regains its fluidity rapidly. This quality is due to thixotropy, enabling the newly formed cast to keep its shape without distortion while wet in the mould. Slip can be used to make test casts, allowing the development of casts that are lump free, do not overly wet the mould and release themselves from the mould without distortion once firmed. If adjustments are necessary, the litre/pint weight of the casting slip should be measured to get a density reading while accurate measurement of fluidity and thixotropy require a torsion viscometer.

After some use, the moulds begin to wear away because of the alkaline quality of the casting slip. This is most notable on precise or angular forms. Frequently used moulds will therefore need to be replaced.

INSECTAPLANT AND FLOWER (55 CM/21½ IN) COMBINED SLIPCASTING AND HAND BUILDING. MOULDS ARE MADE FROM FOUND OBJECTS, SUCH AS STONES AND VEGETABLES, WHICH ARE THEN CAST AND ASSEMBLED AT LEATHERHARD STAGE. HANDMADE ELEMENTS ARE ADDED (JENNY ORCHARD).

## Casting a slip piece

**1** Sieve the prepared casting slip into a bucket. Quickly pour it into the dry mould in one operation. The mould is often spun on a whirler (banding wheel) while it is filled to help disperse the casting slip quickly and to prevent horizontal lines forming on the piece. This also prevents trapped air bubbles, causing another casting fault called pinholing.

CYLINDER (12 CM/4½ IN) SLIPCAST WITH PORCELAIN AND DECORATED WITH YELLOW, JAPANESE RED AND BLACK. THESE PIECES ARE OFTEN FIRED SEVERAL TIMES, RESULTING IN THE CLAY BECOMING MORE TRANSPARENT, AS WELL AS MORE VULNERABLE (BODIL MANZ).

**2** When the wall of the cast piece is sufficiently thick, pour the excess slip away for reuse and leave the mould inverted over a rack or support to let final drips drain away into a collecting tray. Leave the piece in the mould until it is leatherhard. At this point trim away with a knife the excess collar of clay formed in the spare.

**3** Remove the piece from the mould and leave it to dry. Clean it up by fettling away the seam scars with a knife and wiping it with a damp sponge. Wear a mask for large volumes of fettling and hold the work under dust extraction equipment to protect yourself from dust inhalation. Work can be fettled at the leatherhard stage, but you will achieve a less satisfactory finish.

## Materials
A smooth clay
Pottery or Newcast plaster
   for moulds
Plaster for models
   (Keramicast/Crystacal R)

## Equipment
Thin plastic for cottle
String
Soft soap and sponges
Flat steel tool
Hacking knife
Indelible pencil for marking
   out the model
Metal carving tools
Bandsaw or coping saw
Plaster bat for cutting
   around the handle profile
Wet and dry sanding paper
Round plaster bat
Whirler (banding wheel)
Plastic location natches
Plaster base, side sets
   (retaining walls) and spacers

## For casting and glazing
Gloves for glazing
Pre-prepared semi-porcelain
   casting slip
Fettling knife and sponge
Glaze Sneyd Oxide L/S
   Transparent (commercial
   glaze)
Glaze tongs

## Firing
Biscuit (bisque) fire to 1120°C
   (2048°F)
Glaze fire to 1120°C (2048°F)

# Mug with Handle

Making a drop-out mould from a clay model is the easiest type of mould to produce. The first stage is to create a plaster model from a clay original. A mould is then made from this plaster model and this is used to reproduce forms by slipcasting. Many simple forms, such as dishes, bowls and vases, can be created with this type of mould. Adapt your own design to this method, remembering that for a shape to drop out of a mould, the widest diameter must be at the top. The shape must narrow or taper continually from this point onwards so that the form will release easily.

**1** The clay original for this design was thrown on a wheel, although a handbuilt form will work just as well. When leatherhard, place it upside-down on a throwing bat so the model can be easily lifted off. Allow enough excess clay at the base to form a clay bat against which to set the cottle wall at stage 2. A former, cut from thin plastic, will smooth the surface and finalize the shape.

**2** Cottle around the clay model to make the waste mould. Secure it with string and cover the entire clay model with pottery or fine casting plaster. Remove the cottle when the plaster has set.

**3** Face up (size) the internal area and top edge of the waste mould at least three times with soft soap (see facing up). Pour the model plaster inside the mould until exactly level with the top edge and allow to set. Scrape excess plaster flat with a flat steel tool. Split the mould with a hacking knife to remove the model (see steps 2 and 3 of the Open Vase Form project).

**4** To make the plaster handle model fit the shape of the mug exactly, cast a solid piece of plaster onto the attaching face of the plaster model of the mug, which has been faced up (sized). It is important to cut location natches and mark the location points of the handle in indelible pencil. Do this before setting up the clay cottle for pouring the handle piece onto the side of the mug model. Then separate the solid plaster piece and carve it into shape with carving tools.

**5** Cut out the handle shape with the bandsaw or coping saw, leaving the location natches intact. Model the outside of the handle model with metal carving tools until it is very nearly finished, then carefully model the inside surface and smooth it with wet and dry sanding paper. Carving a handle is a delicate process, but if it breaks you can glue it together with polystyrene cement.

**6** Face up (size) the model and a round bat. Set up the model and bat on a whirler (banding wheel) (see the Lidded Container project) and fill any gaps between the seam line and the bat with clay. Also fill the handle location natches level with clay to prepare for the modelling of the handle. Position a plastic location natch on the bat, hold it in place with clay and face up (size) the top edge. Set up a cottle around the bat and fill it with plaster. Run (pour) the plaster carefully over the entire model, until covered to a depth of about 2 cm (¾ in) above the footring (foot).

**7** When the plaster is set remove the cottle and cut location natches. This will register the two parts of the mug mould. Then turn the feed spare (a truncated cone that creates the correct hole diameter through which the casting slip will be fed) on a whirler (banding wheel) (see the Lidded Container project). Having faced up (sized) the feed spare, set it up on top of the mug model that is sitting inside the mould. There should be a gap of around 3–4 mm (⅛ in) between the edge of the model and the feed spare. This allows for the thickness of the cast wall.

**8** Face up (size) the top edge of the mould and tie the cottle into position. Ensure that it is high enough to pour in the next section of the working mould.

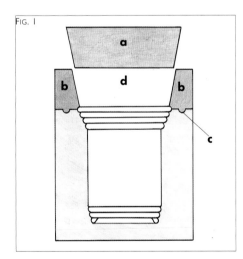

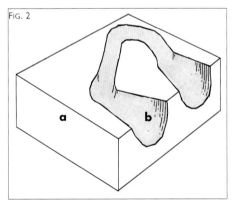

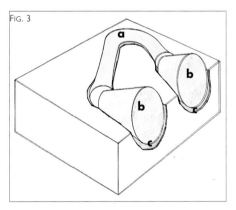

**9** To create the working mould, pour the plaster level with the top of the feed spare (see Fig. 1).
**a** feed spare
**b** verge
**c** natch cut
**d** the hole created by removal of the feed spare from the verge acts as a reservoir for excess slip while the mug is being cast

**10** To make the mould of the handle, draw an outline of the handle model onto the plaster base set and then scoop out a recess with a carving tool (see Fig. 2). Set the handle in this cavity and face up (size).
**a** base set
**b** scooped out recess

**11** Model clay feed spares and set them into the recess and fill any gaps up with clay level with the base set between the model and the set to the seam line (half way from each handle edge). Face up (size) again.
**a** handle set in recess
**b** feed spares placed in recess
**c** gaps between the model and base set filled with clay

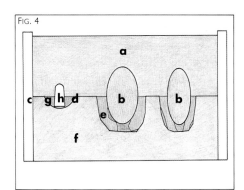

Fig. 4

**12** This cross section of the handle mould illustrates the drawing out of the recess and how the handle mould is made half way up to a middle seam.

**a** plaster poured to make first half of mould

**b** handle model

**c** cottle wall

**d** clay filled level

**e** recess filled with clay

**f** base set with recess cut to house handle model

**g** natch cut

**h** plaster locator natch (optional)

**13** Build up a frame of plaster bats around the profile of the handle (the base set). Fill any gaps around the profile of the handle model with clay from the inside.

**14** Use spacers to secure and tighten up the side set bats (retaining walls) firmly to the base set. Once the first half of the handle mould is run and set, remove the frame and base set. Clean and face up (size) the mould and cut location natches. These should be positioned a good distance away from the model and the edge of the moulds. Then run (pour) the other half of the handle mould in the same way, but this time without profile bats.

**15** When the working moulds are dry, use them to slipcast the mug and handle with casting slip. Trim off any spare clay formed by the feed spare with a flat, steel tool, fettling knife or potter's knife once the clay is dry to the touch. Sponge the trim line with the verge  (see step 9, Fig. I) in place on the mould. Fettle and sponge all seams before fixing the handle in place. Attach the leatherhard clay cast of the handle to the mug with a drop of casting slip while the cast mug is still leatherhard.

**16** Biscuit (bisque) fire the mug and then, wearing gloves glaze it, immersing the entire piece into the glaze with glazing tongs. Use a damp sponge to wipe away any excess glaze off the footring (foot) before glaze firing.

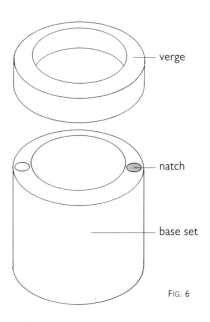

— verge

— natch

— base set

Fig. 6

**Completed two-part working mug mould**

Fig. 5

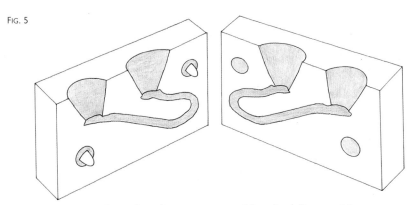

**Completed two-part working handle mould**

# Open Vase Form

This model is an asymmetrical, hand sculpted form. A waste mould is made from a clay original and then a hard plaster original is formed. A seam line in clay (see mouldmaking techniques) is created to make a three-part split seam mould. This process can be used to make moulds for complicated sculpted forms that are then used to create hollow slipcast work.

## Materials

Pottery or Newcast plaster for moulds
Plaster for models (Keramicast/Crystacal R)

## Equipment

Plaster base, side sets (retaining walls) and spacers
Indelible pencil
Cottle
String
Saw
Splitting or hacking knife
Hammer
Wet and dry sanding paper
Soft soap and sponges
Shock absorber disc (solid steel disc)
Metal modelling tools
Surform blade
Potter's knife
Fettling knife
Plastic mould natches

## For casting and glazing

Gloves for glazing
Pre-prepared semi-porcelain casting slip
Glaze Sneyd Oxide L/L Apple Green and Turquoise (commercial glazes)
Glazing tongs

## Firing

Biscuit (bisque) fire to 1120°C (2048°F)
Glaze fire to 1120°C (2048°F)

**1** To make the waste mould, place the flat face of the clay model on a faced up (sized) plaster base set of a suitable size and shape to cottle around the model (see the Lidded Container project). Mark the intended seam line onto the base set with an indelible pencil (see using seam lines, mouldmaking techniques). Wrap the cottle around the edge of the base set and secure it with string before pouring the plaster for moulds over the entire model.

**2** Use a saw to score a deep seam line around the outer wall of the waste mould where the intended seam line is to run. Remove the marked base set.

**3** Lay a splitting or hacking knife along the scored seam and give it successive sharp blows with a hammer to split the mould at the intended seam line. Do this until the shock blows have caused the waste mould to fracture right around the form.

**4** Clean any plaster debris from the inside of the split waste mould and finish the internal surface as required, rubbing down any inconsistencies with wet and dry sandpaper if you want the surfaces to be smooth. Next, face up (size) the internal faces with soft soap. Tie the waste mould back together again and pour in the model plaster mix level with the upper edge of the cavity.

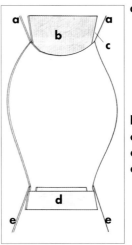

**a** clay cottle walls are secured to a height of 25 mm (1 in) above the top of the model
**b** feed spare
**c** cast thickness
**d** foot spare
**e** clay cottle walls

FIG. 1

**5** Once the model plaster has set, tap open the waste mould with a hammer and shock absorber disc. It will not matter if the swell (or expansion of the plaster as it sets) fractures the waste mould or if undercuts of the model cause the waste mould to come away in broken pieces. What is important is that the plaster model emerges from the waste mould intact, as this part is the one that is needed for the next stages of the mouldmaking.

**6** The new plaster model can now be worked in a number of ways. You can carve its surface with metal modelling tools or finish it with wet and dry sanding paper. Positive clay sprigs can be stuck to the surface of the faced up (sized) model with water, or a footring (foot) can be carved into the form to ease the glazing and firing process (see above). Any slight undercuts can also be dealt with by altering the plaster model surface with carving and finishing tools. Once any alterations are finalized, the plaster model should then be faced up (sized) in preparation for the next stage.

**7** Now make a feed spare and a foot spare – these truncated cones are used to create the correct hole diameter through which slip will be fed (see Fig. 1). Spares are cast directly onto the model and fit exactly on the faced up (sized) plaster surfaces. The clay cottled walls are pared and modelled back with a surform blade (see step 9). Ensure the right measurements are used by marking lines on the model (see step 8) so that the feed spare creates the correct thickness of cast wall.

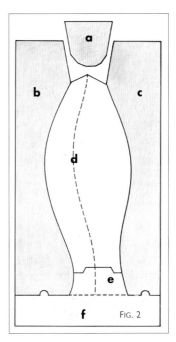

**8** To make the feed spare, mark a continuous line with indelible pencil the slipcast thickness (about 4 mm (⅛ in) in from the top edge of the model). This line will be imprinted by the plaster that is poured into the cottle that has been formed from clay. It is useful as a guide when modelling the spare at step 9 with a surform, built and secured to about 2.5 cm (1 in) at the top of the model.

**9** Repeat this process for the foot spare, but exclude the slip cast thickness. Remove the spare lump of plaster (created in step 8) and model the foot spare and the feed spare with a surform. Both spares should flare out continuously from the point where the line is drawn and imprinted to their top edges.

**10** As this model is asymmetrical and therefore cannot be split in a straight line, you need to allow for undercuts by setting up a point where the mould divides as the seam or parting line (see Fig. 2). First mark the line out on the model with an indelible pencil. Rest the model on clay supports and use an end face as a guide to rest the model at 90° to its base (see the Lidded Container project).

**11** Next, build clay around the model, to block off the areas that will be cast later and model it to a smooth surface.

**12** Face up (size), run (pour) and locate notches for the two vertical split sides.
**a** feed spare is removed from the mould and discarded
**b** first side of mould is run on to clay spare
**c** second side of mould is run once natches cut and first side has been faced up (sized)
**d** seam line
**e** the foot spare forms a trap at the base of the mould
**f** third side of mould is run (plaster is poured) last and released from the mould first

FIG. 2

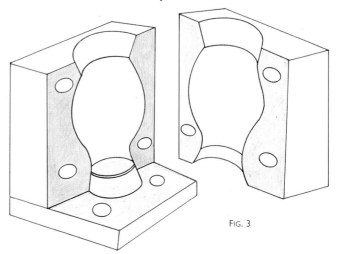

**General view of open vase form mould**

FIG. 3

**13** Once the two vertical split sides have been run, turn the mould upside down. Cut at least two natches into either side of the base of the working mould, then clean and face up the base surface. Frame the base with plaster bats tied with string and tightened with spacers. Remove the foot spare (see above). Face up (size) the indent created between the base of the mould and the foot of the model. Then run (pour) the third and final side of the mould.

**14** To remove the model from the mould, take away the feed spare to open the mould, first tap the foot piece, then one side of the mould with a shock absorber disc.

**15** Once the mould is dry, you can use it to slipcast your open vase form (see slip casting).

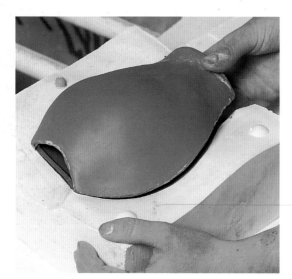

**16** Once the finished slipcast form is ready in the working mould, drain off the excess casting slip and trim away the excess clay from the feed spare. The walls of the feed spare are used to help guide the fettling or potter's knife around the irregular top. Sponge back any coarse edges after cutting off the feed spare. To remove the freshly cast piece from the mould, remove the base first, then one side of the mould. Once the mould has been disassembled the cast can be lifted out by levering out the foot first to avoid distorting the opening of the freshly cast piece.

**17** Biscuit (bisque) fire the piece, and wearing gloves, dip it into a large container of glaze using glazing tongs. Wipe the footring (foot) clean with a sponge and then place the piece in the kiln for glaze firing.

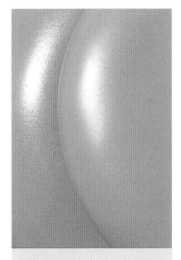

# Lidded Container

This lidded form is particularly suited to slipcasting. It involves a collar on the lid, which drops into the opening of the container. Solid clay models are used for the basic shapes and a whirler (banding wheel) is used to make an accurate fitting lid collar and feed spare in plaster (see steps 2 and 3). The lid collar makes the lid fit snugly in the opening, so consider the relationship between the feed spare and the maximum width of the collar at the design stage.

## Materials

A smooth clay
Pottery or Newcast plaster
   for moulds
Plaster for models
   (Keramicast/Crystacal R)

## Equipment

Whirler (banding wheel)
Bracing stick for whirler
Setting-up plaster bat
Callipers
Cottle
String
Soft soap and sponges
Hacking knife
Indelible pencil
Steel square
Shock absorber disc (solid
   steel disc)
Saw hammer
Polystyrene cement (rubber)
Plastic natches (optional)

## For casting and glazing

Gloves for glazing
Pre-prepared semi-porcelain
   casting slip
Fettling knife
Sponge
Glaze tongs
Sneyd Oxide L/L Turquoise
Sneyd Oxide L/L Apple green
   (commercial glazes)

## Firing

Biscuit (bisque) fire to 1120°C
   (2048°F)
Glaze fire to 1120°C (2048°F)

**1** Model the form of the lid and body shapes from a solid piece of clay and keep the clay wet. Turn a lid collar on the bat on the whirler (banding wheel): mix plaster and pour it onto the whirler inside a rough clay cottle wall (see step 3). It should ease off the whirler (banding wheel) as the plaster sets. Measure with callipers to ensure the measurements are correct and attach this to the clay lid before you make the waste mould. Make the waste moulds (hard plaster originals) from your container and lid design, split them horizontally with a hacking knife and face up (size) inside. Tie the waste mould back together and pour in a modelling plaster mix.

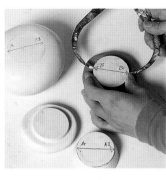

**2** Turn two feed spares, one for the lid and one for the container. First turn the feed spare for the container. In order for the lid to fit, ensure that the line B–B1 (the maximum diameter of the lid collar, see Fig. 1) is smaller than line A–A1 (the minimum diameter of the feed spare into the container, see Fig. 1).

**3** Turn the second feed spare for the lid on the whirler (banding wheel) with the maximum diameter approximately 8 mm (⅓ in) smaller than the line B–B1. Measure these relative distances carefully with callipers. Remove the feed spare from the whirler (banding wheel).

**4** To establish the horizontal seam line on the lid and the container, mark the side of the square with an indelible pencil (see Fig. 1). Having placed it onto a flat surface, touch it up to the model. Join the dots this creates to form the seam line.

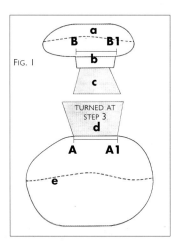

FIG. I

TURNED AT STEP 3

**a** horizontal seam line
**b** lid collar
**c** feed spare to lid
**d** feed spare to container
**e** horizontal seam line

**5** Turn a plaster bat with a central recess for the second feed spare and face this up. Place the lid into the recess and apply clay up to the seam line. Then place a cottle around the bat and tie with string.

**6** Pour plaster on the whirler (banding wheel) and turn the setting up bat for the plaster container form. Tap lightly with a knife to release it. The model will drop into this collar once it has been faced up (see Fig. 2).

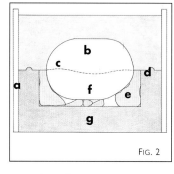

FIG. 2

**a** cottle wall
**b** container model sitting upside down on a turned base set
**c** seam line
**d** natches cut and plastic locator natches inserted
**e** clay
**f** top of model
**g** faced up (sized) base set

**7** Set the lid and container up as two separate sets and face up (size) both models. Drop the container and the lid into their respective sets and apply clay to the gaps. Tie the cottle around the sets and pour in plaster for the bottom half of the moulds, ensuring that it covers the base.

**8** Remove the base set. Set the feed spares into place on top of the container and cut the natches in the first side of the mould (see step 7 of the Mug with Handle project). Use the small non-serrated end of the natch cutter and spin the first side of the mould to cut the natches. One plastic natch can be included (optional). Face up (size) the first side of the mould, secure the cottle around the outside with string and run in plaster (pour plaster) for the second side. Repeat this process for the lid.

**9** Once the plaster has set, place the shock absorber disc onto a flat outside surface of the mould and hit it with a hammer a few times. This will release the surface tension and the two halves of each mould (one for the lid and one for the container) will come apart.

**10** Glue a small disc with polystyrene cement to create the footring to the flat base of the mould. This is made out of plaster, either turned or hand carved. Surform the shape to fit exactly in the curve of the mould. Any negative shapes can be glued quite successfully into dry moulds in this way.

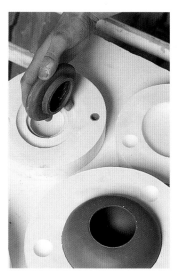

**11** Slipcast the two forms and once they are cast and drained, sponge back sharp edges, which may have formed by cutting off the spare. Remove the lid and container from the moulds.

**12** Glaze the pieces. Fire the lid on the container for the initial biscuit (bisque) firing, but separately for the glaze firing.

# Equus Vase

This project integrates a press-moulded horse form with a thrown form. Combining these two methods gives a multi-disciplinary art form through which Chris Bramble finds that he can express his ideas with endless possibilities. The gas reduction process gives the clay body and the glaze surface unique effects that continue to inspire further work.

## Materials
Iron-based stoneware clay

## Equipment
Wheel and cutting wire
Soft plastic
Metal kidney
Callipers
Turning (trimming) tool
Two-piece mould
Rolling pin
Sponge
Potter's knife
Toothbrush
Needle
Fettling knife and paintbrush
Steel tool
Banding wheel
Face mask (respirator)
  and gloves
Glaze rack and basin
Gas fired kiln

## Glaze
Manganese dioxide
DRY BLUE GLAZE

| | |
|---|---|
| Feldspar | 13% |
| Whiting | 27% |
| China clay | 53% |
| Soda ash | 6.5% |
| Copper | 0.5% |
| Cobalt | 1/10% |

## Glaze firing
Best result for this glaze is
  1260–1280°C
  (2300–2336°F) gas
  reduction firing
Reducing from 1000°
  (1832°F) to 1200°C
  (2192°F)

**1** Throw the cylinder keeping the rim thick enough to collar in the rim. Make sure the cylinder is tall enough because the vase will lose height when forming the bell of the vase. Leave a wide base to support the bell of the vase when it is thrown. Use a piece of soft plastic to compress the rim rather than chamois leather as it will give you more detail and flexibility. (See Throwing, cylinder sections.)

**2** Use your two fingers on the inside of the cylinder to push the body outwards. Start from the base, easing off as you get to the rim, collaring the rim so you can keep the mouth of the vase under control until you reach the desired form. Finish off the surface with a kidney to give a smooth drawing surface for later. This will save time and you will not have to do it at the turning stage.

**3** Next, throw the lid upside-down off the hump or stack. This will save you weighing and centring small lumps of clay if you are making more than one jar. Cup a portion of clay in your hand to throw a 25 cm (10 in) flange. A tall flange will help balance the figure on top and give good clearance for your fingers when you stick the lid on to the wheelhead for turning. Gently squeeze out the lid rim with your fingertips then use callipers to measure the flange of the lid on to fit the mouth of the vase.

**4** Groove the inside of the lid lip with your fingertips. Avoid doing this too deeply or the lid will rest on the shoulder of the vase and you will not be able to fire the vase all together. Finish off the rim and flange with a piece of soft plastic.

**5** Turn the lid and vase when the clay is leatherhard; use stiff coils of clay to attach the lid and vase to the wheelhead. Little turning is needed for the lid. Finish off the base with a turning (trimming) tool and a kidney to achieve a smooth surface.

**6** Use a two-piece mould to make the figure. Make the figure hollow to cut down drying time, decrease the chance of explosion and reduce weight on the lid. Roll the clay flat with a rolling pin then press it into the mould with a damp sponge or your fingertips. Trim away the excess clay then add an extra coil of clay to the inside rim of the mould for strength. Score and slurry the rim to be joined and then paint on the slip. Score and slurry the edge then join the other half.

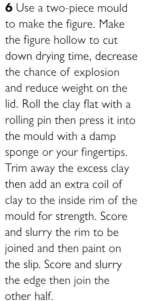

**7** Leave the clay in the mould for an hour to stiffen up, then take it out of the mould and leave it to stand for two hours. When the horse is leatherhard, make a needle hole so that air can escape in the drying-out process or it may crack or blow up in the biscuit (bisque) firing.

**8** Fettle off any waste clay and finish off with a paintbrush. Try to complete any detailed modelling before attaching the horse to the lid because there are certain angles you cannot get to once it is assembled.

**9** Use a steel tool to cross hatch the hooves and the place on the lid where they are to meet. Apply some slurry with a toothbrush and press them firmly together. Clean the joins with a paintbrush.

**10** Incise the design on the vase with a steel tool. Horizontal guidelines can be drawn while it is standing on a banding wheel. Leave the assembled horse vase to dry for about a week before slow biscuit firing to 1000°C (1832°F) or 06 cone.

**11** A protective face mask (respirator) and gloves should be worn when making up the glaze. Paint on manganese dioxide and sponge off the surplus when it is dry. This will leave enough to melt though the covering layer of glaze. Pour the glaze inside the jar first and wipe the rim.

**12** The dry blue glaze can be sprayed or poured on. If you would like to keep the horse a natural clay colour, mask it off with masking tape or wax resist (see Glaze and Decoration, using paper resist and wax resist). Fire the lid on the vase to prevent it warping. The reduction within this firing cycle will bring the iron speckle to the surface of the clay, giving a blue, green and yellow dry-to-satin matt surface.

# Lady Daisy Jug

This press-moulded and sprigged crystalline-glazed jug (pitcher) for Kate Malone assumes the character of a fine, strong young lady. For her, jugs are a symbol of celebration and sharing and are used at gatherings and to mark special occasions. The original piece from which the mould was made was hand coiled. One new mould can be used to press perhaps 20–30 different jugs. This jug's restrained surface shows the shape of the jug with clarity.

## Materials
T-material clay

## Equipment
Two-piece plaster of Paris
    mould made from coiled
    original body shape
Metal serrated-edge kidney
Thick rubber kidney
Craft knife
Sponge
Plastic sheet
Hacksaw blades of varying
    tooth size
Two-piece plaster of Paris
    handle mould made from
    carved original clay handle
    shape
Banding wheel
Sprig mould of daisy (cast
    from child's earring)
Electric kiln and controller
Large mop-head brush
Gloves for glazing

## Glazes
GREEN CRYSTALLINE GLAZE,
ADAPTED FROM EMMANUEL
COOPER BASE GLAZE

| | |
|---|---|
| Alkaline frit P2962 | 58 g |
| Zinc oxide | 23 g |
| Flint | 17 g |
| Bentonite | 2 g |
| Red iron oxide | 3 g |
| Copper carbonate | 2 g |

CREAMY YELLOW-GOLD HEAVY
BLANKET CRYSTALLINE GLAZE,
ADAPTED FROM A DEREK
CLARKSON BASE GLAZE

| | |
|---|---|
| Ferro frit 3110 | 44 g |
| Zinc oxide | 26.5 g |
| Flint | 20.4 g |
| Titanium dioxide | 7.8 g |
| China clay | 1.4 g |
| Ceramatech high firing colour | 2 g |

## Firing
Biscuit (bisque) fire to 1000°C
    (1832°F)
GLAZE FIRING
60°C (140°F) per hour up to
    180°C (356°F)
80°C (176°F) per hour to
    300°C (572°F)
100°C (212°F) per hour to
    600°C (1112°F)
Then as fast as possible
    to 1260°C (2300°F)
Then cool as fast as possible
    down to 1090°C (1994°F)
Soak there for 90 minutes
Then cool to 1080°C
    (1976°F)
Hold for 60 minutes
Cool to 1069°C (1956°F)
Hold 45 minutes
Turn off kiln for normal cool

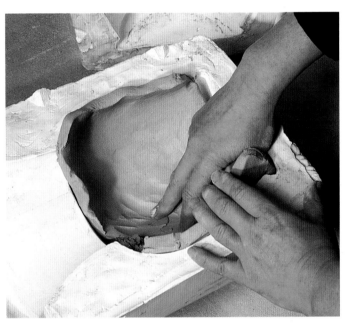

**1** Roll out or wire-cut enough slabs of clay to patchwork fill the mould. Lay them in small pieces, filling the mould like crazy paving, overlapping and joining the edges well. This ensures an even, unstretched layer of clay.

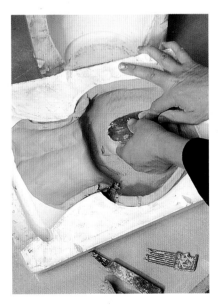

**2** Work the inside first with a metal kidney and then a rubber kidney to ensure segment bonding and create a smooth interior. You need to perfect the insides now because this will be too difficult when the two halves are joined. Score and slurry the edges to be joined. A good bonding is crucial.

**3** Push the two halves of the mould and clay together. Work inside the central seam now, scratching, filling and smoothing. The piece should be as beautiful inside as it is outside.

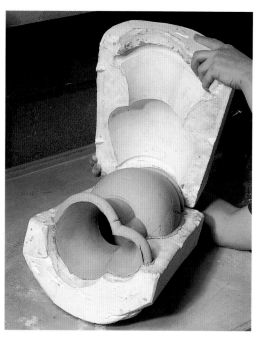

**4** Lie the jug on its side and carefully remove half of the mould leaving the piece created in one half.

**5** Scratch and fill the joint area. Use water from a brush then re-scratch to build a slurry from the body itself.

**6** Fill, but do not overfill, as this creates more work for removal later. The seams between the sections are now strong.

**7** Lift the whole jug from the mould and complete the scratching and filling, paying particular attention to the seam where the two halves join. Wrap it well in plastic and leave for at least 24 hours so the moisture becomes even throughout. It is very difficult to perfect the surface of an unevenly moist piece.

**8** Clean back the pot surface to a perfect, smooth shape by using a series of hacksaw blades from coarse to fine.

**9** Finish off with a rubber kidney, moving it in long, firm sweeps over the form. This stage can take up hours of time so be patient.

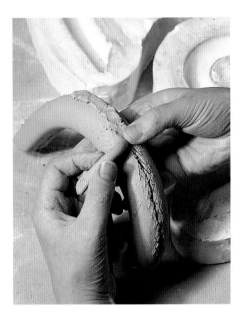

**10** Fill both halves of the handle mould. The hollow centre must be clear to avoid an explosion in the kiln. Score and slurry the seams before joining both halves.

**11** Remove the handle from the mould. Check the hollow channel is clear all the way through by making a hole at each end and blowing down the handle.

**12** Scratch and fill the join then wrap it in plastic and leave it to even thoroughy. Next work with hacksaw blades and kidney to perfect the surface.

**14** Press out a few daisy sprigs from the mould.

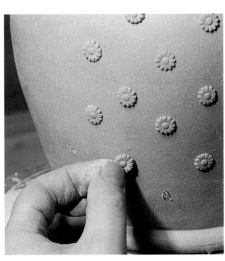

**13** Put the main jug form on the banding wheel and then join the handle to the body when they are both of the same firmness by scoring and slurrying the contact areas and pushing them together firmly. Put a hand inside of the jug and press against it. If necessary, use a temporary pillar of clay to support the handle.

**15** Join them to the pot on scratched, wet areas and bond them well by even pressure. Wrap the whole piece in plastic and leave to even the moisture for a week. Dry very slowly, especially at the start. Biscuit (bisque) fire in an electric kiln to 1000°C (1832°F).

**16** Glaze the inside by pouring in the glaze, swirling it around. Glaze the outside by painting with a large mop-head brush. Crystalline glazes run during firing so apply about three times as much glaze towards the top than at the base.

The raw glaze is so thick it might crack and fall off in chunks when placing in the kiln so take care. Each pot must have its own homemade kiln prop and tray to collect glaze drips during firing. After firing, chisel the pot from its stilt and polish the base. With luck, crystals will have formed on the surface of the pot, which will have grown during the cooling and soaking cycle of the firing.

# THROWING

**ONCE, DURING A SUMMER HOLIDAY** ON THE GREEK ISLAND OF NAXOS IN THE AEGEAN SEA, RICHARD PHETHEAN VISITED A SMALL MUSEUM THAT HAD A COLLECTION OF MINOAN POTTERY UNCEREMONIOUSLY DISPLAYED IN SEVERAL LARGE GLASS CABINETS. THERE BEFORE HIM STOOD ROW UPON ROW OF THE MOST EXQUISITE THROWN POTTERY VESSELS. BOTTLES, VASES, BOWLS AND CUPS WITH DELICATE RIMS AND HANDLES, BEAUTIFULLY PROPORTIONED FORMS, SIMPLE OXIDE DECORATION AND SANDY, UNGLAZED SURFACES. RICHARD PHETHEAN HAD BEEN POTTING FOR TEN YEARS. ALL THESE POTS HAD BEEN MADE OVER 4,000 YEARS AGO. IT HIT HOME INSTANTLY HOW WONDERFULLY TIMELESS THE CRAFT OF POTTERY WAS AND HOW INSPIRATIONAL SIMPLE, CLASSICAL SHAPES CAN BE.

# EQUIPMENT
# THROWING

The earliest type of potter's wheel was simply a heavy, flat turntable – like a mill wheel – which was pushed or kicked around by the potter (or a hapless potter's assistant!). This method is still successfully employed in remote areas where only simple technology is required or available. Now the electric wheel is widely used, but many potters still prefer the gentler pace of the kick wheel.

### Kick wheel

Many throwers who use the kick wheel prefer its unhurried pace, which provides a more contemplative experience and results in less machine-like pots.

Modern kick wheels use much the same basic flywheel with a shaft mounted on free running bearings and a "wheelhead" on which the pots are thrown. Some kick wheels have a crank and treadle, and a relatively small flywheel.  Momentum kick wheels have a heavy flywheel whose weight provides the power to keep the wheel turning. This is maintained with a kick directly onto the flywheel. The one pictured has a special notch on the wheelhead into which a stick is lodged to wind up the speed.

### Electric wheel

An electric wheel is operated with a foot pedal to speed or slow the wheelhead. These use a variety of drive mechanisms and are controlled with a foot pedal. A smooth transition from slow to fast speed is important, and a steady slow speed is essential. Motor output can vary according to the weight of clay the potter is going to use and are usually between ¼ to 1 horsepower. The slip tray catches the water and slurry as you work, but should not be allowed to overflow otherwise the bearing housed beneath the wheelhead will rust. It is a good idea to place a shelf above the wheel on which to place boards or individual pieces of work as they are thrown. Keep water for throwing inside the wheel tray and ensure the throwing area is well lit.

### Bats

Circular plywood or other composite material bats are used for throwing large or open ware. These are fixed onto the wheelhead in several ways:

**1** A thrown clay pad or disc is made on which to stick the bat.
**2** Bats may be drilled with two holes to correspond with pins screwed onto the wheelhead.
**3** A "lotus" wheelhead is spoked and has a retaining lip into which a bat may be slotted.

## Throwing tools

1 Callipers for measuring widths of galleries (seats), lids and other fitted shapes.

2 A needle to cut top edges level while throwing and also to test the thickness of a base section.

3 A dottle or sponge on a stick to remove water from the inside base of a tall, narrowly enclosed shape.

4 Ribs for applying pressure while throwing, to smooth, compress and refine.

5 Metal kidneys to use in a similar way to a rib, but these pare away the surface rather than smooth it.

6 Wires (twisted and smooth) for cutting thrown shapes from the wheelhead.

7 An angled knife or bamboo tool for making a clean, angled base edge or bevel and making an angled notch to slide a cutting wire or twisted cotton into. These are also used for scribing lines on thrown shapes.

8 A chamois leather for compressing, smoothing and refining rims.

9 A pointer gauge for production throwing repeat shapes to a specific height and breadth.

10 Turning (trimming) tools for turning and paring the leatherhard shapes.

11 A hole cutter for cutting circular holes for teapot lids or straining holes.

12 A table knife for using like a metal kidney in tight corners.

13 A toothbrush is used for scoring and applying slurry.

14 A toggle and twisted cotton for cutting lids and small objects off a hump when throwing (not shown).

# TECHNIQUES
# BEFORE YOU START To begin with throwing can seem frustratingly bound in

impenetrable techniques, so an ordered preparation is vital. Approach the subject in logical steps, and with

patient practice your confidence will grow and tangible progress will be achieved.

No other pottery technique requires the clay to be quite as well prepared for successful progress as throwing (see preparing clay). Have a good supply of homogenous, de-aired, soft plastic clay balled up into 300–500 g (10 oz–1 lb) pieces stored in an airtight container, such as a lidded bucket. Also have a large sponge, a bowl of water, a basic tool kit, including a rib, needle, chamois, bevelling tool, dottle or sponge on a stick, cutting wire, and a hand towel within easy reach.

### Wheel speed
Electric pottery wheels spin at up to 300 rpm. This top speed is only useful to experienced, fast production potters. In principle it is advisable to throw at much slower speeds, especially if you are a beginner, as the resulting pots will have more personality. The whole experience will also be less intimidating and frenetic, and much more contemplative and enjoyable. Throwing is a decelerating process from start to finish. Start at a top speed of between 100–150 rpm, a medium speed of between 50–100 rpm and a slow speed of between 10–50 rpm.

### Body position
Do not be afraid of the clay. Sit closely into the slip tray and lean over the wheel-head in a dominant position. Always look for comfortable and effective methods to brace and control your hands and arms. Your hands should always be working together and preferably linked as if they are the hinged parts of one tool.

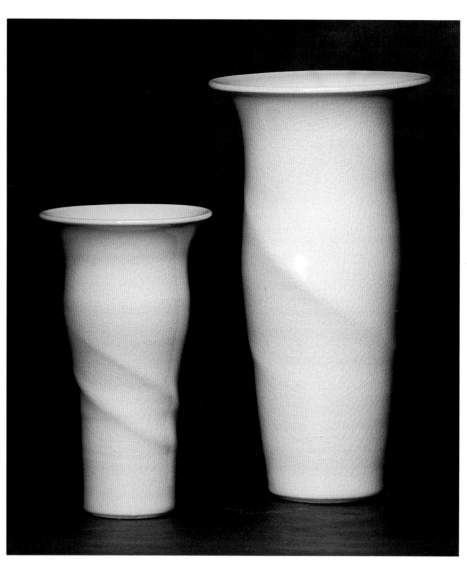

VASE FORMS (16 CM/6¼ IN AND 19 CM/7½ IN)
LIMOGES AND AUDRY BLACKMAN CLAY, POT RIMS ARE DRIED WITH A HOT AIR
GUN TO KEEP THEM SYMMETRICAL WHILE THE SOFT CLAY IS ALTERED, REDUCING
THE RISK OF COLLAPSE. THE MOVEMENT MARKS ARE MADE WITH A SMALL
ROUND STICK (JOHN DAWSON).

### Water
This is your all-important lubricant throughout the throwing process. A container of water is therefore needed for all throwing work. Use too much and the clay will become saturated and weak. Use too little and the clay will stick, twist and tear. The right prescription is "little and often" – and

should be sponged on, rather than poured. Ensure that you re-wet both your hands and the clay before each move and that there is always a film of lubrication between your hands or fingers and the clay surface. Lastly, ensure your finished pots are free from any pools and puddles of water before you remove them from the wheel.

The information in this chapter reflects an individual style and approach. Ask 10 different potters how to carry out a single technique and you will get 10 sometimes conflicting answers. This only proves that there are no hard and fast rules. You must simply regard all advice as personal. Try all methods and eventually you will develop a personal style of your own.

# TECHNIQUES
# CREATING A SIMPLE CYLINDER The common, basic shape to a whole

family of pottery vessels, the cylinder is a simple form to practise. This exercise will give you the most

valuable lesson in the basic throwing techniques of hollowing, opening out and raising walls.

## Centring (fast speed 100–150 rpm)

This action will form your rough ball into a smooth dome, which will spin without the slightest oscillation in the centre of the wheelhead. This is the foundation of successful throwing.

**1** Ensure the wheelhead is clean and dry. Slap your ball of clay onto the centre so it sticks securely. Cup the first hand around the clay with your fingertips like a claw and rest your thumb on top, creating a "mould".

**2** Bring your second hand to overlap the first and squeeze the clay into the 'mould'. Note how the arms are resting securely on the slip tray at 90° to each other. Now gently, but firmly, tug the clay towards you. As the wheel spins, the wobbling clay should begin to settle down. Always release your grip with a gentle relaxation, never with a jerk. Remember to re-lubricate with water regularly to prevent drying out.

**3** This next action, which is called "coning-up", is a way of fine tuning the clay's preparation. One theory suggests that it orientates the clay particles into a spiral mode, thereby adding a little more evenness to the throwing process. Using the bottom edge of your palms and overlapping your fingers, squeeze and draw the clay up into a cone.

CUPS AND SAUCERS (8 CM/3¼ IN AND 10 CM/4 IN) STONEWARE CLAY, MATT WHITE AND CREAM GLAZES, REDUCTION FIRED (RUPERT SPIRA).

**4** Keep your "mould" hand on the clay and move your second hand to press down onto it causing the clay to settle back into the desired flattened dome. Repeat moves 1 and 2 as necessary.

## Hollowing (medium/fast speed 50–150 rpm)

At this stage the aim is to utilize all the available clay to create a vessel with walls and base of an even thickness. Walls that are even in any pottery making technique are perhaps the key to success.

**5A** In the orthodox method, a steady thumb is pressed down into the clay. It must be perfectly still otherwise the pot will become off-centre. Leave a base thickness of about 4–5 mm (⅛ in).

**5B** Alternatively, use your fingers to create the same result. Note how the other hand offers support and control in both methods.

**6** An even base is created as the fingers open out the bottom of the form – this creates a 'doughnut' ring. The orthodox method would be to use the thumb as a logical progression of step 5A. Note how the fingers of the other hand provide counterpressure to maintain the width of the cylinder.

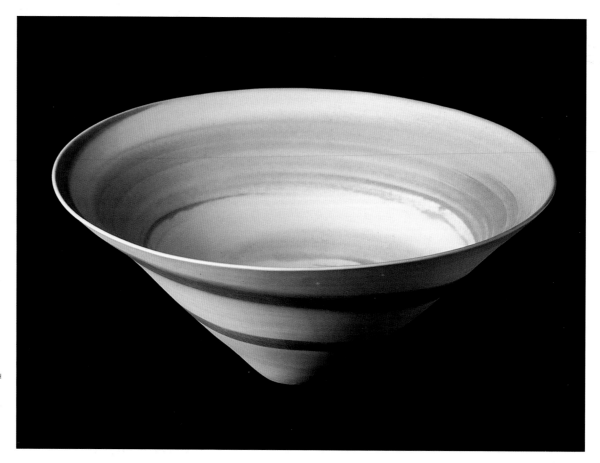

COPPER SPIRAL FLARED VESSEL (14 CM/5½ IN) THROWN PORCELAIN WITH A COPPER STAINED SPIRAL CREATING INTEGRAL LINES, EMULATING THE DECORATION OF PEBBLES (SUE PARASKEVA).

## Pinching and lifting (slow/medium speed 10–100 rpm)

Essentially, the clay is pinched (pulled up) creating a narrow aperture through which the clay must pass as you draw your hand upwards, thereby reducing the thickness and increasing the height of the wall.

**7** Now begin raising the wall. A simple and secure basic technique for beginners is a one-handed method with the thumb inside, the fingers outside and the other hand used for support. Each lift should be a steady glide from bottom to top. Lubricate before each lift. Here the fingertips are forming the pinch while the thumb makes a link. The potter's body should be forward with the forearms braced on the abdomen.

**9** The wall is now taller and requires a more sturdy grip. Pinch your fingers into the knuckle and use your thumb to form the link (known as knuckling or pulling up). Lubricate and lean forward so your forearms can once again use your body for support. Lean backwards slowly to raise the grip in a nice, controlled lift.

**10** Refine the finished cylinder with a rib. Use a chamois leather strip to smooth the rim by draping it over the rim and pinching lightly through the leather. A 325 g (11½ oz) ball should make a coffee mug-sized cylinder about 10 cm (4 in) high and 7 cm (2¾ in) wide when it is fired and finished.

**8** The "doughnut" is now converted into a good, evenly thick, slightly tapered cone. You may find it helpful to use the rib, as shown here. Push gently from inside against the rib in a rising action.

TALL JUG (58 CM/23 IN)
ST THOMAS CLAY, THROWN
AND ALTERED, TITANIUM
CREAM GLAZE WITH BRUSHED
OXIDE DECORATION.
(KYRA CANE).

## Cylinder sections

These pictures illustrate how the cylinder grows in cross-section, as the throwing process develops. This gives a clear visual demonstration of how potters adjust the form in clay as they are throwing. The subtle thickening is the secret to success in all thrown forms. It provides both wet and fired strength, helping to control distortion during the making processes and warping in the kiln.

**1** You can check the basic thickness of the hollowed clay by pushing a needle through the clay to the wheelhead and resting your fingertip on the surface of the clay base. A thickness of 4–5 mm (⅙–¼in) is ideal.

**2** The fingers open out a flat, even base creating the "doughnut". This puts all available clay in the right place for making the wall. Do not undercut too deeply.

**3** The first lift creates a solid, even wall. See how the fingers are positioned to face each other through the clay.

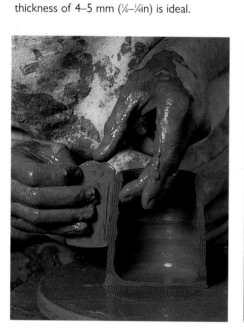

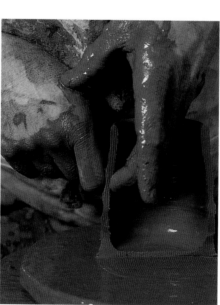

**4** The rib consolidates and prepares the wall for further thinning.

**5** Knuckling up (pulling up) to the final height thins the wall even further.

**6** The chamois refines the rim. If you examine this cross-section closely, the wall is even, but notice how the rim carries a little extra weight.

## Making cylinder refinements

These pictures show how a basic thrown form can be refined into a neat, finished vessel and then removed from the wheel.

Refining all your pots at this early stage is a good habit to get into. It preserves a lively freshness that can be progressively dulled

during subsequent leatherhard trimming and tidying. With practise, this method can be used to lift tall, cylindrical or bellied forms.

**1** To maintain the correct development of a form, it is often necessary to decrease the diameter. "Collar in" by encircling the wall with your thumb and fingers, then slide the fingers across each in a scissors action.

**2** Use a needle to trim an uneven or damaged rim by cutting through the slow turning pot towards a fingertip and lifting off the unwanted ring of clay.

**3** Ensure that any water is sponged out before the pot is removed.

**4** Make a neat angled undercut, or "bevel", at the bottom of the wall, otherwise you will be left with a jagged skirt. This bevel also aids accurate cutting off with a wire.

**5** Hold a thin, taut cutting wire flat on the wheelhead or bat and pull or push it cleanly through underneath the pot.

**6** Stop the wheel. Towel dry your hands and gently encircle the pot so the clay lightly sticks to your fingers and palms. Lift the pot off and gently place it down on a waiting board or bat.

## Common cylinder-making problems

By cutting your pots in half you can learn a great deal, especially in diagnosing problems.

Each of these four cross sections shows the problems that can occur when developing a

cylinder form. Twisting may occur if the clay is insufficiently lubricated during throwing.

In this example the pot is short, thick and heavy because the clay is underused. The base hasn't been thinned or flattened enough, so the clay on the bottom cannot be used to heighten the wall.

This pot was off-centre when hollowing began, or was hollowed off-centre. As you start to raise the walls, the rim undulates markedly as the thick side grows more than the thin side.

This pot has been made fatally weak or has even been torn during the initial pinching and lifting (pulling up). The grip was too vigorous and/or the hands did not rise soon enough. Any thin or weak point within a wall will ultimately undermine your ability to further thin or stretch the form.

This cross-section shows the initial centred width of this pot. The wall has collapsed outwards forming a wider, shallower shape, but the corner is now so thin and weak that the base will probably crack or tear away from the wall.

BLACK OVAL BOWL (5 CM/2 IN) PORCELAIN, THROWN AND GENTLY BENT WHILE STILL SOFT. THE LEATHERHARD FORM IS ATTACHED TO A NEW HAND-ROLLED BASE AND SLOWLY DRIED (PRUE VENABLES). PHOTOGRAPH BY TERENCE BOGUE.

# TECHNIQUES
## CREATING BOWL SHAPES
The open shape of a bowl demands a switch of focus from the exterior silhouette to the interior's concave line. A second, distinct procedure called "turning" (trimming), carried out when the bowl is leatherhard, is used to trim away the surplus weight and create a footring (foot) on which the bowl form is cradled. Whether your shape is steep sided and enclosed like a cup, or shallow and open like a saucer, if it is curve-based, it is a member of this family.

**1** The centred clay begins a little lower and wider than for a cylinder. Hollow it down to a clay depth of about 1 cm (⅓ in), then open out a curved base, gathering the clay into the familiar "doughnut" ring.

**2** Pinch and lift the wall upwards and slightly outwards like the straight side of a "V", remembering to leave weight in the rim.

**3** As the form grows, slow down the wheel speed. It should be slower than when you are working on a cylinder, because the rim of this wider shape is travelling faster and will therefore be more effected by the centrifugal force.

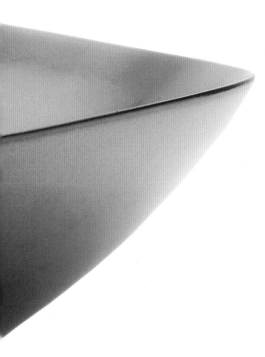

**4** Now, in a stroke that begins in the centre of the form and rises up to the rim, the concave curve of the bowl is delicately pressed out, creating a smooth transition from base into wall. Hold your fingers either side of the clay, guiding the line of the shape, but no longer pinching. Use the rib to smooth and refine the form further if you wish.

**5** The rim is refined on the finished form. Should you wish to make the form shallower, fold the rim gently out into a trumpet shape clasping your hands over the clay in a "praying" position, then regain the concave curve again using the method that has been described above.

## Bowl sections

These pictures illustrate how the bowl develops in cross section. A bowl shape grows outward simultaneously, so a considerable thickness is left around the rim and immediately below it, as this will build up as the bowl swells outward.

**1** Note that the curve and width of the bowl's base are already established, and how the doughnut ring is poised to be drawn up and outwards.

**2** The initial bowl form is taking shape. Note the weight of clay at the rim.

**3** The "V" shaped wall is further raised and thinned. The thorough throwing keeps the trimming and turning to a minimum.

## Common bowl-making problems

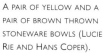

**4** The rib is used to refine the all-important curve of the form's interior. Ensure that as the rib rises into the wall, the fingers outside the wall provide gentle counter pressure.

If the bowl wall becomes too thin and/ or too shallow the upper half of the wall can easily begin to slump. This is quickly exaggerated if the clay is a little off-centre to begin with or if the width of the clay is too narrow after centring.

A PAIR OF YELLOW AND A PAIR OF BROWN THROWN STONEWARE BOWLS (LUCIE RIE AND HANS COPER).

## Repetition throwing

As your skills develop, you will find that your methods will settle into a pattern and rhythm. You can use this to establish your own style of work. Should you then wish to repeat shapes accurately, you must measure each one. When designing a piece of functional work for volume production, keep notes on the weight of clay used and its overall dimensions.

**1** To make a run of pieces to the same size, weigh and shape the clay into balls ready to put onto the wheelhead. Beginners should take 12 or so pieces to the wheel to allow for uninterrupted practise. For a coffee mug, you need balls of 275–350 g (10–12 oz). Store them in plastic to prevent air drying the surface, and do not let them come into contact with a porous surface as this will also dry the outer surfaces of the clay.

**2** Having weighed out your balls of clay, centre each piece to the same width using callipers.

**3** When you are happy with the size and shape of the pot, use a point gauge to set the height and width without actually touching the pot. A gauge with a hinged tip is the most useful as you can swing the tip out of the way to remove the last pot and begin the next. Ultimately though, the character and personality of your pots will do more to give them a "family" resemblance than a pure measurement.

## Turning a footring

Before turning a footring (trimming a foot), the bowl must be left to dry evenly to a leatherhard firmness. There are varying degrees of softness and stiffness within leatherhard, so it is useful to apply a simple test: is the bowl stiff enough to be stood on its rim and fixed to the wheelhead without it becoming distorted? And is the base soft enough to mark easily with a thumbnail, but too hard to make a thumbprint? If the answers are "yes" to both questions, then you are ready to proceed.

**1** First, assess where to begin trimming the clay on the wall and the base. Above all, your aim should be to follow as accurately as possible the curve of the bowl's interior, creating an even balanced thickness and balanced weight.

**2** Centre the upturned bowl, using the rings of the wheelhead to guide you. Revolve the wheel to check it is centred and then stop and correct if necessary. Fix the bowl using three coils of stiffish plastic clay on the wheelhead, evenly spaced around the bowl.

**3** The width of a footring (foot) will vary according to the shape and width of the bowl, but will invariably be a third to a half of the rim's diameter. Use your aesthetic judgement and callipers to establish this measurement and mark the base accordingly.

SOUP TUREEN (38 CM/15 IN)
THROWN AND DECORATED
EARTHENWARE (FENELLA
MALLALIEU).

**4** Use the turning (trimming) tool to trim the clay from the edge of the base. The first cut establishes the height and width of the footring (foot). Note how the blade of the tool is controlled with both hands. Rest your finger lightly on the spinning pot to prevent the bowl from dislodging suddenly. The pace of this technique should be "brisk".

**5** The shape of the form is now trimmed out. A misjudgement of the bowl's shape at this point can lead to a bad weak point at a critical place where the wall meets the footring (foot).

**6** The final trimming should be made inside the footring (foot).

**7** Take care to examine the form as a whole. Regard the footring (foot) as extraneous and visualize the complete dome shape. This should correspond well to your memory of the bowl's interior. The footring (foot) itself needs to have a quality and weight to reflect the rim of the bowl.

**8** You may need to remove the bowl and check progress once or twice during trimming. Mark one fixing coil and the bowl with a locating scratch, remove another coil and slide out the bowl. Reverse this and the bowl will return to its centred position. Finally, cradle the bowl in your hands to assess its weight and balance.

## Trimming an upright form

**1** Measure the base width and wall thickness. Assuming the pot's base is flat and even, trim the lower portion of the wall. Note the taller, fatter coils used to fix this pot in place on the wheelhead.

**2** Trim the wall while keeping your other hand hovering over the pot to catch it should it dislodge.

**3** The next stage is to add a neat bevel to the bottom edge.

## Throwing on a bat

There are many occasions when it is preferable or even essential to use a bat. Bats can be made from a sheet material, such as plywood or chipboard. There are numerous systems to fix a bat to a wheel, but the method illustrated here requires no precision cutting or drilling – you simply stick the bat onto the wheelhead using a pad of plastic clay.

   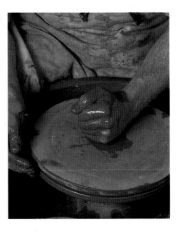

**1** Centre about 300 g (11 oz) of clay for a 20–25 cm (8–10 in) bat. Use the side of your hand to flatten the clay into a shallow disc about 6–8 mm (¼ in) thick.

**2** Use a rib to ensure it is perfectly flat, smooth and dry. Lie a ruler or straight stick across the pad to check it is not even the slightest bit thicker at the centre or the bat will not adhere properly.

**3** Cut a groove into the surface and score a cross. This prevents the pad surface from becoming wet and slippery. It must remain tacky, but not wet.

**4** Take a clean, dry bat and wipe the underside lightly with a damp sponge. Centre it into position and thump it in the middle to stick it down. Push it to test how well the bat is attached.

# TECHNIQUES
# CREATING FLAT FORMS This is the last of the three basic forms in throwing. Here,

base-making becomes the main and most critical part of the process. The clay you use can be

considerably softer than that used for upright forms. It does not need to stand up in a thin wall, so a

softer consistency helps with centring and flattening. A different, but equally demanding, set of skills and

techniques have to be learned.

## Making a plate

Use about 1.2 kg (2½ lb) of clay to make a 25–27 cm (10–10½ in) dinner plate.

**1** Centring is the dominant part of the whole process. Note how as the top hand compresses and widens the clay, the fingertips of the hand underneath control its growth. The edge of the clay must not be allowed to fold over onto the bat like a wave, it must grow from below, pushing the water and slurry before it.

**2** A wide, shallow disc is formed utilizing the width of the bat.

**3** Make a hollow by hooking a thumb over the outside edge of the disc and drawing your fingertips across, creating a base thickness of 5–7 mm (¼ in). Use the fingers of your other hand to both support the move and compress the edge of the hollow as it grows to prevent the clay peeling away.

**4** The desired width is achieved leaving the familiar doughnut ring at the circumference.

**5** Here the base is put under compression as the thickness of the base is refined and subtly moves from the centre outwards or vice versa. This action compacts and binds the clay's particles, thus increasing crack resistance. The evenness of the base thickness is crucial as plates are particularly vulnerable to splitting or cracking as they shrink during drying and firing.

**6** Use a rib to further refine the surface in a sweep from the centre to the rim. It is advisable to leave 1–2 mm (¹⁄₁₆ in) more thickness at the base's centre than at the rim.

**7** Finally, pinch out and refine the rim into a suitable weight and width. When cutting off with a wire keep the cutting wire taught, level and on the surface of the bat.

# TECHNIQUES
# MAKING LIDDED FORMS There are numerous ways to make a pot with a lid.

Essentially there are two thrown elements, one of which has a retaining edge whereas the other is plain. Which method you choose depends on the function of the finished pot. This casserole dish form has a shelf or "gallery" (seat) on which the lid can sit.

**1** Centre the clay and partially thin the wall before you form the gallery (seat). You will need a generous rim thickness.

**2** Hold the rim gently just underneath, while using an index finger to cut a groove into it at a roughly 45˚ angle. Note how the thumb forms a link between the two hands.

**3** Knuckle up (pull up) the wall of the pot to its finished height, taking care not to interfere with the gallery (seat).

**4** Use the blade of a table knife to give the gallery (seat) a crisp refinement. Avoid making the gallery (seat) either too wide or too thin.

**5** Stop the wheel to measure the gallery (seat) width with callipers. Do not be afraid to actually touch the clay surface to do this accurately.

**6** The lid is a simple saucer shape. Centre and flatten as before, but not as wide as for a plate, and throw as if you are making a very shallow bowl. At the centre the thickness need only be about 6–7 mm (¼ in). Once again, actually touch the clay with the callipers to ensure you get an accurate measurement of the lid's diameter.

**7** Trim the lid. When leatherhard, it becomes a gentle dome on which a knob or, as shown here, a strap handle, can be applied to create the finished form. The lugs are made from the same extrusion of clay used to make the handle (see handles).

## A flange-lidded pot

Here the jar shape is plain, but note the weight and roundness of the rim.

The lid is thrown exactly like a saucer, but with an upstanding flange. The aperture of the pot is measured to fit the outside edge of the flange. The slight overhang of the lid creates a good dust cover.

## A cap-lidded pot

This "ginger jar" form is more enclosed so is suited to this cap lid, which needs a shoulder to sit on. Callipers are used to measure the

outside edge of the raised lip on the jar as well as the outside edge of the cap to ensure a snug fit.

BISCUIT BARREL (20 CM/8 IN)
THROWN FORM WITH A
MIXTURE OF GRANITE, IRON,
ASH AND CLAY GLAZE
(MIKE DODD).

# TECHNIQUES
# HANDLES

It is necessary to develop other skills than throwing in order to enhance the piece and extend the potential of wheel-thrown forms. Handles can be both a practical necessity on a pot and a way of giving further character, and they can be pulled or extruded.

## Pulling handles

Of the many ways you can make coils or straps to shape into handles and lugs, pulled handles are the strongest and arguably the most akin to throwing. They are drawn from a stem of clay, giving them both the inherent strength and character of thrown pots.

**4** Lie the strap on a clean board, taking care not to kink, bend or otherwise spoil it. Cut it cleanly from the stem with a chopping action using your fingertips over the edge of the board.

**3** Refine the surface and edges of the strap by drawing your thumb down against a crooked finger.

**1** Several straps can be drawn or "pulled" from a tapered stem of well prepared clay. Wet your pulling hand and form a hole between your thumb and finger. Now draw downwards in swift strokes. Do not squeeze the clay, but rather let the friction do the stretching as you pull down.

**2** Keep re-wetting your hand, otherwise the strap will tear prematurely. An elliptical section will give the strap strength down its centre and refined edges. Alter the size and shape of the hole in your hand to make handles suit the scale of the pot or pots you are working on.

CURL KNOB (DETAIL)
EXTRUDED, TEXTURED
AND MODELLED, SALT
GLAZED OVER COBALT
AND TITANIUM SLIPS
(JANE HAMLYN).

## Extruding handles

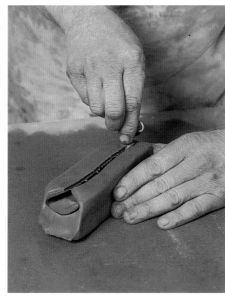

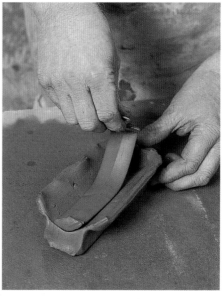

**1** Extrusions are usually made by using a wad box (extruder) that forces clay through an aperture cut into a metal die (see Handbuilding, equipment). Here is a quick alternative. Make a wire loop with a suitable shape and size. Prepare an oblong block of good, soft carefully de-aired clay.

**2** Hold the end of the loop in an upright position and draw it cleanly through the clay.

**3** Do not allow the loop to exit from the rear of the clay block. Leave it in place while you carefully fold back the encasing flaps. Then lift out the strap using the loop.

**4** Lie the straps on a clean, dry surface, ready for use. If you are not going to use them immediately, wrap them carefully in plastic – if they are too dry when you loop them onto the pot, they will crack or split.

LARGE DISH (33 CM/13 IN) HIGH SILICA BODY CLAY WITH ADDED FIRE-CLAY, THROWN AND ALTERED, MOUNTED ON FEET WITH A CENTRAL HANDLE ATTACHED, REDUCTION FIRED AND SALT GLAZED (MICHAEL CASSON).

# TECHNIQUES
# ALTERED FORMS
Simple functional forms can possess great beauty and you may be happy to focus on the technique of throwing bowls or cups. However, even the process of developing a jug or a teapot that pours, involves an element of manipulation of the thrown form. The potential of altering thrown forms is quite vast, and this approach often characterizes a particular style of thrown work.

■ Examples follow of how to approach functional forms in a range of throwing projects including a cup and saucer, a plate, a jug, a teapot and a sectional vase that uses two joined thrown elements. The classic vessel forms created in these throwing projects illustrate how, with relatively simple manipulation, your basic throwing skills can be extended to produce pieces that have a quite specialized function.

Inevitably, as your throwing skills improve, your standards rise, and your ambition to make ever larger or complex forms also increases. While many contemporary makers enjoy the technique of throwing to endlessly explore the character and simplicity of familiar everyday pots, such as bowls, cups, jugs, containers and dishes, others seek to extend the boundaries of the vessel and of functional form by using the potter's wheel as a tool to create

OPEN MANDALA (88 × 101 CM/34½ × 40 IN)
THROWN AND ALTERED, SINGLE FIRED IN LOW TEMPERATURE
SALT PROCESS. TERRA SIGILLATA SLIPS DEVELOPED FROM RED
AND WHITE CLAY (NEIL TETKOWSKI).

STONEWARE JAR (50 CM/20 IN)
THROWN AND ALTERED, WITH THICK, HIGH-SHRINKAGE
SLIPS TO CREATE SURFACE TEXTURE AND COLOUR, BARIUM
MATT GLAZED (ASHLEY HOWARD).

more organic and sculptural forms. Arguably, the successful distortion and deconstruction of thrown forms is dependent on a thorough understanding and considerable mastery of the basic craft. This will make a difference both aesthetically and technically. Such experimentation can make your work more versatile and involves calling on other methods of forming clay, such as pinching or joining slabs.

Having mastered the basic techniques, your freshly thrown pots may then be pulled, stretched, faceted, pinched, squashed, torn and even dropped to distort their circular symmetry in a soft, organic way and enhance the surface with textural "distressing". Once stiffened, thrown shapes may also be cut and reassembled, carved and creased to build more angular "slab" or metal-like objects and vessels.

The most accomplished practitioners of this method manage to combine extraordinary and radical object making, while at the same time retaining the unique and quite unmistakable character and subtlety of the throwing method.

ABOVE: STONEWARE CYLINDER VASE (37 CM / 14½ IN) STONEWARE CLAY WITH GROG AND FIBRE MESH, THROWN IN SECTIONS WITH THE WINGS COMBED, CARVED AND ATTACHED (COLIN PEARSON).

BELOW: BOWL OF DRY WATER (31 CM / 12½ IN DIAMETER) THROWN AND ALTERED FORM WITH STONEWARE MIXED CLAYS, MULTIPLE SLIPS AND GLAZES (AKI MORIUCHI).

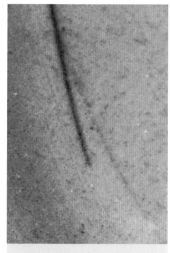

# Cup and Saucer

The generous scale of this breakfast cup and saucer by Richard Phethean is perfect for the French morning habit of drinking café au lait from a bowl, or just for a refreshing cup of tea. Throwing both a flat saucer shape and an enclosed cup form will automatically extend your skills. A slip decoration technique is used, with wax resist applied to certain areas that will then avoid coverage by the slip and show the natural colour of the earthenware clay.

## Materials
Spencroft sanded red
    earthenware 'green dot'

## Equipment
Wheel and cutting wire
Rib
Callipers
Toothbrush
Turning (trimming) tool
Wax resist
Brushes for slip

## Slips
White – white Devon ball clay
Light blue – add
    5% cobalt oxide
Dark blue – add
    20% cobalt oxide
Green – add 10% copper
    oxide and 1% chrome oxide
Thin lines – neat cobalt oxide

## Glaze
CLEAR
| | |
|---|---|
| Lead bisilicate | 72% |
| Potash feldspar | 13% |
| Ball clay | 10% |
| Borax frit | 5% |
| Bentonite | 2% |

HONEY
Powdered red earthenware
    clay is substituted for ball
    clay in above recipe.
Red iron oxide            ½%

## Firing
Biscuit (bisque) fire to 1050°C
    (1922°F)
Glaze fire to 1125°C (2057°F),
    cones 03/02

**1 The Cup** This shape is very similar to the bowl illustrated earlier (see creating bowl shapes), but the base width is narrower and the footring (foot) depth taller. Take 450 g (1 lb) of clay and hollow and create a narrow curved base with a depth of about 1 cm (½ in).

**2** Pinch and lift the wall into a steep-sided, V-shape, taking care to leave ample weight at the rim. If the rim is made too thin the handle's weight will pull the cup shape into an oval during drying and firing.

**3** Refine the rim and subtly conceal the weight just below it.

**4** Use the rib to refine and finish the curve of the cup's interior.

**5** When leatherhard, measure and turn the cup's footring (foot) the same way as you would a bowl (see turning a footring). Then measure the exact width of the finished footring (foot) with callipers.

**6** Make a pulled or extruded strap for the handle to a scale to suit the size and refinement of the cup (use a strip of paper and fold it against the cup to measure for length). Prepare the cup with a toothbrush where the handle will begin and end. Apply a blob of slurry to either end of the strap. Offer up and pinch the strap on the top end (good side facing the cup).

**7** Place a finger above and behind the top join, loop the strap over and stick the other end lightly to the lower prepared area. Check that the handle is correctly aligned before joining (the cup can be stood on its rim allowing the strap to stiffen while it overhangs the surface).

**8 The Saucer** Centre and flatten the shape. Take 800 g (1¾ lb) of clay and hollow out the subtle curve of the saucer by leaving a clay depth in the centre of between 5–8 mm (¼–⅓ in). Draw the weight to the edge of the shape.

**9** Pinch and pull out the full width of the saucer, taking care not to overthin the rim or flatten the shape too much.

**10** When leatherhard, centre the saucer, right side up, and mark the well to take the cup's footring (foot).

**11** Fix the saucer lightly in place and trim a very slight well into the surface.

**12** Assess how much trimming the saucer requires and where the footring (foot) should come (its width should be approximately half that of the total saucer width). Allow the pieces to dry to leatherhard.

**13** Mix the white slip base to a single (light) cream consistency. Half fill the tea cup with slip and empty it with a "tip and turn" action to coat the inside. Leave to stiffen, then dip the cup, held by the footring (foot), to coat the exterior. Wax the saucer around the rim's underside and coat on the top only, by tipping and turning. Once the white slip is dry, apply the coloured slips. Make long spiral strokes using a banding wheel. Biscuit (bisque) fire and glaze and fire.

# Jug

This jug (pitcher) by Richard Phethean must be one of the most enduring and timeless forms since pottery was first made on the wheel. Once you become competent at making good, even cylinders, it is a natural and logical step to greatly increase the volume of the pot simply by stretching and swelling the wall. Today, large jugs are much more often used as vases, but as a form, with its handle pulled from the neck, it provides endless design possibilities.

## Materials

Spencroft sanded red
  earthenware "green dot"

## Equipment

Wheel and cutting wire
Rib
Toothbrush
Serrated metal kidney
Wax resist
Brushes for slips

## Slips

White – white Devon ball clay
Light blue – add 5% cobalt
  oxide
Dark blue – add 20% cobalt
  oxide
Watery green – add 10%
  copper oxide and 1%
  chrome oxide
Thin blue/black lines – neat
  cobalt oxide

## Glaze

CLEAR

| | |
|---|---|
| Lead bisilicate | 72% |
| Potash feldspar | 13% |
| Ball clay | 10% |
| Borax frit | 5% |
| Bentonite | 2% |

HONEY

Powdered red earthenware
clay is substituted for ball clay
Red iron oxide ½%

## Firing

Biscuit (bisque) fire to 1050°C
  (1922°F)
Glaze fire to 1125°C (2057°F),
  cones 03/02

**1** Use 1.8 kg (4 lb) of clay to throw the basic form. In order to gain height rather than width, centre the clay into a narrow dome. Carry out hollowing, hand over hand, for increased force. Lean your body into the slip tray with your forearms braced against your abdomen for extra control.

**2** Create a smooth, even base to the form before knuckling up (pulling up) the primary wall. It is important to gain significant height with each lift, taking care not to weaken or overthin the wall. Note the characteristic "chimney-pot" shape. The creation of this shape is crucial to your success at gaining maximum height. If need be, use the collaring technique to keep to the classical form.

**3** Smooth and dry the pot's surface by pressing out towards a rib in an upward stroke between lifts. This is very helpful to reinforce the wall in preparation for further lifts.

**4** Now that you can no longer link hands, assume a standing position and stoop over the wheel, with your arms braced against your body. This will provide the control and stability you require. For subsequent lifts, lubricate the wall, make a firm grip and lift initially by straightening up your body. Always ease off your grip towards the top of the form in order to allow the neck to retain its crucial strength.

**7** Establish clearly where the neck of the form will begin. Collar in if required.

**5** Create the belly by stretching rather than pinching. Use the minimum of lubrication and a gentle wheel speed. Stroke out the form with a very slow, rising push from the inside with fingertips against fingertips, or fingertips against a rib, moving up in parallel on the outside. The rib can also simultaneously smooth the surface of the pot if that is what you want. Tilt your head to watch the silhouette of the form develop.

**6** Gently increase the volume with successive strokes from bottom to neck, allowing the form to distend naturally, as a balloon would inflate. Take care not to cause the belly to swell too much too low down, and not to create any odd corners or angles in the form's line, as this may cause it to collapse.

**8** Refine the shape and character of the neck and rim.

**9** Stop the wheel. Dry the thumb and forefinger of one hand and lightly place them against the rim to form the pouring lip aperture and width of the lip to suit the scale of the pot. Wet the index finger of your other hand and gently stroke out the lip with a waggling side-to-side action. Hold the finger vertically at first to create the throat, and then progressively more horizontally to create the "pout".

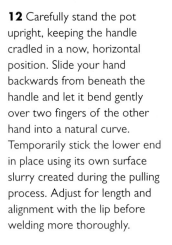

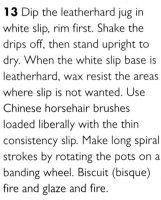

**12** Carefully stand the pot upright, keeping the handle cradled in a now, horizontal position. Slide your hand backwards from beneath the handle and let it bend gently over two fingers of the other hand into a natural curve. Temporarily stick the lower end in place using its own surface slurry created during the pulling process. Adjust for length and alignment with the lip before welding more thoroughly.

**10** Prepare the jug rim to attach the handle, and a pre-made tapered stem of plastic clay, with a wet toothbrush. Then, stick the end of the stem firmly into place.

**11** The form must be just stiff enough to hold its shape. Cradle the belly in one hand and refine the weight and length of the handle with the other and pull the handle from the rim. Add the combed detail with the serrated kidney. Place your hand lengthways behind the handle with your fingertips touching the neck, and the handle end resting on your wrist.

**13** Dip the leatherhard jug in white slip, rim first. Shake the drips off, then stand upright to dry. When the white slip base is leatherhard, wax resist the areas where slip is not wanted. Use Chinese horsehair brushes loaded liberally with the thin consistency slip. Make long spiral strokes by rotating the pots on a banding wheel. Biscuit (bisque) fire and glaze and fire.

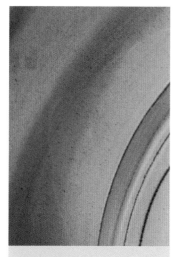

## Materials

Spencroft sanded red
   earthenware "green dot"

## Equipment

Wheel and cutting wire
Bat
Rib
Turning (trimming) tool
Wax resist
Brushes and banding wheel

## Slips

White – white Devon ball clay
Light blue – add 5% cobalt
   oxide
Dark blue – add 20% cobalt
   oxide
Watery green – add 10%
   copper oxide and 1%
   chrome oxide
Thin blue/black lines – neat
   cobalt oxide

## Glaze

CLEAR

| | |
|---|---|
| Lead bisilicate | 72% |
| Potash feldspar | 13% |
| Ball clay | 10% |
| Borax frit | 5% |
| Bentonite | 2% |

HONEY
Powdered red earthenware
clay is substituted for ball clay
Red iron oxide   ½%

## Firing

Biscuit (bisque) fire to 1050°C
   (1922°F)
Glaze fire to 1125°C (2057°F),
   cones 03/02

# Wide-Rimmed Dish

During the 17th century, when the Staffordshire potteries in England began to rise in importance, huge versions of this form, known as "chargers", were produced with bold, slip-decorated patterns and motifs. This presumably means they were used to carry food from the kitchens to load or "charge" the dining tables in the large homes of the wealthy. Richard Phethean considers them a great canvas on which to experiment with colour and pattern.

**1** This wide-rimmed dish will take 4–5 kg (9–11 lb) of clay. Place your clay lightly on the bat, turn the wheel and adjust the clay into a roughly centred position before patting the clay into a rough cone. With elbows out and hands facing in towards each other, gather the soft clay into a tallish cone.

**2** Brace the forearm of your lateral centring hand on the slip tray or tuck it into your hip. Bear down on the clay with an upright forearm and let the fingers overlap and reinforce the centring hand. Do not allow the clay to "mushroom" over at the edge as this may cause air and/or slurry to become trapped in the clay.

**3** Continue this process downwards and outwards, creating a shallow disc which utilizes the full width of the bat.

**4** Hollow the centred disc to a base thickness of between 8–10mm (⅓–½ in). Claw out the base width using the fingers of one hand with the thumb hooked over the outside edge of the clay. Reinforce this move with the other hand and simultaneously compress the edge of the hollow to prevent it peeling away excessively.

**5** Compress and refine the subtle curve of the base (this is vital to avoid cracking during drying). The pressure of both hands can move the weight either from the centre to the rim or vice versa.

**6** Turn the wheel very gently, throw the wall upwards and outwards, but do not overthin it as it has to support itself during the final stage. Refine the weight and quality of the rim. Use the rib to dry, compress, smooth and refine the base and create the step before the rim.

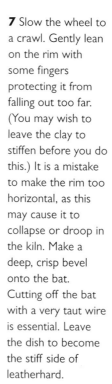

**7** Slow the wheel to a crawl. Gently lean on the rim with some fingers protecting it from falling out too far. (You may wish to leave the clay to stiffen before you do this.) It is a mistake to make the rim too horizontal, as this may cause it to collapse or droop in the kiln. Make a deep, crisp bevel onto the bat. Cutting off the bat with a very taut wire is essential. Leave the dish to become the stiff side of leatherhard.

**8** Assess where the footrings (feet) have to come and how much weight can be trimmed away. Overturn your leatherhard dish onto a bat wide enough to take the rim. (Here the bats are used to raise the wider one above the height of the slip tray, or if you can, remove the slip tray first.) Rest the centre of the dish on a flattened lump of stiff clay during turning (trimming).

**9** Now you should establish both the width and the depth of the outer footring (foot), and then centre up and fix the dish with three coils of clay.

**10** Trim between the rim and the outer footring (foot).

**11** Establish the width of the inner footring (foot) and trim away to the outer footring. Use the corner of the tool to create a spiral of concentric furrows as this causes less pressure on the base. Shave off the furrows.

**12** Shave the very centre of the dish. Take care not to overthin the base at any point as flat forms are prone to cracking during drying or firing. Create the combed detail with a serrated metal kidney on the freshly-thrown clay.

**13** At leatherhard stage wax the rim's underside and coat with white base slip on the top side, using the tip and turn method. When the white slip is dry, apply the coloured slips, with brushes and a banding wheel. Biscuit (bisque) fire and then glaze and fire.

# Oval Baking Bowl

This oval bowl, designed by Nick Membery, is another example of a combined form using the techniques of throwing and handbuilding. The main form is initially thrown on a potter's wheel, then altered into an oval shape and finally joined onto a slab-rolled base.

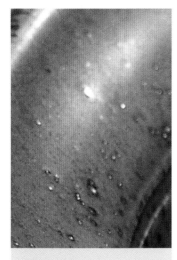

## Materials

Stoneware clay

## Equipment

Wheel and cutting wire
Circular throwing bat
Straight-sided throwing rib
Strip of thin plastic
6 cm (2½ in) oval nail with
   rounded end
Sponge
Rolling pin
2 rolling guides 5 mm (¼ in)
   thick
Rolling cloth
Patterned plaster slab
Banding wheel
Knife
Needle
Plastic comb
Toothbrush
Round-ended wooden dowel
Profile beading tool
Water sprayer
Gas kiln
Gloves for glazing

## Glaze

BLUE GLAZE

| | |
|---|---|
| Potash feldspar | 50% |
| China clay | 30% |
| Whiting | 10% |
| Talc | 10% |
| Cobalt oxide | 0.75% |

## Firing

Biscuit (bisque) fire to 990°C
   (1814°F)
Reduction fire to 1280°C
   (2336°F)

**1** Centre 1.2 kg (2½ lb) of wedged clay onto a throwing bat and open the clay straight through to the bat leaving no base. Continue opening the clay to a diameter of about 14 cm (5½ in). Do this fairly slowly and push the clay firmly onto the bat throughout, otherwise there is a tendency for the clay to work loose when making pots without a base.

**2** Cone the opened clay upwards and inwards with your thumb and forefinger, preparing to pull the wall up to the required size. Leave the clay slightly thicker where it joins the bat while you are pulling it upwards. This will help when joining the wall to the base later on. Once you have pulled up the wall start to fold over the rim from the inside using your right hand outside for support.

**3** Refine the shape of the pot with a straight-sided throwing rib by pushing from the inside outwards onto the rib. This will also remove any excess slurry and the drawing rings (rims) from the outside of the pot.

**4** Finalize the rim shape. The rim is smoothed and compressed by holding a flat piece of plastic across it as it turns on the wheel. Use a steel nail to emphasize the start of the rim and the change of direction in the pot wall, both inside and out. The thrown wall of the pot should measure 10 cm (4 in) high by 25 cm (10 in) wide. Remove any water from inside the pot with a sponge. Lift the bat with the pot from the wheelhead, put to one side and leave to stiffen.

**5** Roll out a clay slab onto a cloth using guide sticks for the thickness. This slab should be oval and big enough for the base of the thrown pot. Dry it out for a couple of hours. When it has stiffened slightly, place it face down on a patterned plaster slab. Place the rolling cloth over the clay slab and roll it once more to impress the pattern into the base. Remove the clay slab from the plaster slab and leave to dry until leatherhard.

**6** Place the bat with the thrown wall of the pot onto a banding wheel. Take a thin knife and cut the clay from the bat all the way around and then use both hands to gently push the bowl into an oval shape. The pot should be altered before it is leatherhard, but when it has dried enough to be handled easily.

**7** When both the thrown wall and the base are leatherhard they are ready to be joined. Put the base onto the circular bat and then both onto the banding wheel. Position the oval pot wall on the base. Check the oval shape is symmetrical and mark the outline of the wall onto the base both inside and outside with a potter's needle. Remove the wall. Leave about 1 cm (½ in) extra all the way round the outside of the larger of the two marked oval shapes and cut away the excess clay from the slab with a knife.

**8** Take a piece of plastic comb about 2.5 cm (1 in) long and score the bottom edge of the thrown wall and the section of the base to which it will be joined. Slurry the scored wall of the pot and press the wall firmly into position on the base. Wriggle the bottom of the wall slightly all the way round to ensure that it is tightly stuck onto the base.

**9** Support the inside of the pot wall with your left hand and move around pressing the excess clay from the base up and onto the outside of the pot. Turn the banding wheel and smooth the clay with two fingers, softening it with water if necessary.

**10** Run a round-ended piece of wooden dowel all the way Around the inside of the pot where the wall joins the base This will help to seal and compress the join and will also add an attractive finishing mark to the inside.

**11** Finish the outside base of the pot with a profile beading tool made from thin plastic or metal. Run the tool smoothly around by holding it in a fixed position and turning the banding wheel. This will remove the excess clay and finalize the beading at the base of the pot. Spray water around the bottom of the pot, as it turns to lubricate the beading tool.

**12** Leave the finished pot to dry before biscuit (bisque) firing it to 990°C (1814°F). Then, wearing gloves, dip it into the glaze and reduction fire it to 1280°C (1236°F) in a gas kiln.

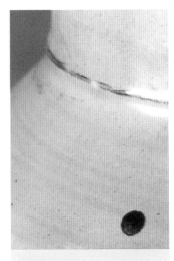

# Sectional Vase

Richard Phethean advises that the degree of difficulty in throwing this shape in one piece easily outweighs the technical skill required to make and join two sections. This is because the tall neck of a single form would cause the belly to distort or collapse. The two smaller thrown sections are easier to make accurately and evenly, and the resulting pot will be lighter and more elegant. This working method will also increase the scale and diversity of your work.

## Materials

Spencroft sanded red
   earthenware "green dot"

## Equipment

Wheel and cutting wire
Bats
Callipers
Rib
Sponge
Needle
Table knife or metal kidney
Serrated metal kidney
Wax resist
Brushes for slips
Electric kiln

## Slips

White – white Devon ball clay
Light blue – add 5% cobalt
   oxide
Dark blue – add 20% cobalt
   oxide
Green – add 10% copper
   oxide and 1% chrome oxide
Thin blue/black lines – neat
   cobalt oxide
Make up the coloured slips to
   a thin, watery consistency

## Glaze

CLEAR
| | |
|---|---|
| Lead bisilicate | 72% |
| Potash feldspar | 13% |
| Ball clay | 10% |
| Borax frit | 5% |
| Bentonite | 2% |

HONEY
Powdered red earthenware
   clay is substituted for ball
   clay in above recipe
| | |
|---|---|
| Red iron oxide | ½% |

## Firing

Biscuit (bisque) fire to 1050°C
   (1922°F)
Glaze fire to 1125°C
   (2057°F), cones 03/02

**1** Make a clear, visual plan of the form so that each section may be accurately thrown. The bottom section has a flat base and is thrown and bellied in a very similar way to the Jug (pitcher) project. It will use 1.25 kg (2¾ lb) clay. Good centring is vital for this technique to work well. Here, the rim of the section is being squared off at an appropriate angle.

**2** Carefully measure the inside edge of the neck with callipers. Do not wire off the pot from the bat. Leave it to stiffen.

**3** The top section, which uses 800 g (1¾ lb) clay, is made "upside down". The width at the base of the centred clay will determine the width at the top of the finished form. Hollow the clay right down to the bat and open out in the usual way.

**4** Raise the primary wall into a narrow cone.

**5** Achieve the final height and rough form.

**6** Refine the concave top section with a rib. Measure and square the rim with callipers in a corresponding way to that of the bottom section.

**7** When it has stiffened sufficiently, recentre the bottom section onto the wheel with its bat restuck lightly onto a clay pad. Wet the rim with a sponge and score thoroughly in preparation for joining. Similarly prepare the top section's rim and apply a coating of slurry (see Handbuilding, using slurry for joining slabs).

**8** Invert the top section and bring it down onto the bottom section, aligning the joins carefully. Now slowly revolve the wheel to check if the top section is on centre. If not, quickly lift it off and realign before it sticks too well.

**9** Turn the wheel and seal the join between the two sections with a table knife or kidney.

**10** Release the bat from the top section of the pot with a cutting wire, using your breastbone as counter pressure.

**11** Trim the top section with a needle and preserve it in a state just soft enough to wet and re-throw.

**12** Rethrow the new rim and refine as required.

**13** Once leatherhard, wax resist the areas where slip is not wanted. Dip the vase rim first in white slip to a single (light) cream consistency. Once it is dry and leatherhard, brush the coloured slips onto the white slip base. Biscuit (bisque) fire and then glaze and fire.

# Three-Footed Bowl

This pot was inspired by a collection of 14–16th century bronze tripod pots made by slaves of the Shang culture in China. Unearthed in 1955 at Chengchow, Honan Province, the pots were often decorated with animal masks and dragons and mainly used for cooking. This pot is constructed with four thrown forms and the maker, Chris Bramble, is intrigued by the visual dynamic of the three individually thrown pointed legs.

## Materials

Iron-based stoneware clay
Manganese dioxide

## Equipment

Wheel and cutting wire
Metal kidney
Plastic credit or phone card
Toothbrush
Sponge
Metal tool
Paintbrush
Needle
Gloves for glazing
Glaze rack and basin
Banding wheel
Gas kiln

## Glaze

Manganese dioxide
DRY BLUE GLAZE

| | |
|---|---|
| Feldspar | 13% |
| Whiting | 27% |
| China clay | 53% |
| Soda ash | 6.5% |
| Copper | 0.5% |
| Cobalt | 1/10% |

## Firing

Best result for this glaze is
1260–1280°C
(2300–2336°F) gas
reduction firing
Reducing from 1000–1200°C
(1832–2192°F)

**1** Throw a bowl with straight, almost upright, sides, 25 cm (10 in) taller than you require, leaving a wide base. This bowl should have a thick rim and base because at a later stage it will be turned over and rested on its rim while you work on the base.

**2** Throw the rim to a surface depth of 25 cm (10 in) leaning 45 degrees towards the centre of the bowl. Flatten the rim with a kidney, supporting it from the inside. Draw a line around the bottom of the rim. This will stop the manganese dioxide, applied later, from running down the side of the bowl. Finish off with soft plastic – an old credit or phone card will not get rusty or cut you when it gets worn.

**3** While throwing leg cylinders, keep the base narrow and the rim quite thin. Slowly collar in from the base upwards. Do not close the opening because air inside may distort the shape.

**4** When you have the desired angle, smooth with a kidney. Compress the tip to close the cone. Draw horizontal guidelines and then cut the leg off the board for drying. Repeat twice.

**5** When the bowl is leatherhard, turn the base into a dome reflecting the shape inside. It is best to turn this shape from the rim to the base.

**6** Draw guidelines for the decoration of the bowl and legs. This process is much more easily executed on the wheel.

**7** Measure the correct position for the legs. Stick on the legs temporarily with slip. Mark around them with a tool. Remove the legs then score and slurry the bowl and legs where they are to meet. Replace and fix the legs firmly and finish off with a paintbrush.

**8** Draw the surface decoration on the bowl. Then put a needle hole in each of the legs, otherwise they may crack when drying or explode during biscuit firing. Leave the bowl to dry upside-down to stop warping then slow biscuit (bisque) fire it to 1000°C (1832°F) or 06 cone.

**9** Paint on the manganese dioxide and when it is dry, sponge off the surplus. There will be enough left in the grooves to melt the covering layer of glaze.

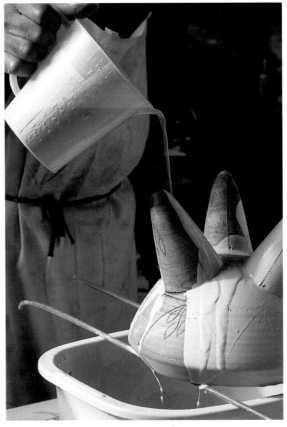

**10** Pour the glaze inside the bowl first. Try to get different thicknesses with the glaze. This glaze breaks into three colours, so the colours can be very dramatic.

**11** Place the bowl upside-down over a glaze rack and basin. Pour glaze on the outside, again varying the thickness for the best effects.

**12** When the glaze has dried clean off the rim with a kidney and sponge. Apply manganese dioxide to the rim with a brush using a banding wheel. Wipe the feet and put sand on your kiln shelves to stop the bowl sticking to their surface. Fire the bowl. The reduction within this firing cycle will bring the iron speckle to the surface of the clay, giving you a blue, green and yellow dry to satin-matt surface.

# Lemon Squeezer

This lemon squeezer is thrown in two halves on a potter's wheel. The bottom piece is a juice-collecting bowl with a pouring lip, which has decoration added using a plaster mould. The top piece is thrown and turned (trimmed) with the addition of a press-moulded centre. The press-moulded element allows the quick production of a form when producing a range of repeating domestic forms, but this element could also be created by handbuilding.

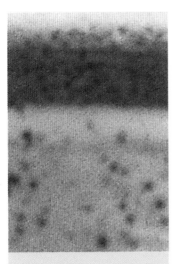

**Materials**

HT stoneware clay

**Equipment**

Wheel and cutting wire

Profile beading tools

Callipers

Straight-sided throwing rib

6 cm (2½ in) oval nail with rounded end

Strips of thin plastic

Sponge

Boards

Plaster mould for squeezer section (this can be cast using an existing lemon squeezer as the model)

Plaster lip mould (optional)

Turning (trimming) tool

Toothbrush

Needle

Hole cutter

Round-ended wooden dowel

Gloves for glazing

Gas kiln

**Glaze**

WHITE GLAZE

| | |
|---|---|
| Potash feldspar | 38% |
| China clay | 18% |
| Whiting | 7% |
| Talc | 7% |
| Flint | 28% |
| Bone ash | 2% |
| Zirconium silicate | 6% |

**Firing**

Biscuit (bisque) fire to 990°C (1814°F)

Reduction fire to 1280°C (2336°F)

**1** Centre 425 g (15 oz) of clay on the wheelhead and open into a small bowl shape. This will form the bottom half of the lemon squeezer.

**2** Pull the wall of the bowl upwards and outwards, undercutting at the bottom initially to form a narrow base. Leave a roll of clay at the top of the pot wall starting to form a fairly thick rim.

**3** Take a profile beading tool made from either thin plastic or metal, and cut inwards at the bottom of the pot to form a bead around the base. Once in position, push the lemon squeezer bowl from the inside outwards to form a rounder shape.

**4** When you have finalized the shape of the bowl it should measure 8 cm (3¼ in) high by 14 cm (5½ in) wide. Remove the throwing rings (rims) from the outside of the pot with a straight-sided throwing rib. Add lines to the inside and outside of the pot with the end of a steel nail to emphasize the chunky rim. Lastly, smooth and compress the rim with a thin strip of plastic and remove any water from inside the pot with a sponge. Cut through between the base of the pot and the wheelhead with a wire and place the bowl on a board.

**5** Centre 300 g (11 oz) of clay into a wide, flat shape on the wheelhead. Open the clay straight through to the wheelhead forming a hole, about 2.5 cm (1 in) in diameter. Continue to open out the clay leaving a thin base. Once opened, cone the wall of the top half of the lemon squeezer upwards and inwards with your left forefinger and thumb.

**6** Pull the wall of the pot once and fold it over from the inside with your left hand. Use two fingers of your right hand, outside and underneath, to help shape and support the forming of the folded-over rim. Push downwards onto the edge of the rim with a profile beading tool to continue to shape it. Measure the diameter of the top half of the lemon squeezer at this stage. It should be about 14.5 cm (5¾ in) wide so that when it sits inside the lemon squeezer bowl, it hangs just slightly over the edge. Smooth and compress the rim with a thin strip of plastic and remove any water from inside the pot with a sponge. Undercut at the base of the pot with the sharp end of a throwing rib, then cut through with a twisted wire. Remove the pot from the wheelhead and place it on a board.

**7** Take a piece of clay about the size of an egg to form a simple pinch pot, which should roughly echo the shape of the inside of the plaster drop-out mould. Use this to make the centre of the top half of the lemon squeezer.

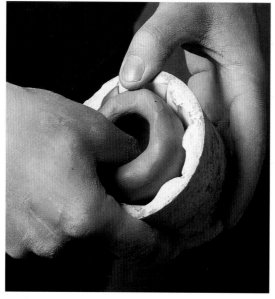

**8** Put the pinch pot inside the plaster mould, pressing in the clay firmly with your thumb. Start at the bottom and work outwards towards the top edge, turning the mould continuously with your other hand as you do so. Take particular care to press firmly where the mould has any relief detail. Cut off any excess clay, which is forced outwards beyond the edge of the mould, with a twisted wire.

**9** Leave the clay in the mould until it starts to dry and shrink away from the edge. Then tap sharply on the side of the mould and a lemon squeezer centre will drop out.

**10** Wait until the thrown bowl of the lemon squeezer has stiffened enough before you create the pouring lip, formed from the thick rim. Wet a thumb and forefinger and pinch straight upwards thinning out the clay.

**11** Hold a patterned plaster lip mould, if using, outside the rim with one hand and work the clay into the mould with your other forefinger. Remove the mould from the lip and wet your forefinger. Smooth and refine the shape of the lip while supporting it on either side with your other thumb and forefinger.

**12** Trim the bowl of the lemon squeezer with a loop-ended metal turning (trimming) tool once it is leatherhard. Position the bowl upside-down on a thrown chuck which you have centred and stuck to the wheelhead with a small amount of water. The next stage is to add two secondary details of beading next to the original bead at the bottom of the bowl.

**13** When it is leatherhard, centre the top half of the lemon squeezer and stick it upside down straight on to the wheelhead with a little water. Trim it with a metal turning (trimming) tool.

**14** Wait until the press-moulded centre of the lemon squeezer is leatherhard then apply slurry to its bottom edge with an old toothbrush. Score the corresponding position on the top half of the lemon squeezer with a potter's needle. Place the thrown piece on a flat surface and then join the two pieces by pushing the press-moulded part firmly onto the thrown part.

**15** With a hole cutter make the hole, through which the squeezed lemon juice will fall, at the base of the press-moulded lemon squeezer centre. Finish off the holes very neatly at both the top and bottom with one twist of the end of a rounded piece of dowel. The top of the lemon squeezer should sit neatly inside the bowl. Leave the two halves to dry.

**16** Biscuit (bisque) fire the lemon squeezer to 990°C (1814°F). Then, wearing gloves, dip the bottom half of the lemon squeezer into the glaze.

**17** Dip the top half of the lemon squeezer into the glaze. Then reduction fire both halves to 1280°C (2336°F) in a gas kiln.

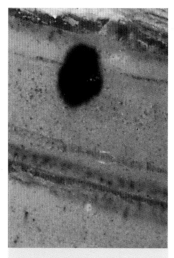

# Teapot

Tea drinking originated in the Far East and beautiful variations of the teapot's ergonomic form, with handles made from clay, cane or metal can be seen in many museum collections. The three thrown elements of body, lid and spout in this piece by Richard Phethean combine harmoniously to create a lightweight, functional and aesthetic form. The same basic process can be adapted to follow different teapot designs.

## Materials
Spencroft sanded red
  earthenware "green dot"

## Equipment
Wheel and cutting wire
Bat
Rib
Callipers
Metal tool
Wire or tough cotton
Round stick
Metal kidney
Tool to bore straining holes
Serrated metal kidney
Toothbrush
Plastic
Potter's knife
Wax resist
Gloves for glazing
Brushes for slip
Electric kiln

## Slips
White – white Devon ball clay
Light blue – add 5% cobalt
  oxide
Dark blue – add 20% cobalt
  oxide
Watery green – add 10%
  copper oxide and 1%
  chrome oxide
Thin blue/black lines – neat
  cobalt oxide
Make up the coloured slips to
a thin watery consistency

## Glaze
CLEAR

| | |
|---|---|
| Lead bisilicate | 72% |
| Potash feldspar | 13% |
| Ball clay | 10% |
| Borax frit | 5% |
| Bentonite | 2% |

HONEY
Powdered red earthenware
  clay is substituted for ball
  clay in above recipe

| | |
|---|---|
| Red iron oxide | ½% |

## Firing
Biscuit (bisque) fire to 1050°C
  (1922°F)
Glaze fire to 1125°C
  (2057°F), cones 03/02

**1** Centre 900 g (2 lb) of clay into a shallow dome about 16–18 cm (6¼–7 in) wide to make the body. Open out the base as you would a flat plate with a thickness of 4 mm (⅙ in). Lift the wall into a tall, even cone leaving a little weight on the collar rim.

**2** At a gentle speed, keep the aperture of the neck just narrow enough to admit your hand and gently stroke out the form into a cylinder against the rib. Collar in the top third of the form to a quarter of the cone.

**3** Support under the shoulder while the rib leans down on top, closing the diameter of the neck and creating a subtle step to the rim. Then create combed detail with a serrated metal kidney.

**4** Cut a decorative, "spiral" crease with the corner of the rib. Finally, measure the neck's aperture with a pair of callipers with the points facing each other. Dry to leatherhard.

**5** The lid is thrown "off the hump" so centre 1 kg (2¼ lb) of clay into an upright cone, then create a "waist" below sufficient clay to make your lid. Hollow "off-centre" with one finger to create a knob and tuck the other finger into the waistline to pinch out a shallow "saucer".

**6** Refine the knob with two fingers of one hand, and fold over the rim of the saucer creating a flange to sit on the rim of the teapot. Use the callipers to check the width of the lid underneath the flange.

**7** Cut a V-shaped groove to clearly divide the lid from the hump. Cut the lid from the hump with either a cutting wire or a length of tough cotton looped around the groove and held at one end as the wheel rotates slowly. The latter always makes a neat horizontal cut. Wait until the lid has dried to leatherhard.

**8** Use the same hump to recentre and recreate a "waisted" ball for the spout. Hollow and deeply undercut the base of a small cone to make quite sure that all the available clay is utilized.

**9** Pinch and lift with your fingertips into a concave, tapering cone. (Avoid making the walls overthin at this stage or buckling will occur during subsequent procedures.)

**10** Use an upward, collaring action to close up the spout a little, creating a wide skirt and a long, narrow neck.

**11** Pinch against a round stick to further raise and thin the spout's neck. The slender, parallel neck should be almost as tall as the flared cone it sits on.

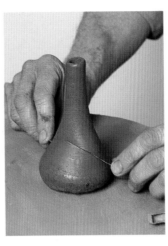

**12** Refine the line and surface of the spout with a rib or metal kidney, then underscore the completed spout. Cut through with a cutting wire and remove it with its own base. Preserve the spout in a softer state than the teapot body and lid.

**13** Trim and refine the teapot body and the lid. Then cut the spout from its base at a diagonal angle with a cutting wire. Gently pick up the soft spout and, with a wet finger, moisten and slightly flare the joining edge. Offer the spout up to the pot and lightly touch it into position.

**14** Replace the spout on its base while you bore the straining holes within the mark left by the spout. Make as many holes as you can. Textured decoration can be added with a serrated metal kidney.

**15** Use a wet toothbrush to roughen the pot around the straining holes. Pick up the spout and roughen its joining edge as well. Position the spout directly over the strainer and gently press into place. Carefully blend the spout seamlessly into the wall of the teapot.

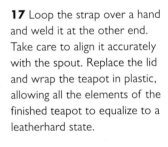

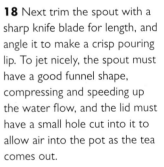

**16** Extrude a strap handle (see extruding handles), allow it to stiffen and trim it to the desired length. Score and slurry the ends of the strap and teapot where the handle will be fitted (see Handbuilding, using slurry for joining slabs). Hold the strap vertically and pinch and weld the front end into position. Add a decorative finish to the handle with the serrated metal kidney.

**17** Loop the strap over a hand and weld it at the other end. Take care to align it accurately with the spout. Replace the lid and wrap the teapot in plastic, allowing all the elements of the finished teapot to equalize to a leatherhard state.

**18** Next trim the spout with a sharp knife blade for length, and angle it to make a crisp pouring lip. To jet nicely, the spout must have a good funnel shape, compressing and speeding up the water flow, and the lid must have a small hole cut into it to allow air into the pot as the tea comes out.

**19** Allow the pot to dry, ensuring that the handle and spout equalize to the same condition as the pot, by covering them in plastic for a day or so. Brush areas to be protected from slip coating with wax resist. Dip the teapot, rim first into the white slip. Gently shake the drips off and stand upright to dry. Apply the coloured slips. Biscuit (bisque) fire and glaze and fire.

# Porcelain Bowl

Sue Paraskeva, the maker of this thrown porcelain vessel, sees the stick-driven momentum wheel as an important part of the making process as it is beautifully simple and encourages good pottery. After throwing, the vessel is slowly dried and carved, reshaping the base and altering the balance. Inspired by the natural form of pebbles, particularly their decoration and the shadows they create, some of her pieces are raw glazed with classical porcelain glazes, others are thrown with various oxides, grogs and other decoration materials.

## Materials

1 kg (2¼ lb) Limoges Porcelain

## Equipment

Stick-driven momentum wheel
Strong cutting wire
Fine cutting wire
Sponge
Firm rubber kidney
Strip of chamois leather
Metal tool
Wooden bat
Newspaper squares
Small surform blade
Plastic sheet
Hacksaw blades
Old-fashioned razor blades
Paintbrush
Gloves for glazing
Wax resist
Large bowl
Jug (pitcher)
Gas-fired kiln

## Glaze

Celadon glaze based on a
   recipe by John Davis
| | |
|---|---|
| Potash feldspar | 42% |
| Quartz | 27% |
| Wolsanite | 17% |
| China clay | 13% |
| Red iron oxide | 2% |

## Firing

Reduction fired to 1260°C
  (2300°F)

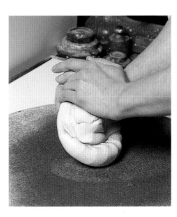

**1** Make sure the clay is well mixed with an even consistency. Spiral wedging is a good final preparation before going to the wheel. Pat the porcelain into a ball, place it firmly in the centre of the wheelhead then wind up the wheel.

**2** Once it is spinning, wet both hands and place them firmly on either side of the ball. Apply downward pressure and a cone will begin to rise in the centre. Press the cone harder and it will spiral upwards.

**3** Place your hands, interlinked, over the top of the cone and push gently downward. Apply some inwards pressure to keep the clay central and bring the clay down into a mushroom shape. Now it is centred and ready to make into a pot.

**4** Splash some more water onto the clay with one hand around the back of the pot. Then, with your other hand over the top, place your thumb over the centre. Push your thumb down into the middle of the clay, making sure to use enough water so that it doesn't get too sticky.

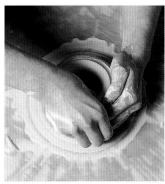

**5** Push down, leaving enough clay at the bottom for the base, and swing your thumb firmly from side to side to define the curve of the pot. Use the other hand for support so that the porcelain does not flare out.

**6** Next, pull up the wall of the pot. With one hand inside and one outside, use your fingertips to lift (pull) a collar of clay from the base of the pot to the top. Do this steadily and repeatedly. If you are using a non-electric wheel make sure you are not pulling up the clay faster than the revolutions of the wheel.

**7** Repeat this process until the walls are as high as required, then begin to flare out the pot. Always start at the bottom and work up to the very top. Use a sponge or a kidney-shaped tool to use all the clay and to reveal the smoothness of the porcelain.

**8** Slow down electric wheels considerably at this stage (momentum wheels will have slowed down naturally at this point). Using a rubber kidney on the inside, continue flaring out the pot, concentrating particularly on the inside of the form. Because you are making a fine bowl, the outside shape will follow the inside form.

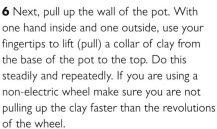

**9** Check that the rim is smooth and even. Do this very gently with your fingers and then use a small slither of wet chamois leather to finish.

**10** The pot is finished. Clean the base with a sharp tool, cutting in slightly, then stop the wheel. Sponge some water on the wheelhead at the back of the pot and pull a fine cutting wire through under the pot to release it from the wheel. Always use clean water and pull the wire through three times to make certain of a clean release. Cover a bat with newspaper then pick up the pot and place it on the bat. This facilitates even drying and eliminates the need for further cutting.

**11** Leave the pot to dry overnight and when it is firm enough to handle, begin to carve back the base using a small surform blade. As soon as you feel the softer clay underneath, stop work. Wrap the pot in plastic and leave it overnight to firm up. Wrapping the pot in this way ensures a slow and even drying process.

**12** The next day, when the pot has firmed again, carve it back with a more delicate hacksaw blade to get the detail of the final shape. Again, leave it wrapped overnight.

**13** Take a razor blade or a sharp metal kidney to get rid of the texture lines. Make the base flat, or angle the pot as desired. Allow the pot to dry fully when finished.

**14** Brush wax-resist inside the rim and on the base. This will repel any glaze on areas to be left unglazed. Because the pot is unfired or raw, sponging back will only disturb the form.

**15** Wearing gloves, hold the pot very carefully, upside down, over a large bowl then pour the glaze evenly all over the pot. The piece is at its most fragile at this point, so carefully wipe back any drips before gently setting it down to dry.

**16** Pack the pot into the kiln when it is dry. Create the green celadon glaze from iron oxide by firing in a reduced atmosphere. No biscuit (bisque) firing is needed as the pot is fired raw. The firing takes 11 hours to reach 1260°C (2300°F).

# Undulating Vase

This throwing project is inspired by the quote by Lao Tzu, "it is written the water that flows into the earthenware vessel takes on its form". Nicholas Arroyave~Portela's interest in this form lies in the accentuation of throwing lines, the rethrowing the pot at various intervals to make the clay walls as thin as possible, drying it out with a paint stripper gun in order to continue working it and, finally, its tactile manipulation.

## Materials
1 kg (2¼ lb) ball white St Thomas clay

## Equipment
Electric wheel and serrated wire cutter
Wooden bats
Sponges of different sizes
Needle
Wooden tool
Paint stripper gun
Water spray
Plastic sheet
Spray booth
Face mask (respirator)
Gloves for glazing
Sandpaper (medium-coarse)
Banding wheel
Newspaper
Compressor
Spray gun
Electric kiln and controller

## Slip
TERRA SIGILLATA
3 litres (5¼ pt) warm water
1 kg (2¼ lb) dry white ball clay hymod
15 g (½ oz) Hexametaphosphate
8%–10% commercial stains
1%–10% oxides
Ball mill the Hexametaphosphate with the water, oxide and/or stain.

## Glaze
Ready-made transparent glaze CT2330, range 1110–1180°C (2030–2156°F)
Oxides 1%–4% (different coloured glazes on different slips will have different effects)

## Firing
1000°C (1832°F)
60°C (140°F) an hour until 300°C (572°F)
120°C (248°F) an hour until 1000°C (1832°F)
5 minute soak at 1000°C (1832°F)

1180°C (2156°F)
60°C (140°F) an hour until 300°C (572°F)
120°C (248°F) an hour until 1180°C (2156°F)
10 minute soak at 1180°C (2156°F)

**1** Have a bowl of water, a sponge, cutting wire, a needle and a sharp wooden tool ready before you start work. Put the clay on the wheel and centre it. Begin to spin the wheel.

**2** Start to draw up the clay. Try to even out the clay walls by continual throwing, starting upwards from the thickest at the bottom, but be very careful not to tire the clay out too quickly.

**3** Once you have some height, start to define the shape of the vase by pushing out the main body, then pulling it back in at the shoulder before flaring out the rim.

**4** Now the clay probably needs some drying out with the paint stripper gun. Carry this out evenly while the wheelhead turns slowly. Slightly wobble the appliance up and down so that no patch of the pot is overly exposed to the direct heat.

**5** Take away some of the excess clay at the bottom of the pot with a sharp wooden tool. This clay usually proves difficult to lose completely in the throwing process.

**6** Use the water spray when rethrowing the pot so as not to oversaturate it. Push out the final shape of the main body, making sure that the clay walls are thin enough to manipulate.

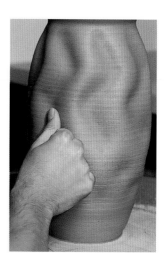

**9** Join the undulations with your thumb and start to create a zigzag definition.

**7** Refine the rim by softening any sharp edges with a sponge at a slow and constant speed. This is the final stage of throwing the vase.

**8** Touch the pot to see that it is not too wet nor too dry, then lightly indent the surface of the pot with your thumbs, maintaining a regularity around the whole pot from the top to the bottom.

**10** This pattern is effective when viewed from the inside too. Free the bottom of the pot from the bat with serrated wire and cover it lightly with some plastic for a day. Then remove the sheeting to allow it to dry. This may take up to a week.

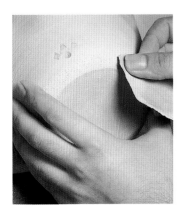

**11** Place the bone-dry pot on its side on a large sponge in the spray booth then, while wearing a face mask (respirator), gently remove any sharp edges with a piece of medium-coarse sandpaper. Be sure to sand away the same amount around the whole pot to maintain its regularity. Aim also to taper the line in at the bottom. This will give the desired effect of lift to the pot once it is standing.

**12** Place the pot on a banding wheel covered with newspaper. Then, while wearing your face mask, spray the slip evenly around the pot from top to bottom, turning the wheel intermittently.

**13** Give the piece about three coats of slip with a break of a couple of hours between each layer. Remember – the pot is not fired so it will crack if oversaturated.

**14** Place the pot back on its side once it has dried sufficiently after its three layers of slip. Take a different coloured slip, spray it across the bottom of the pot and let the contrast catch on the throwing lines and shape. Make sure you keep turning the pot after each spray so that the same effect can be seen all the way round. Leave for a day to dry, then fire the piece to 1000°C (1832°F).

**15** Pour the slip into the fired pot and give the inside a good coating, making sure that all the areas are covered. Pour out the slip to ensure that the inside rim gets coated as well. Let the pot dry for a day, then do the same with the glaze, being careful not to spill any on the outer surface. The glaze must have a thin consistency so that it does not go on too thickly.

**16** Finally, clean any spillage off the outside of the pot with warm water and a sponge (you will have to change the water regularly). Wipe the edges clear with a small sponge to reveal a clear line between glaze and slip. Leave your vase for a day before firing to 1180°C (1976°F).

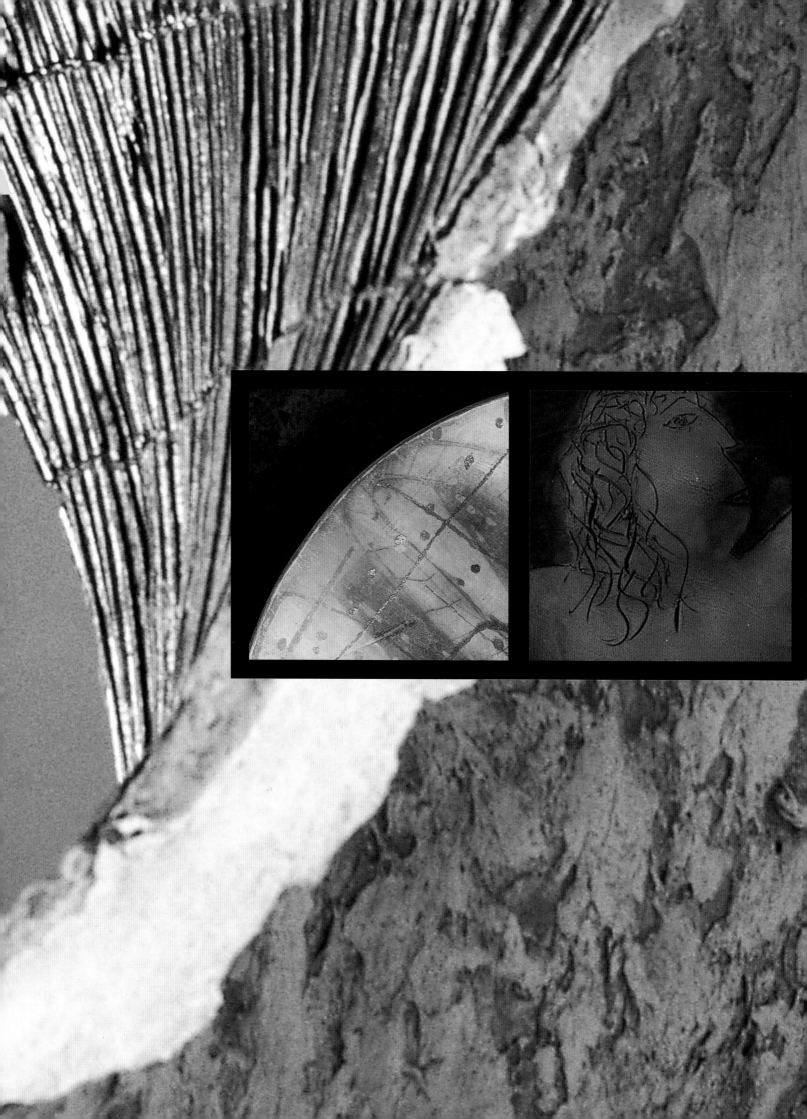

# GLAZE AND DECORATION

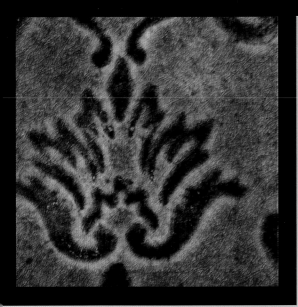

**GLAZE AND DECORATION PRESENT** A BROAD, EXCITING AREA FOR CONTINUAL LEARNING AND PLAY. THE ONLY RESTRICTIONS ARE TECHNICAL, SUCH AS WHEN TO APPLY A GLAZE OR DECORATION AND AT WHAT STRENGTH. GLAZE AND DECORATION OFTEN WORK HAND-IN-HAND. NOT ALL WORK, HOWEVER, NEEDS TO BE GLAZE FINISHED AND, AS IN THE CASE OF BURNISHED SLIP, DECORATION CAN ALSO BE USED IN ISOLATION. GLAZE, TOO, CAN WORK AS A SEPARATE STAGE OR WITHOUT OTHER APPLIED DECORATION – MAYBE CREATING A DECORATIVE SURFACE IN ITS OWN RIGHT, OR AS A MORE PRACTICAL APPLICATION OF A PROTECTIVE COVERING.

THERE IS NO EXACT FORMULA FOR APPLYING GLAZE OR DECORATION – LIKE ALL DESIGN, IT IS A PERSONAL CHOICE OF WHAT METHODS AND RECIPES ARE USED TO PRESENT AN IDEA. AS YOU TRY OUT EACH NEW AREA OF DECORATION, OR EACH NEW GLAZE RECIPE, KEEP A RECORD OF WHAT YOU DO AND OF THE FIRED RESULT TO HELP TO BUILD UP A REFERENCE OF SURFACE EFFECTS TO DRAW ON WHEN PLANNING NEW WORK.

# EQUIPMENT
## GLAZE AND DECORATION Both the basic glazing and decoration equipment,

such as brushes or buckets, and the more specialist equipment, such as sieves or masks (respirators), are

available from ceramic suppliers. Spraying equipment involves a greater financial outlay, and is

unnecessary if your preferred methods of applying glaze and colour are by brush, dipping or pouring.

### Equipment for preparing ceramic colour and glaze

Even if buying your glaze as powders ready made, there is often a certain amount of weighing and preparation involved. All the equipment listed here is a standard range, which will be essential for this stage of work.

**1**  Accurate scales and weights for large (1a) and small (1b) quantities are used for weighing glaze ingredients, particularly colour additions or small quantities of test ingredients. When weighing out, check items off as you go in case of interruption.

**2**  Sieves are used for sieving ceramic colour. Mesh sizes vary, measured by holes per square inch. An optimum for ceramic colour is a 60–80 size mesh. Test sieves (2a) are used for smaller amounts and large sieves (2b) for larger quantities.

**3**  Sieve brush for pushing materials through a sieve.

**4**  Support slats for supporting sieves over a bucket.

**5**  Mortar and pestle for crushing stubborn materials before passing through a sieve and returning them to the mix.

**6**  Bucket and a range of plastic ware suitable for safe, airtight storage and for transferring materials.

**7**  Indelible pen for labelling buckets, as many mixed recipes look very similar once in slop form.

### Equipment for applying glazes

**8**  A spray gun (8a) and compressor (8b) are used with a spray booth to apply colour or glaze when a flat, even application or a diffused quality is required. They are useful when you have only a small quantity of glaze. A spray gun is linked to a compressor via a flexible air hose. Airbrushes can also be used to spray small areas of decorative colour.

**9**  Glazing claw for gripping work when using a glaze that is susceptible to pouring and finger hold marks.

**10**  Safety mask or respirator (see health and safety) and gloves (not shown).

**11**  Brushes for applying glaze colour.

**12**  Measuring jug (cup) for pouring or transferring glaze.

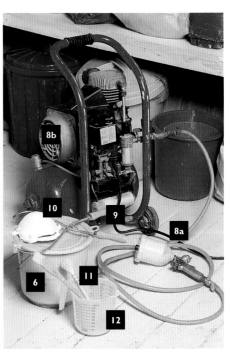

## Equipment for printing

Equipment for screen printing on ceramics is essentially the same as for screen printing on paper or fabric.

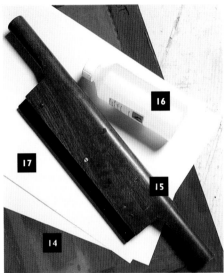

**13**    Screen with hinged frame – using a screen attached to a board makes the screen printing process much easier to control.

**14**    Silk screen.

**15**    Squeegee for pulling colour across the silk screen.

**16**    Liquid mediums, thinners and covercoats for oil-based colours.

**17**    Thermoflot paper for making screened decals (or transfers).

## Lino cutting equipment

**18**    Lino (linoleum block).

**19**    Lino (linoleum) cutter

**20**    Interchangeable blades for the lino (linoleum) cutter.

**21**    Potter's tissue (ceramic tissue) for transferring a lino (linoleum) print to a clay surface.

## Brushes

There is a vast array of brushes on the market. Every brush has its own quality in terms of precision, spring, versatility of stroke and loading capacity, ranging from generous to resilient.

When decorating and applying colour, have a selection of different brush sizes and shapes at hand to choose from. To be able to select the right brush for the stroke, get to know the brushes that are available. Test a brush's load and stroke on a porous surface to find its "personality". Newspaper or a wooden board is good for this, and closely resemble the "draw" that biscuit (bisque) ware or powdered glaze exerts on a brush. What a flat test area will not give, though, is the feel of painting onto a curve.

Look after your brushes carefully and wash them after each use. This is essential when using wax resist and latex resist solution, which should never be allowed to dry on a brush. Store brushes with their heads straight.

**22**    One stroke brushes can be used flat for laying on wide areas or can be drawn on their edge to make a fine line.

**23**    Pointed writer for fine lines.

**24**    The glaze mop's full, soft body will hold large quantities of colour.

**25**    Traditional Japanese brushes are used for fine decorative work or calligraphy.

**26**    Fine Japanese calligraphy brush.

**27**    The traditional hake brush is soft haired for laying on large, flat areas of colour or slip.

**28**    Fine liner brush.

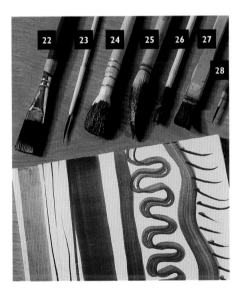

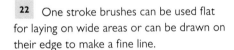

The different brushes are used according to the types of stroke that they perform. All the brushes shown here are available in a variety of sizes.

# MATERIALS

## DECORATING

Decoration can be applied to plastic, leatherhard, dry, biscuit (bisque) fired, raw glaze or glaze fired clay depending on the effect you desire and the materials used. So that the decoration works as a whole with the ceramic piece and that it looks convincing, plan your approach to materials and how to apply them right from the beginning.

**Colours for decorating ceramics come in many forms:**

1 powders.

2 liquid form.

3 tubes.

4 pencils, felt pens and crayons.

5 pans.

### Clay for decorating

The colour and texture of the clay you use will affect your decoration – a light clay will give a better colour response than a dark clay. A covering of white or light slip can also be applied to any of the darker clays and will respond to colour in a similar way to a light clay. Remember when applying clay as decoration (for example with modelling or inlay) it should be applied when the clay is still plastic or leatherhard. Clay can only be joined to dry clay when using fibre clay.

### DECORATING SLIPS

Not to be confused with casting slip, which is liquid clay, decorating slip is applied to clay at the leatherhard stage. A base white slip can be stained or coloured to whatever colour you require (see sources of glaze colour).

### ENGOBES

A mixture between slip and glaze, an engobe contains clay and a fluxing material, such as borax frit. Engobes can be applied in the same way as slips at the leatherhard or the biscuit (bisque) stage.

### Colour for decorating

Oxides, underglaze colours and stains are available in many forms. They can be applied to leatherhard, dry, biscuit (bisque) fired clay and to raw glaze surfaces.

### METALLIC OXIDES

Naturally occurring metallic oxides, such as cobalt, iron and rutile, are sold in powdered form and can be mixed together or used singly. They can be used to stain light-bodied clays and slips or glazes (see sources of glaze colour). Used as painted colour, powdered oxide should be mixed with water to the required strength, to approximately watercolour paint consistency. As metallic oxide particles are heavy, however, they settle quickly in water, which can cause application problems. To overcome this, they are often mixed with a little painting medium to keep them in suspension, or other mediums, such as china clay, glaze, oil or milk, making them easier to apply.

Metallic oxides have a softer quality than commercial stain colours. Each metallic oxide requires a specific strength of painted application which can only be learnt by initial trial and error and assessing the fired results.

Colour applied on top of a raw, unfired glaze surface while it is still powdery is known as "inglaze" because the applied colour sinks into the fired glaze, becoming soft and diffused as it melts in the heat of the kiln. This technique is also referred to as "maiolica" decoration when used in conjunction with a white glaze. Painted colour is often applied underneath a transparent glaze covering or a glaze with which the colour can interact.

### UNDERGLAZE COLOURS AND STAINS

Commercially produced and sometimes intermixable, these are made up from a controlled blend of colour oxides. Suppliers refer to underglaze colours and stains respectively as UG and BS. They are available in a huge colour range in a number of forms and can be used for the same techniques as oxides. Underglazes, not in powdered form, contain carrying mediums, binders and fluxes. The colours are more stable and predictable than naturally occurring oxides and are often used as a means of obtaining reds or yellows, which are difficult to achieve with oxides.

There is an often overwhelming array of underglaze and stain products available from ceramic suppliers, so always read their catalogues carefully to make sure that you get what you need. Check that colours, particularly reds and yellows, can achieve the right firing temperature for the clay you are using and the effect you require, as some will burn out at high temperatures.

- Powdered underglaze colours and stains are prepared in the same way as oxide powders either by mixing in water or with a specific medium. They can be used for staining slips, engobes and glazes.
- Liquid underglaze colours and stains are available in 56 ml (2 fl oz) to 568 ml (1 pt) jars. They can be thinned, but are thixotropic (see glossary) so they should be stirred before thinning. They are often intermixable and come in various guises such as one-strokes, which are transparent, or velvets, which are opaque and can be thinned for transparency or left unglazed for a velvet surface. Some can be applied to leatherhard clay, while others can be applied to both leatherhard and biscuit (bisque) fired clay. They can also be used to stain slips, engobes, glazes and clay, but powders are a more economical way of doing this.
- Paste underglaze colours and stains are available in 15 ml (¼ fl oz) tubes. Mix with water and a brush.
- Pan underglaze colours and stains should be mixed with water for painted application.
- Pencil, felt pen and crayon underglaze colours and stains are available in crayon, pencil and felt tip. They require pressure to apply, so they can be applied only at the biscuit (bisque) fired stage.

ONGLAZE

Also known as overglaze or enamel, onglaze colour is applied on top of a shiny, fired glaze and requires a separate firing. It is a strongly coloured, low-temperature glaze used for painting china. It is often laid on using various types of oils as a medium, but is also available in water-based formulations. They generally use lead as a flux and should therefore be handled carefully.

## Commercial products

You can buy commercially prepared slips and glazes in powdered or liquid form from ceramic suppliers. The glazes can be selected from a catalogue in the same way as selecting paint from a colour chart. Ensure that the glaze is in keeping with the temperature range of the clay, with other glazes in the same piece and with other pieces in the same firing.

## Base glazes

Commercial white or transparent glazes and white slips can be used as a base and varied by adding stains or oxides while in their dry state. Test the slips and glazes altered in this way before use (see simple testing and line blending). A small tile of clay is adequate for test samples fired to their maturing temperatures, but applying glaze to a vertical piece of clay

will give a better indication of its fluidity. To prevent spoiling a kiln shelf with unwelcome drips of molten glaze, fire test pieces on old or broken pieces of kiln shelf.

## Single-fire decorating and glazing

Glaze is commonly applied to clay at the biscuit (bisque) stage of the clay cycle. Many potters, however, choose to single fire their work, applying all decoration and glazes up to and at the leatherhard or bone-dry stages. If the piece to be glazed is in two states, such as dry at the top and leatherhard at the bottom, cracking can occur between the two states so the work must be of an even consistency. Specific, single-fire glazes of a tested and suitable shrinkage rate should be used to fit these methods of working.

Single firing is a technique that has obvious time-saving, economic and ecological advantages, as well as allowing a spontaneous affinity to work that can be lost when work "reappears" in its biscuit (bisque) fired state. One potter who single-fires work refers to the break in continuity for the biscuit (bisque) firing as leaving makers "feeling alienated from the abrasive altered beasts that came back". (See Kilns and Firing for the effect the type of kiln and kiln firing has on a glaze.)

GEO-VECTOR
(35 × 54 × 36 CM/14 × 21¼ × 14 IN)
PORCELAIN WITH MOLOCHITE, SLAB MADE,
SURFACE COLOURED WITH SLIPS, OXIDIZED
FIRING (JENNY BEAVAN).

# TECHNIQUES
## PREPARING CERAMIC COLOURS AND GLAZES

This stage can be labour intensive, but thorough preparation is essential to ensure that all ingredients are evenly distributed within the slop of a glaze, slip or engobe mixed recipe. This is the case even if using commercial glazes with no colour additions. Take especial note of health and safety requirements, as many of the substances are hazardous. When preparing glazes, wear protective clothing, with gloves and a mask (respirator) and avoid making unnecessary dust.

### Mixing and sieving

A mesh number on a sieve denotes how many holes are present in the sieve per square inch. The higher the number, the finer the mesh and the slower the sieving will be. A 60–100# is an optimum mesh size for most materials, a 200# would be best for a final sieving for something like a terra sigillata slip, which is made up from extremely small precipitated particles.

**1** When making up a glaze, slip or engobe, place the dry ingredients in a lidded bucket that is at least twice the size of the volume you are mixing. Add approximately 100 ml (3½ fl oz) of water to every 100 g (3½ oz) of dry materials and allow the water to soak in thoroughly before then sieving the ingredients. If stubborn materials, such as flint, refuse to break down, pull them out and pound them in a mortar and pestle and return them to the bucket.

**2** Support the sieve securely with slats on the bucket rim and sieve the wet ingredients at least two to three times. Push the ingredients through with a sieve brush or washing-up brush.

**3** Use a rubber kidney to clean off the ingredients from the sides of the bucket and to help any stubborn lumps through the sieve mesh.

**4** After the mixture has been sieved, check its consistency by stirring it and then dipping in a dry finger and checking its cover. The correct consistency and thickness of the sieved mix, or slop, will vary according to the technique you use and the particular characteristics and nature of the recipe.

### Getting the consistency right

The thickness of any ceramic medium can only be established by testing and assessing its consistency once it has been fired.

Generally glaze should have a single (light) cream consistency, but there are plenty of instances that break this rule. Most transparent glazes, for example, are applied milk thin, and trailed slip should be yogurt thick.

If a mix is too thick, add a little water little by little until it feels right. If it is too thin, leave it overnight to settle. Next morning, pull or scoop off all the water on the top and take it back to the required consistency by again stirring in a little water at a time. For an accurate consistency use a glaze hydrometer to measure the water content of a slop mix.

To keep a constant consistency, measure the volume of water added to a known quantity of glaze as each fresh batch is mixed. Ensure that glaze kept over a period is stored in a container with an airtight lid to prevent water evaporation.

Stir a slop material well before use. Most glazes settle to the bottom of their container because of the weight of the particles in suspension. Adding a small amount of bentonite (1–2%) to a glaze that is prone to settling will suspend the glaze. Bentonite should be added to the dry materials when weighing them out as it is difficult to mix into a glaze already in slop form. If a glaze has settled in a bucket, an electric mixer will quickly return it to an even consistency.

# TECHNIQUES
# DIRECT DECORATING

Illustrated here are the main, and some lesser used, traditional methods of applying glaze, slip, engobes, colour, and onglaze as mediums of decoration. Each technique is detailed with an indication of which medium is suitable for which technique. All of these techniques can be used on their own or combined with any number of the techniques on the same piece.

## Applying a slip background

Pouring slip as a base coat or ground covering over the leatherhard piece can be nerve wracking because the clay wall expands as it takes on moisture from the slip. This expansion often causes the clay wall to split apart. To minimize this risk, the wall section of the work must be even in its consistency and in the thickness of its section.

The slip should be of single (light) cream to milk consistency and the piece at the firm stage of leatherhard. Mugs or teapots assembled once slip has become leatherhard to prevent them pulling and distorting can be retouched with slip using a soft brush.

Apply slip first to internal or upper faces. Allow the slip to firm to leatherhard before applying slip to external or under faces. Once a piece has had an overall covering it should not be touched until the slip and the piece itself have returned to a firm, leatherhard state.

A slip background can also be applied with a brush, giving a less even effect, but creating a pleasing broken quality. If applied in layers, it will become opaque. A brushed slip should have a slightly thicker consistency to a poured slip.

## Using paper resist

Suitable for: slip, glazes, engobes and onglaze. Dampen resist shapes cut from newsprint and apply them flat to a leatherhard surface. Then brush on your colour with a soft, flat brush using strokes away from the edges of the paper shapes (see first picture). Paper resist using slip and engobes gives hard, clean edges, which can be picked up at the biscuit (bisque) stage with a wash of colour.

PORCELAIN VASE (20 CM/8 IN) PORCELAIN, WHEEL THROWN, DECORATED WITH CERAMIC STAINS AND UNDERGLAZE COLOURS USING PAPER RESISTS. TRANSPARENT CERAMIC GLAZE AND REDUCTION FIRED (PETER LANE).

## Using wax resist

Suitable for: glaze, slip, engobes and colour. Apply a wax resist to create a soft, broken edge dotted with random droplets of colour. The wax must be completely dry before any colour is applied in a milky to single (light) cream consistency. Lines scratched through the wax can be painted over with colour to give an etched line effect, which makes a good contrast to the mottled wax resist effect. Wax can be painted on leatherhard clay, biscuit (bisque) fired clay and on a raw glaze surface. Once applied, wax resist can only be removed by burning it out while firing.

## Using latex resist

Suitable for: glaze, slip, engobes, colour and onglaze. Unlike wax, latex resist has the advantage of being removable to allow for further additions of colour or glaze to the blocked areas before firing. A latex resist must be completely dry before applying colour of any consistency. It leaves a sharper edge and cleaner finish than wax resist. It can be used to block out tight, graphic or fluid, painterly shapes. Remember to rinse brushes in warm water before the latex resist dries.

## Feather combing

Suitable for: slip, but can also be tried with single fired glazes applied to leatherhard clay. The technique of feather combing is executed in two stages. The first is to trail a series of contrasting colour lines, which must sink into a wet, previously laid slip ground. Then use a bristle or feather tip to pull across the trailed lines on the wet ground. The slips should be a single (light) cream consistency and the decorating should be carried out as soon as the slip ground and trailed lines are laid.

## Spraying

Suitable for: glaze, slip, engobes, colour and onglaze. A spray gun or air brush can be used to spray an overall covering of glaze or to create soft, blurred areas of colour (see glazing techniques). Spraying can be used in conjunction with stencils or with other resist methods.

The spray gun nozzle should be wide enough to suit the particle size of the medium being sprayed without blocking it. Remember to always wear a face mask (respirator) and avoid spraying work unless you have suitable extraction equipment or a spray booth (see glaze and decoration equipment). Colour and glazes are often toxic and inhalation and ingestion should be avoided at all times.

## Combing

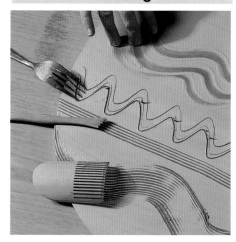

Suitable for: slip and glaze. Applied with fingers or any toothed tool on wet or dry mediums, combing creates lines, which can be straight or curved. Burrs of clay caused by combing into leatherhard or wet slips should be removed when the work is bone dry to prevent sharp fired edges of clay.

## Banding

Suitable for: glaze, slip, engobes, colour and onglaze. Banded straight lines can be applied by centring a piece on a throwing wheel or heavy banding wheel and holding a loaded brush in a steady position while the work rotates.

SOFTLY-THROWN DISH (30 CM/12 IN) SLIP TRAILED AND BRUSHED WITH COPPER OXIDE AND PINK GLAZES (SANDY BROWN). PHOTOGRAPH BY JOHN ANDREW.

## Marbling

Suitable for: slip but can also be tried with engobes, single-fired glazes applied to leatherhard clay and onglaze. Applied to leatherhard clay, marbling consists of laying trailed lines of fluid slip onto a contrasting ground of wet slip and tilting the work, traditionally an open form. As the wet slip begins to run down, the work is turned and tilted to allow the lines to run in a different direction. As the name indicates, the effect simulates the striations of marble.

## Slip trailing

Suitable for: glaze, slip and engobes. Slip trailing and tube lining use the same method of drawing a fluid or raised piped line of slip. Slip trailed lines or dots are applied with a slip trailer at the leatherhard stage. The slip should have a double (heavy) cream to yogurt consistency and can be used in single or contrasting colours (the Throwing, Cup and Saucer and Teapot projects for use of slip trailing technique).

## Slip trailing and tube lining

Tube lining is always raised and involves defining areas that are then filled with colour. It varies from slip trailing in that the tubed line can also be applied at the biscuit (bisque) fired stage when an engobe or glaze slip mixture is used. The areas defined by the raised lines are then coloured in or filled with oxides and underglazes which are further covered by a transparent glaze. Alternatively the glaze can be applied first and colours then applied to the defined areas.

## Mocha decorating

Suitable for: slip only. Originating from 19th-century English ware with tree-like motifs, mocha ware was produced by mixing manganese dioxide with tobacco juice. The stain is applied to the edge of freshly dipped or banded slip and allowed to spread, tilting the piece to move the stain downwards. The slip ground must be wet.

## Working with sgraffito

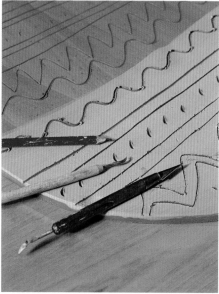

Suitable for: glaze, slip, engobes, colour and onglaze. The technique of scratching through one layer to reveal another underlying, contrasting colour is known as sgraffito. The quality of line produced depends on the tool you use and the state of the medium scratched through. Burrs caused by scratching through slips should be avoided by catching the slip at the correct state of leatherhardness, but they can also be removed before firing when the work is bone dry.

## Washing back

Suitable for: glaze, slip, engobes, colour and onglaze. Wiping back washed colour is effective for revealing any texture or relief applied to clay. Colour is washed onto and into the surface of a textured biscuit (bisque) fired surface with a brush and wiped back using a damp sponge or stiff wet brush.

## Brushing

Suitable for: glaze, slip, engobes, colour and onglaze. Brushes can be used to apply any type of ceramic colour. Brush strokes will be accentuated by the application of glaze over or under any brush mark in the glaze firing process, so work boldly and be in control of your brush strokes. Brushing will perform only to the skill of the decorator. The angle at which you hold a brush and the amount of colour loaded will affect the shape, length and cover of a stroke (see also glaze and decoration equipment).

Unless you are aiming for short stop-and-start strokes, continue the stroke for as long as the brush and load will allow. Brushwork is varied according to the mood of the work created and can be controlled or free, painterly or flat.

For an opaque, flat covering of slip, apply two or more thin layers allowing the first layer to become dry to the touch before applying the next.

PORCELAIN THROWN PLATE (39 CM/15½ IN DIAMETER) THE INITIAL DESIGN IS MARKED OUT WITH UNDERGLAZE BLUE IN BISCUIT WARE. THE BRIGHT GLASSY ENAMELS ARE PAINTED ON WITH A BRUSH AFTER A REDUCTION FIRING AND THE PIECE IS THEN FIRED AGAIN (RUSSELL COATES).

# TECHNIQUES
# PRINTING Combined with the appropriate ware, printed ceramic techniques have an exciting

creative potential far exceeding that of print on paper. Whether they are used commercially or not, the

fired finishes, textures, styles and application methods are all open to adaptation and personalization.

Success will depend on your choice of materials and colour medium.

■ Here are just a selection of the printing techniques that are available for use with ceramics. Photocopy transferral, lithography, gelatine and powder pick-up techniques are just a few of those not mentioned. The print area is vast and like all ceramic techniques, each needs to be explored and experimented with to be used effectively. Some of these direct and indirect methods require specialist ceramic materials.

### Indirect printing

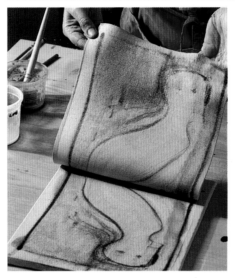

Suitable for: slips, engobes and colour. Monoprints using wet colour can be made from damp fabric, such as canvas, that is held flat and tight over a board. Colour used for the print is held together by placing a rolled sheet of soft clay over the surface and gently rolling with a rolling pin. Mono printing from fabric can be used for any colour that will pick up on a sheet of unfired clay.

### Direct printing

'NINI'S CORNER' (48¼ × 48¼ × 7½ CM/19 × 19 × 3 IN)
VIDEO STILL OF STREET LIFE PRINTED USING AN INDIRECT SILK-SCREEN
METHOD (WARREN MATHER).

Suitable for: glaze, slip, engobes, onglaze and colour. The technique of sponging colour to a surface can be used with the above materials in their liquid states. The sponge should not be overloaded on detailed prints. Sponges can be cut with a sharp knife or a heated tool or blade. The principle of sponged decoration extends to the use of rubber stamps, which can be used for applying lustres and onglaze colour directly on to a glazed, fired surface.

## Methods of transferring a lino print

Suitable for: slips, engobes, colour and onglaze, but can also be tried with glaze. Rubber stamps and lino (linoleum) block cuts can be used to transfer colour to potter's tissue (ceramic tissue) to make monoprints to glazed, fired glaze, leatherhard dry or biscuit (bisque) fired clay surfaces. Oxide, underglazes, stains and onglazes can be mixed with copperplate oil using a palette knife and then spread evenly on a glass sheet using a plastic phone or credit card. The ink should not be so thick that it is sticky and lumpy, but not so thin that it runs off the palette knife. Stamps and lino blocks then pick up the colour which is transferred to the potter's tissue. The printed tissue is then transferred to the work (see above).

Lino cut and rubber stamp prints can be transferred to a curved surface by indirect printing using potter's tissue or printed directly on a flat clay surface.

## Transferring a drawn design on potter's tissue

Suitable for: colour only. Using a brush, apply a water-based ceramic colour as an opaque covering to a sheet of glass with a brush and allow it to dry. Cover the dried area of colour with a piece of potter's tissue, taping it to the clean areas of glass to prevent it moving. Draw the image with a pencil directly onto the tissue freehand or with the guide of a traced design. To transfer the design to clay, carefully unstick the tissue and press the underface that has made contact with the colour onto wet or damp clay. This gives a well defined print. When combined with biscuit (bisque) fired or dry clay, this technique gives a print with a hazier effect.

## Etched and engraved plates for printing

Suitable for: colour and onglaze. Etchings, dry points and engravings are printed using copperplate oil mixed with colour (see methods of transferring a lino print). Plates are inked up using a plastic card, also used to wipe away excess ink on the plate. Give the plate a clean with newsprint before printing. Fibre clay slabs (see handbuilding, fibre clay slabs) can be printed directly on the plate under an etching press or by rolling the clay onto the plate with a rolling pin. Alternatively the ink in the plate can be transferred to potter's tissue and then to clay by rubbing the tissue by hand on to a plate to pick up the print. Potter's tissue can also be used to transfer the print to a curved clay surface.

NATURE/STRUCTURE (DETAIL)
(360 × 360 × 360 CM/12 × 12 × 12 FT)
PRINTING CAN ALSO BE USED TO SHAPE THE SURFACE OF
CLAY (SEE HANDBUILDING, DECORATING INTO CLAY).
HERE, ORGANIC LAYERS SEPARATING CLAY LAYERS ARE BUILT
WITHIN A MOULD AND BURNT AWAY IN THE FIRING,
LEAVING THEIR PRINT IN THE FIRED CLAY
(JANET WILLIAMS).

## Intaglio printing from plaster

Suitable for: slip, engobes and colour. To prepare a design for intaglio printing, carve lines or areas into a smooth block of flat, damp plaster (see Making and Using Moulds, running plaster and facing up). Apply your colour with a brush into and over the carved image. The applied colour is then scraped back with a plastic card to remove excess colour, leaving the indented image. Areas inside or around the drawn, infilled image can be painted with contrasting colours.

This intaglio print method can also be used to make a raised line on sheets of clay without the application of colour. Lines can be varied according to the tool you use to carve the plaster and the amount of pressure you apply.

Textured plaster sheets can also be used for printing. To make up textured plaster blocks plaster can either be poured on a flat sheet of textured clay or on textured surfaces such as textiles or wallpaper.

**1** To pick up the print clearly, cover the applied colour with a layer of fibre clay slop or casting slip poured inside a retaining wall of plastic clay. The image can also be picked up with a sheet of plastic clay for a hazier printed effect.

**2** Once the slop or casting slip has firmed to leatherhard, or the plastic clay has been rolled over with a rolling pin, it can be pulled back.

PRINTED PLATE (32 CM/12½ IN)
PRESS-MOULDED, SURFACE PRINTED WITH LINOCUT USING BODY
STAINS AND PRINTING MEDIUM, PAINTED UNDERGLAZES AND
CERAMIC TRANSFERS (MARIA DONATO).

## Screen printing

Suitable for: glaze, slip, engobes and colour. Images can be screen printed directly or indirectly onto any flat clay surface. The most obvious choice of surface for direct screen printing is an unfired, bisqued or glazed tile. Indirect screen prints can be made using ceramic colour on thermoflot (decal paper). The coloured print is held together with a screen of emulsion called a covercoat. The dry "decal" is soaked in water, allowing the held print to slide off and be transferred to a piece of work. Apply a decal to a dust and grease free, fired, glazed surface using a rubber kidney to remove any trapped air bubbles. Oil- or water-based onglaze or inglaze colours contained in the decals require a separate firing to fuse to or into the glaze.

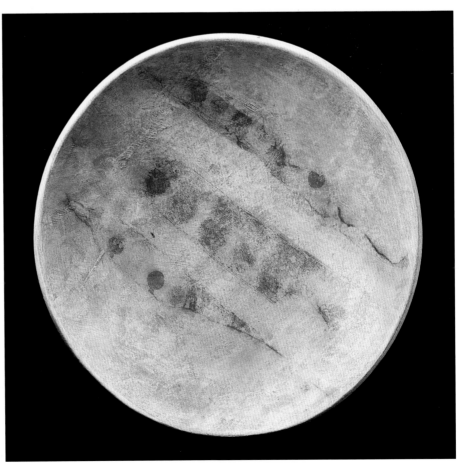

# TECHNIQUES
## GLAZING
The sensitive application of glaze will enhance the colour, texture and design of a piece of work. However, the main practical reason for coating the entire surface of a domestic clay piece with glaze is to ensure that it is watertight, so that it can be cleaned easily and is safe to use for storing or presenting food or drink. The glazing technique you choose will depend on what you are glazing and how much glaze is available. The most suitable technique and the thickness of application is also dictated by the nature of the glaze you are using.

### Glazing the inside of an enclosed shape

Enclosed internal surfaces should be glazed before any external glazing or colour decoration is undertaken. This prevents any unnecessary handling of applied external, unfired powdery materials or marring of carefully applied, unfired designs and glaze.

**1** First stir the glaze thoroughly and check its consistency. Fill a jug (pitcher) and pour the glaze into the piece of work. Pour in enough glaze to fill the vessel as quickly as possible.

**2** While turning the work in both hands, immediately pour out the excess back into the bucket making sure you have covered the entire surface of the inside wall. Any small spots you miss can be touched up using a soft brush or glaze mop and any excess spilled over onto the outside wall can be wiped back with a damp sponge.

The reason for performing this task with speed is to prevent the wall from becoming saturated. If this happens the glaze applied to the outer wall will not adhere. The wall will act like a wet sponge that cannot take up any more water, and the capillary action caused by the porosity of the bisqued wall will cease, therefore preventing the glaze particles forming an even covering to the surface of the work. If a piece does become over saturated either leave it until dry and then continue with the glazing or speed dry the work with a heat source, such as a paint stripper gun.

JUG (23 CM/9 IN)
PORCELAIN THROWN AND
MODELLED, WITH SLIP AND GLAZE
(EMMANUEL COOPER).

## Glazing the outside of an enclosed shape

The work should be held in as few places as possible – at the foot or base to prevent unnecessary fingermarks of omitted glaze. Alternatively, and where possible, use a glazing claw (see glaze and decoration equipment) particularly if a piece is awkward to hold or the glaze is susceptible to marking because it does not "flatten out" in the firing.

**1** Hold the work upside down and level to the surface of the glaze as it is submerged so a pocket of air is trapped inside, preventing a double build-up of glaze to the inside wall. Immerse it in the glaze quickly for no longer than three seconds to the point to which you want the glaze to reach.

You could also dip the piece base down, holding onto the dry inside wall. This enables you to use a different or contrasting glaze on the external wall, which will finish to a clean line at the rim edge. Plunge the piece in to the required depth of glaze for a maximum of 3 seconds being careful not to let glaze cascade over the top edge.

When removing the piece, tilt it to let any excess glaze drip back into the bucket giving it a slight shake to help any last drips fall away.

**2** Slide the wet glazed piece onto the edge of a board or table rim being careful not to touch the wet glaze, and allow it to dry before it is handled again. If there are any missing spots, fill them in using a soft brush.

**3** When the glaze is bone dry, you can pare away any touched-up finger marks or glaze drips with the edge of a metal kidney or rub them down with a dry finger tip bringing the powdered glaze to an even level. Pinholes in the powdery glaze surface can also be rubbed down with a dry finger once the glaze is thoroughly dry, but this is often unnecessary for fluid glazes will smooth out in the firing.

**4** If required, a second overlapping layer of glaze (or selectively dipped areas) can be applied in the same way. This double dipping technique will affect the fired result and such overlapping glazes should be test fired first to ensure that one glaze does not cause the other to overly flux and run in the firing.

THROWN SKIRTED BOWL
(25.5 CM/10¼ IN)
A CLAY MIXTURE OF RED
EARTHENWARE AND STONEWARE
WITH VERY COARSE GROG. GLAZES
ARE DIPPED AND SPRAYED AND THE
PIECE IS THEN OXIDATION FIRED
(RAY SILVERMAN).
PHOTOGRAPH BY HOWARD SHOOTER.

## Dipping a tile or small object

Small objects are dipped using the same technique as glazing the outside of an enclosed shape. If glazing a number of small objects ensure the glaze is stirred frequently as glaze allowed to settle, even for a short time, will not give an adequate covering.

Eggcups, for example, can be dipped with a quick once up and down jerking action while under the glaze to dispel the trapped air pocket and pull glaze over the internal walls.

## Pouring glaze for external walls

It is often easier to use a pouring technique for glazing ceramic pieces. This might be suitable if there is insufficient glaze to fully immerse a large piece of work, if spraying equipment is not available or if the glaze is inappropriate for brushing.

Invert the piece, resting it on level slats over a large container. Pour glaze down the side of the piece, covering as much of the surface as possible. Try not to overlap the glaze unless this is effect you desire. Small, missed areas can be spot patched rather than making the applied glaze overly thick.

Glazing external walls in this way tends to cause drops of dried glaze to accumulate at the rim and around any points that are resting on the slats, so it can be a laborious technique that requires careful scraping once the glaze is dry to level the surface. To avoid unnecessary handling, wipe the bases clean of glaze while the piece is still inverted. The powdered glaze will damage when dry, particularly at the top edge or rim if it is knocked.

Pouring is used for the Three-Footed Bowl throwing project because overlapping the glaze gives a multi-coloured effect where the thicknesses vary.

## Glazing open shapes

**1** Glaze the top face of a plate, saucer or any other flat shape first. If you do not have a glaze claw and there is not enough glaze to fully immerse the open shape, the glaze should first be poured on the front face, tilting the edges and using a swilling motion to cover the surface. The excess is poured out and splashes to the back face wiped back after the piece has been allowed to become dry to the touch.

**2** To glaze the bottom face of an open shape, immerse it by holding the rim in two places and supporting the back with your thumbs.

If there is a foot rim you can hold, this is the better alternative, leaving fewer fingermarks to be retouched. Alternatively the back face can be poured one section at a time allowing the first to become dry to the touch before moving onto the next.

**3** Alternatively, glaze claws are particularly useful for glazing flatware, such as plates and saucers, which cannot be easily held. Hold the piece with a glazing claw and sweep it with one motion through the glaze.

## Spraying Glaze

Spraying is normally used to apply a "difficult" glaze that will not fire flat or that needs to be applied extremely thinly in a controlled manner. It is also often used when a soft, blurred, "disappearing" effect is required to edges of areas of coloured glaze. This is also a useful method of applying glaze when the work is too heavy or awkward to lift, or when there is insufficient glaze for individual, large pieces of work.

As with all glaze application, spraying should be done only when wearing an appropriate mask (respirator) and using extraction equipment (see glaze and decoration equipment and health and safety) as particles of airborne glaze materials should never be inhaled. Build up the glaze evenly, turning the piece of work on a banding wheel and holding the gun at an adequate distance to allow a wide spray that does not spot patch. After use, ensure that you wash spraying equipment with water to prevent the nozzle clogging up with glaze.

This shows the spraying of the Wicker Wave Vase project, where a transparent glaze is applied to the textured interior. This enables a thin, even application, which suits the nature of a transparent glaze. Pouring glaze on this piece would have resulted in pools of glaze collecting in the low points of the texture. Other "difficult" types of glaze that should be applied by spraying include those with a matt-fired finish.

## Brushing a glaze

There are many brush-on glazes sold commercially in many colours, surfaces, fired effects and temperature ranges. They have a similar consistency to non-drip emulsion (latex) paint and are therefore easier to apply with a stiff brush. For a covering equivalent to poured or dipped glaze you will need to apply at least two coats, allowing the first to dry first.

These glazes are useful when using a small amount of glaze or if you require a particular colour or effect. Many slop glazes can be applied with a soft brush as an overall covering or as decoration. Glazes made up from dry materials should be tested for brushing as the technique can appear patchy and uneven.

## Wax resist

Wax resist solution or hot candle wax melted with equal parts of paraffin oil (or kerosene) can be banded (see banding) onto footrings (feet), bases and lid galleries to give a clean edge to the applied glaze and to make the important task of wiping back less laborious. Ensure the wax resist solution is completely dry before applying the glaze so it will repel the glaze. Candle wax and oil is an inflammable mixture and can easily catch fire if it gets too hot. If this happens smother flames with a fireproof material and remove the heat source immediately. Do not pour on water or use a fire extinguisher.

## Cleaning back glaze

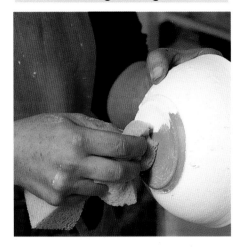

Any glaze must be cleared away from lid fittings where lids are to be fired in place to ensure a good fit. Bases, edges or points that will touch a kiln shelf should also be wiped clean with a damp sponge. This process is crucial to avoid the fired piece becoming stuck to a kiln shelf.

Spout strainer holes and lid air holes for teapots should be cleared of glaze before firing to prevent the fired gaze permanently filling holes that should be open. Do this, once the glaze is dry, with a needle or hole cutter.

Glaze can be left on a base if the piece to be fired is set on a stilt (see Kilns and Firing). Razor-sharp stilt scars can be removed using a carborundum stone (kiln brick bits) after firing.

# TECHNIQUES

## DEVELOPING GLAZES

Many potters choose to avoid the science of glaze by working with ready-made glazes or by using tried and tested recipes, and this approach is a perfectly valid one. However, even on the simplest level with a restricted range of ingredients, it is possible to develop an invaluable practical knowledge of the various glaze materials and their effects. Such an understanding of how different effects and colours are created and the ability to experiment with the glaze components extends your glaze range and gives you greater control over the work that you produce. The science of glazing is a vast subject that provides a specialist area of research and development.

## Simple testing and line blending

Glazes, engobes and slips are all combinations of glaze materials that require a degree of experimentation. A line blend is a way of testing colour additions to a base slip, base engobe, or base glaze (any recipe that can have colour or further material added). Colours can be added to the base recipe in gradually increasing intensities. They can also be used to test combinations of colour additions or to alter a glaze recipe by adding one material at a time.

Keeping records of your fired line tests will develop your understanding of the different materials and the roles they play. There follows a base slip recipe tested with a variety of colour additions – stains and metallic oxides used in isolation or in combination with each other. Protect yourself by wearing a face mask (respirator) and gloves while producing line blends.

### Method

**1** Start by preparing a range of leatherhard test pieces of clay. Clay for making test pieces should be considered carefully as the colour of the clay will affect the fired result. Ideally, use the same clay you are using to make your finished piece. If you are unsure about which clay you will be using, use any clay that is corner dipped in white or black slip (see glaze tests). This will give you a good indication of how the glaze will look on most types of clay. It might also influence your decision of the type of clay to use to make your piece. If they are made with a pierced hole, the fired pieces can be displayed on a board or threaded together for easy reference.

**2** Weigh and prepare a base slip recipe to its correct consistency in a known, easily divisible quantity. The recipe shown below uses 1 kg (2½ lb).

600g (1½ lb) SMD ball clay (or 60%) (SMD is a type of ball clay that fires white) 400 g (1 lb) China clay (or 40%)

**3** Divide and pour the kilo (2½ lb) of sieved white base slip into ten equivalent sized containers (such as plastic drinking cups). Measure it into equal quantities to give you ten cups holding a known dry weight of 100 g (¼ lb) in each cup.

**4** Carefully weigh the small amounts of colour additions using accurate scales and tip each into an individual cup (see sample recipe opposite). Mark each cup's contents with an indelible pen.

**5** Using a test sieve, sieve each cup of slip with its additions three times with a 60–100# sieve. Begin with the lower addition of colour for each set so that the sieve only has to be cleaned four times between each set change instead of 10 times for each colour test.

**6** Dip the test pieces into each test pot and mark them as you go with a pointed tool. Remember to mark the recipe and the final firing temperature. You can mark bisqued clay test pieces with iron oxide mixed with water applied with a small brush.

**7** Biscuit (bisque) fire the test pieces to 1000°C (1832°F).

**8** Glaze the slip tests with the same transparent glaze (see recipe below) and fire to the required temperature of the glaze.

## Clear lead glaze

This uncrazed, glossy glaze developed by Nick Ward has a good colour response. Apply the glaze thinly and ensure that the temperature is exact, as it over fires easily.

### Materials

75 g lead bisilicate
4.7 g whiting
17.4 g potash feldspar
1.3 g zinc oxide
1.6 g bentonite (to suspend the glaze)

### Firing

1050°C (1922°F)

All glaze ingredients have a tendency to settle at the bottom of water, but lead glazes more so than others. Bentonite therefore needs to be added to the clear glaze to act as a suspending and binding agent to stop the heavy particles settling. It should be added to the dry glaze materials before water is added, as once wet it will swell and will float around on the water surface. It is this strange swelling property that keeps the other ingredients suspended.

A range of line test results for earthenware and for stoneware clays follow on the next few pages.

LINE BLEND 1:
1 g chrome oxide
1 g cobalt oxide

LINE BLEND 2:
2 g chrome oxide
2 g cobalt oxide

LINE BLEND 3:
3 g chrome oxide
3 g cobalt oxide

LINE BLEND 4:
1 g colbalt oxide

LINE BLEND 5:
3 g cobalt oxide

LINE BLEND 6:
5 g cobalt oxide

LINE BLEND 7:
2 g yellow stain

LINE BLEND 8:
6 g yellow stain

LINE BLEND 9:
8 g yellow stain

LINE BLEND 10:
2.5 g red clay
0.25 g iron oxide
0.05 g cobalt oxide
0.3 g manganese oxide

## Further glaze testing

If you become intrigued by the science of glazing you may like to investigate altering glazes by increasing, decreasing, or substituting, one material at a time. Tri-axial blending is an extended type of glaze testing (beyond the scope of this book) that works along the principle of making up all potential combinations from three ingredients (see bibliography for further reading).

## Glaze recipes

Glaze recipes are generally indicated in the projects in percentages, although some specify grams and ounces. Percentages can easily be converted to grams or ounces and scaled up and down to suit the volume of work you are producing.

DISHES (38 AND 25 CM/15 AND 10 IN)
SLIPCAST EARTHENWARE WITH COLOURED GLAZES,
DESIGNED FOR POOLE POTTERY (JANICE TCHALENKO).

# GLAZE TESTS

## GROUP 1
Here are a range of glaze recipes giving a taste of the infinite number of glaze colours and effects. Use them as a basis from which to start your own glaze experiments. Always keep a careful record of glaze recipes so that you can reproduce the effects again. The glazes below are for earthenware.

### Top row

#### 1 Glossy Pink
980–1040°C (1796–1904°F)

| | |
|---|---|
| Calcium Borate Frit | 33% |
| China Clay | 12% |
| Potash Feldspar | 29% |
| Zinc Oxide | 14% |
| Titanium Oxide | 2% |
| Quartz (flint) | 10% |
| ALSO ADD: | |
| Pink Glaze Stain | 6% |

#### 2 Seagull White
1040–1080°C (1904–1976°F)

| | |
|---|---|
| High Alkaline Frit | 29% |
| Lithium Carbonate | 5% |
| Calcium Borate Frit | 19.5% |
| China Clay | 16% |
| Quartz (flint) | 26% |
| Titanium Oxide | 4.5% |

#### 3 Dark Honey Glaze
1060–1100°C (1940–2012°F)

| | |
|---|---|
| Lead Sesquisilicate | 56.5% |
| Calcium Borate Frit | 17% |
| China Clay | 15% |
| Quartz (flint) | 8% |
| Red Iron Oxide | 3.5% |

#### 4 Glossy Zircon White
1080–1120°C (1976–2048°F)

| | |
|---|---|
| Standard Borax Frit | 40% |
| Lead Bisilicate | 29% |
| Cornish Stone | 4% |
| China Clay | 5% |
| Zirconium Silicate | 22% |

#### 5 Glossy Yellow 1
1040–1080°C (1904–1976°F)

| | |
|---|---|
| Lead Bisilicate | 50% |
| Potash Feldspar | 25.5% |
| Zinc Oxide | 4% |
| Whiting | 6% |
| China Clay | 7% |
| Quartz (flint) | 7.5% |
| ALSO ADD: | |
| Yellow Stain | 9% |

### Second row

#### 6 Barium Matt Blue
1080–1120°C (1976–2048°F)

| | |
|---|---|
| Nepheline Syenite | 19% |
| Barium Carbonate | 40% |
| Petalite | 9% |
| Quartz (flint) | 13% |
| China Clay | 15% |
| Copper Carbonate | 4% |

#### 7 Glossy Blue
1040–1080°C (1904–1976°F)

| | |
|---|---|
| Lead Bisilicate | 49% |
| Potash Feldspar | 25.5% |
| Zinc Oxide | 4% |
| Whiting | 6% |
| China Clay | 7% |
| Quartz (flint) | 7.5% |
| Cobalt Oxide | 1% |

#### 8 Glossy Dark Green
1040–1080°C (1904–1976°F)

| | |
|---|---|
| Lead Bisilicate | 49% |
| Potash Feldspar | 25.5% |
| Zinc Oxide | 3% |
| Whiting | 6% |
| China Clay | 7% |
| Quartz (flint) | 7.5% |
| Copper Oxide | 3% |
| Red Iron Oxide | 1% |

#### 9 Glossy Turquoise
1040–1080°C (1904–1976°F)

| | |
|---|---|
| High Alkaline Frit | 56% |
| China Clay | 17% |
| Quartz (flint) | 21% |
| Copper Carbonate | 4% |
| Bentonite | 2% |

#### 10 Glossy Yellow 2
1040–1080°C (1904–1976°F)

| | |
|---|---|
| Zinc Oxide | 7% |
| Lead Bisilicate | 49% |
| China Clay | 16% |
| Quartz (flint) | 16% |
| Yellow Stain | 12% |

### Third and bottom rows

These are low-temperature earthenware glazes – the colour variations are all listed as additions to the basic recipe, except tile 15 which has a separate recipe.

#### 11–14 and 16–20 Lead Tile Glaze
980–1040°C (1796–1904°F)

| | |
|---|---|
| Lead Bisilicate | 90% |
| Whiting | 4% |
| China Clay | 5% |
| Bentonite | 1% |

Use Lead Tile Glaze base glaze and add for examples illustrated:

#### 11 Apple Green
| | |
|---|---|
| Copper Carbonate | 3% |

#### 12 Dark Green
| | |
|---|---|
| Chrome Oxide | 2% |

#### 13 Mid Brown
| | |
|---|---|
| Manganese Oxide | 2% |

#### 14 Bright Blue
| | |
|---|---|
| Cobalt Oxide | 1% |

#### 15 Alkaline Tile Glaze
980–1040°C (1796–1904°F)

| | |
|---|---|
| High Alkaline Frit | 74% |
| China Clay | 7.5% |
| Quartz (flint) | 15% |
| Bentonite | 1% |
| Copper Carbonate | 2.5% |

Use Lead Tile Glaze base glaze and add for examples illustrated:

#### 16 Rich Green
| | |
|---|---|
| Copper Carbonate | 4% |

#### 17 Mid Green
| | |
|---|---|
| Copper Carbonate | 3% |

#### 18 Dark Brown
| | |
|---|---|
| Red Iron Oxide | 6% |

#### 19 Honey Brown
| | |
|---|---|
| Red Iron Oxide | 2% |

#### 20 Dark Blue
| | |
|---|---|
| Red Iron Oxide | 3% |
| Cobalt Oxide | 1% |

FIVE-STRIPED AUSTRALIAN ANGEL FISH (18 x 22 CM/7 x 8¾ IN) STONEWARE PLATE WITH SLIPS, OXIDES AND STAINS (FRANK HAMER)

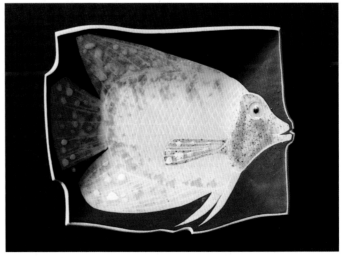

# GLAZE TESTS
## GROUP 2 Some of these stoneware glazes are reduction fired (R) and some have an oxidized firing (O). All glaze tests are fired at 1250–1285°C (2282–2345°F) unless otherwise specified.

### Top row

**21 Celadon**    **R**

| | |
|---|---|
| Whiting | 12% |
| Potash Feldspar | 49% |
| China Clay | 10% |
| Quartz (flint) | 27% |
| Red Iron Oxide | 2% |

**22 Glossy Blue Brown**    **O**
1250–1280°C (2282–2336°F)

| | |
|---|---|
| Potash Feldspar | 27% |
| Dolomite | 19% |
| Whiting | 7% |
| China Clay | 18% |
| Quartz (flint) | 19% |
| Titanium Oxide | 6% |
| Cobalt Oxide | 1.5% |
| Red Iron Oxide | 2.5% |

**23 Tenmoku**    **R**
1250–1280°C (2282–2336°F)

| | |
|---|---|
| Cornish Stone | 71% |
| Whiting | 9% |
| Quartz (flint) | 11% |
| China Clay | 2% |
| Red Iron Oxide | 7% |

**24 Iron Red**    **O**
1250–1280°C (2282–2336°F)

| | |
|---|---|
| Potash Feldspar | 52.5% |
| Talc | 7.5% |
| Bone Ash | 7.5% |
| China Clay | 7.5% |
| Quartz (flint) | 15% |
| Red Iron Oxide | 10% |

**25 High Whiting/ Clay Matt**    **R**
1250–1300°C (2282–2372°F)

| | |
|---|---|
| Potash Feldspar | 18% |
| China Clay | 15% |
| Calcined China Clay | 15% |
| Whiting | 37% |
| Calcium Borate Frit | 3% |
| Yellow Ochre | 12% |

### Second row

**26 Copper Purple**    **R**
1250–1280°C (2282–2336°F)

| | |
|---|---|
| Nepheline Syenite | 62% |
| Wollastonite | 12% |
| China Clay | 8% |
| Quartz (flint) | 11.5% |
| Calcium Borate Frit | 3% |
| Tin Oxide | 1% |
| Copper Oxide | 2.25% |
| Cobalt Oxide | 0.25% |

**27 Copper Purple**    **O**
1250–1280°C (2282–2336°F)

| | |
|---|---|
| Nepheline Syenite | 62% |
| Wollastonite | 12% |
| China Clay | 8% |
| Quartz (flint) | 11.5% |
| Calcium Borate Frit | 3% |
| Tin Oxide | 1% |
| Copper Oxide | 2.25% |
| Cobalt Oxide | 0.25% |

**28 Green Speckle**    **O**
1240–1280°C (2264–2336°F)

| | |
|---|---|
| Nepheline Syenite | 48% |
| Whiting | 19.5% |
| Quartz (flint) | 11.5% |
| China Clay | 11.5% |
| Zinc Oxide | 8% |
| Copper Oxide | 1.5% |

**29 Barium Turquoise**    **O**
1240–1280°C (2264–2336°F)

| | |
|---|---|
| Barium Carbonate | 19% |
| Nepheline Syenite | 39% |
| Soda Feldspar | 36% |
| China Clay | 2% |
| Bentonite | 1% |
| Copper Carbonate | 3% |

**30 Glossy Yellow**    **O**

| | |
|---|---|
| Potash Feldspar | 27% |
| Dolomite | 19% |
| Whiting | 7% |
| China Clay | 14% |
| Quartz (flint) | 19% |
| Titanium Oxide | 6% |
| Yellow Stain | 8% |

### Third row

**31 White Dolomite**    **R**

| | |
|---|---|
| Potash Feldspar | 42% |
| Dolomite | 18% |
| Whiting | 6% |
| China Clay | 28% |
| Quartz (flint) | 6% |

**32 White Dolomite**    **O**

| | |
|---|---|
| Potash Feldspar | 42% |
| Dolomite | 18% |
| Whiting | 6% |
| China Clay | 28% |
| Quartz (flint) | 6% |

**33 Satin White**    **O**

| | |
|---|---|
| Potash Feldspar | 36.5% |
| Dolomite | 16% |
| Whiting | 8% |
| China Clay | 15% |
| Quartz (flint) | 21.5% |
| Titanium Oxide | 3% |

**34 Vanadium Yellow**    **R**

| | |
|---|---|
| Nepheline Syenite | 31% |
| Whiting | 31% |
| Fireclay | 18% |
| China Clay | 12% |
| Vanadium Pentoxide | 8% |

**35 Vanadium Green**    **R**

| | |
|---|---|
| Nepheline Syenite | 31% |
| Whiting | 31% |
| Fireclay | 14% |
| China Clay | 12% |
| Copper Oxide | 2% |
| Vanadium Pentoxide | 8% |

### Bottom row

**36 Frosty Blue**    **O**

| | |
|---|---|
| Nepheline Syenite | 74% |
| Wollastonite | 8% |
| China Clay | 3% |
| Quartz (flint) | 10% |
| Bentonite | 1.5% |
| Cobalt Oxide | 0.5% |
| Titanium Oxide | 3% |

**37 Copper Green**    **O**

| | |
|---|---|
| Nepheline Syenite P3322 | 74% |
| Wollastonite | 8% |
| China Clay | 3% |
| Quartz (flint) | 10% |
| Bentonite | 2% |
| Copper Oxide | 1% |
| Tin Oxide | 2% |

**38 Barium Blue**    **O**

| | |
|---|---|
| Barium Carbonate | 18% |
| Quartz (flint) | 9% |
| China Clay | 9% |
| Soda Feldspar | 47% |
| Dolomite | 4% |
| Titanium Oxide | 3% |
| Zinc Oxide | 7% |
| Copper Carbonate | 3% |

**39 Frosty Blue**    **O**

| | |
|---|---|
| Nepheline Syenite | 74% |
| Wollastonite | 8% |
| China Clay | 3% |
| Quartz (flint) | 10% |
| Bentonite | 1.5% |
| Cobalt Oxide | 0.5% |
| Titanium Oxide | 3% |

**40 Chrome Green**    **O**

| | |
|---|---|
| Nepheline Syenite P3332 | 74% |
| Wollastonite | 8% |
| China Clay | 4% |
| Quartz (flint) | 11% |
| Bentonite | 1.5% |
| Chrome Oxide | 1.5% |

# TECHNIQUES
# THE GLAZE OXIDES
To fully understand how the different characteristics of glazes occur and to get maximum benefit from your line tests, it is useful to have an understanding of the main components of a glaze. It can be helpful to think of the three main consituents of a glaze as comprising blood, flesh and bones, or respectively the flux, the stiffener (alumina) and the glass (silica or another glass forming oxide, such as boric acid).

Although the main component is silica (silicon dioxide), a glaze differs from glass because it also contains alumina (aluminium oxide), which stiffens and stabilises the flow of the melting glass in the intense heat of a kiln. The third component, the flux, completes the triangle of interaction and determines the glaze characteristics – the temperature at which it will melt and how smooth or colourful it will be.

All glazes have a certain viscosity, meaning the liquid quality of a glaze as it melts, and this is altered by various factors. One of these factors is the presence and quantity of alumina. Viscosity is also altered by the presence of the fluxes and any colour additions, which act as catalysts that cause the glaze to melt. Each individual flux has a characteristic and temperature range of its own. One flux that brings about the melting of a glaze at a high temperature stoneware glaze might have no effect at all on a low temperature earthenware glaze recipe.

The three main glaze constituents are oxides. However, do not confuse this term with metallic oxides (see sources of glaze colour), which introduce colour to a glaze. None of the glaze oxides listed below introduce colour to a glaze except lead, giving a slight yellow.

Each glaze oxide is normally identified by a chemical symbol, and these are listed below as well as at the back of the book (see Chemical Formulae) along with chemical symbols of elements. It is useful to get to know these symbols as this will help you understand how other materials, such as frits and feldspars, can affect a combination of glaze oxides.

## The fluxes

LEAD OXIDE (PbO) TOXIC
A lower-middle temperature flux for oxidation only. Bright, glossy, good colour response. More reliable when combined with boron to give a wide firing temperature range. Blisters in reduction firing.

SODIUM OXIDE ($Na_2O$)
Gives strong, brilliant colour. Good with copper, cobalt, manganese and iron when fired above 1080°C (1976°F). Soft finish to glaze. Easily worn and a tendency to craze.

POTASSIUM OXIDE ($K_2O$)
A flux that gives a good colour response.

CALCIUM OXIDE (CaO)
A high temperature flux that has little effect on colour. Used in celadons. Use a high % for matt glazes.

MAGNESIUM OXIDE (MgO)
This high temperature flux gives a smooth, fatty surface. Small quantities harden sodium and potassium glazes.

LARGE PLATTER (45 CM/18 IN)
MAIOLICA AND TIN GLAZE (DAPHNE CARNEGY).

BARIUM OXIDE (BaO) TOXIC

Used in high fired glazes, this flux is not very active and is used for satiny, matt, dry glazes with an excellent colour response particularly with copper.

LITHIUM OXIDE (Li$_2$O) TOXIC

A high temperature flux similar to sodium. which is used to create vellum or smooth quality glazes.

BORIC OXIDE (B$_2$O$_3$)

A low temperature flux with a wide firing range that reduces expansion of a glaze and, therefore, crazing (except when used in large amounts). It intensifies colours and is smooth and hard wearing in lead boro-silicate glazes (see also silica).

ZINC OXIDE (ZnO)

A middle and high range flux used moderately to prevent pinholing. On its own it gives opaque, stiff and not very smooth glazes with a poor colour response. It has a good effect when mixed with copper, cobalt and chrome. With copper it can produce a brilliant turquoise and with titanium it produces crystalline glazes.

## The stiffener (alumina)

ALUMINIUM OXIDE (Al$_2$O$_3$)

Most of the alumina necessary for a glaze is supplied by clay and feldspar. This neutral oxide increases glaze viscosity or stability and prevents the glaze from running off a fired ceramic piece. It is also used in glaze as a matting agent and to resist crystallization. On its own, alumina has an extremely high melting point of 2050°C (3722°F). It can be line-blend tested to reduce the glaze defect of crawling.

TITANIUM OXIDE (TiO$_2$)

An opacifier used widely in crystalline glazes.

## The glass (silica)

SILICON DIOXIDE (SiO$_2$)

Glass forming oxide.

BORIC OXIDE (B$_2$O$_3$)

Glass forming oxide.

## Glaze oxide sources

Oxides are sourced from naturally occurring rocks and minerals. The raw materials do not deteriorate with age and can be stored in powder or in a wet, mixed form (slop) within a glaze, slip or engobe recipe.

There follows a list of some of the more commonly used raw materials that contain the various oxides or components in the composition of glaze, slip and engobe recipes. You can order them from a ceramic supplier in powdered form. Wear adequate protective clothing with a face mask (respirator) and gloves when handling these materials.

FLINT OR QUARTZ (SiO$_2$)

Flint, prepared from calcined flint stones, and quartz, a pure form of silica rock, are the main sources of silica in a glaze. Flint adjustments to a glaze when line blending are often necessary to reduce crazing defects. On its own, silica melts at 1600°C (2912°F) and quartz at 1710°C (3110°F).

CLAYS (VARIABLE)

A high proportion of secondary clays are included in single-fire glazes, also known as slip glazes, allowing for raw clay shrinkage. Local clay referred to in glaze recipes can be assumed to be fine-particle clays that contain from 4–6% iron. They melt at low temperatures so in high temperature glazes they act as fluxes, as well as sources of iron. With such a variable material, line testing is particularly essential.

BALL CLAY (VARIABLE)

Acting as a suspending and binding agent, ball clay introduces silica and alumina to a glaze. Ball clays are usually highly plastic and white firing. They vary from mine to mine. Some are high in silica, others in alumina - no two are the same. Typical UK ball clays are TWVD, SMD Hymod and Hyplas. Ball clay is a main ingredient in decorating slips.

CHINA CLAY (OR KAOLIN)

(Al$_2$O$_3$ 2SiO$_2$ 2H$_2$O)

Pure white clay, which gives no colour to a glaze or slip, china clay also acts as a suspending and binding agent and introduces silica and alumina to a glaze. All china clays have the same theoretical analysis, but there are variations in particle size and plasticity. Grolleg is a high quality plastic china clay produced in the UK. China clay is a main ingredient in decorating slips.

CALCINED CHINA CLAY (OR MOLOCHITE)

(Al$_2$O$_3$ 2SiO$_2$)

Substituted for use in glazes that include more than 12% of clay, calcined china clay reduces the plastic content and therefore reduces shrinkage. It has had the chemically combined water removed.

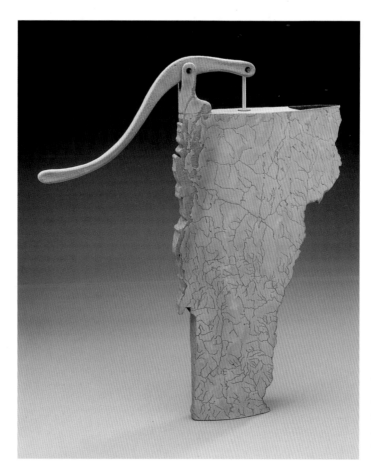

ACCEPTABLE LEVELS
66 CM/26 IN)
SLAB CONSTRUCTION
WITH METAL ADDITIONS,
AIRBRUSHED AND
PAINTED UNDERGLAZES
(NANCY SELVAGE).

## Feldspars

These are the most widely used and important of glaze raw materials and contain all three essential types of glaze materials: fluxes, alumina and silica. They are an economical way of introducing the alkalis sodium and potassium in an insoluble form. The most commonly used include orthoclase (potash feldspar), albite (soda feldspar) and anorthite (calcium feldspar). Feldspars are, in effect, natural frits as most will melt by themselves at approximately 1250°C (2282°F). At temperatures of 1260°C (2300°F) or more, extremely simple glazes can be made with a 5–10% addition of dolomite, whiting or talc.

Each feldspar has a different chemical composition. The feldspars, or spars, below are listed with their theoretical formulas to indicate which glaze oxide is contained in each material. Catalogues often break down how much of each glaze oxide is in a feldspar. This is useful if you need to find a near equivalent for an ingredient.

TEAPOT (28 CM/11 IN) EARTHENWARE CLAY WITH BASE SLIP OF STONEWARE WHITE AND STUDIO WHITE. A RANGE OF OXIDES AND BODY STAINS ARE ADDED, AND AFTER FIRING A TRANSPARENT GLAZE IS APPLIED BEFORE GLAZE FIRING (SOPHIE MACCARTHY).

POTASH FELDSPAR ($K_2O\ Al_2O_3\ 6SiO_2$)
This is used when no specific spar is called for in a recipe. It contains potassium oxide, alumina and silica.

SODA FELDSPAR ($Na_2O\ Al_2O_3 6\ SiO_2$)
Contains sodium oxide.

NEPHELINE SYENITE ($K_2O_2\ Na_2O\ Al_2O_3\ 8SiO_2$)
Varies from a middle to lower temperature-range flux and introduces higher amounts of the alkalis sodium and potassium and less silica than other feldspars. It also contains alumina.

CORNISH STONE OR PEGMATITE STONE
This is a complex and variable material, which cannot be shown as a single formula. It contains a high silica proportion and a wide combination of fluxes for high temperature glazes including sodium, potassium, magnesia and calcium.

DOLOMITE OR CALCIUM MAGNESIUM CARBONATE (typically $CaCO_3\ MgCO_3$)
Glaze testing is necessary with this feldspar as it varies widely in its chemical composition. It is an important high-temperature flux that introduces magnesium and calcium. When proportions of 10–25% are included in a glaze, it imparts a characteristically vellum-smooth quality.

WHITING OR CALCIUM CARBONATE ($CaCO_3$)
By itself, whiting is refractory or high firing, but when combined with feldspars it acts as a major flux in the temperature range 1100°C (2012°F) onwards. It introduces colour development for celadon glazes and is craze resistant. In excess, whiting gives a matt dull or rough surface.

TALC, FRENCH TALC OR SOAPSTONE ($3\ MgO\ 4SiO_2\ H_2O$)
Containing magnesium, this secondary flux gives an opaque, vellum finish.

CALCIUM BORATE FRIT ($2CaO\ 3B_2O_3\ 5H_2O$)
This is used in small quantities as a primary or secondary flux that intensifies glaze colour and reduces crazing. It introduces boron to a glaze.

BARIUM CARBONATE ($Ba\ Co_3$) TOXIC
Provides barium oxide, which gives a characteristic dry glaze of an intense turquoise blue when combined with copper oxide.

LITHIUM CARBONATE ($Li_2\ CO_3$) TOXIC
Gives a good colour response and increases a glaze's firing range.

BENTONITE
This is useful in small quantities (1–2%) in a glaze to suspend glaze particles (see glaze oxide sources).

SPODUMENE ($LiO_2\ Al_2O_3\ 4SiO_2$)
This lithium feldspar provides lithium oxide and corrects crazing.

SILICON CARBIDE (SiC)
This gives a volcanic or pitted quality to a glaze because of gases that escape as it reacts with the molten glaze beyond 1000°C (1832°F). It is used as a 10–15% addition and must be coarse grade.

BONE ASH ($Ca_3(PO_4)_2$)
This gives opalescence and, in high-fired glazes, a source of calcium.

## Frits

A frit is a ceramic material that is fused with glass in a furnace and then crushed in a ball mill to make soluble raw materials (such as borax) insoluble for use in a glaze and, as in the case of lead, safer to use. They introduce a combination of fluxes and silica to a glaze and, if fired high enough, almost form a glaze in themselves. They vary widely in the glaze oxides they introduce and in their temperature range.

Manufacturers produce a wide range of frits, many of which can be easily substituted if the one quoted in a recipe is not available.

### LEAD FRITS

The three types of lead frit are lead monosilicate, lead sesquisilicate and lead bisilicate. The two former are used in glazes melting below 900°C (1652°F), such as raku glazes; lead bisilicate is used in glazes above 900°C (1652°F). Lead frits are almost a glaze in themselves, but should be thought of as fluxes.

### BORAX FRITS

A range of these are available, meaning that glaze tests have to be carried out when the particular borax frit quoted in a glaze recipe is not available.

### ALKALINE FRITS

These are found in alkaline glazes with a high proportion of soda or potash.

## Opacifiers

Additions of 2–15% of the following oxides, known as opacifiers, will make a transparent glaze opaque. Combined with metallic oxides or stains they will make an opaque coloured glaze. Tin used in amounts of 5–10% encourages the iron contained in a clay to speckle or mottle into the white glaze. Tin and zirconium can be combined.

### TIN OXIDE, OR STANNIC OXIDE ($SNO_2$)

Add 2–15% depending on the base glaze and the degree of opacity required. Although tin is an expensive material, its soft blue-white quality makes it popular.

### ZIRCONIUM OXIDE ($ZRO_2$)

Add 12–20% for a generally harsher white glaze. The oxide form contains more zircon, but the silicate form disperses better in a glaze even though it is half as strong. Zircon lends a strength to the glaze surface, which is scratch and craze resistant. It can be used at any temperature and in reduction firing.

### TITANIUM DIOXIDE ($TIO_2$)

Use this in additions of 5–15% to give a creamy white glaze and to soften oxide additions. This opacifier does not respond well in a high alkaline glaze.

The type of white lent by the various opacifiers depends on the colour of the clay to which they are applied.

TOP ROW: DOLOMITE, CORNISH STONE, ALKALINE FRIT, BALL CLAY; BOTTOM ROW: POTASH FELDSPAR, WHITING, BENTONITE, CHINA CLAY

# TECHNIQUES
# SOURCES OF GLAZE COLOUR
Most metallic oxides are mined in the form of ores, which are smelted, ground and precipitated. The oxides used for ceramic colour are sometimes used in different forms. Cobalt, for example, is used as an oxide or a carbonate. If used in combination with a glaze the ingredients in the glaze recipe will also affect the colour produced by that oxide.

Some oxides are heavy or coarse, while others will disperse more readily. With a few exceptions, such as copper, all the oxides are stable at low temperatures, but some, such as copper, become volatile at higher temperatures and can affect other work in the kiln. Stronger oxides should be used in small quantities or very weakly. They should be tested when used in colouring slips and glazes.

Metallic oxides are added to glazes in measured amounts and each produces a characteristic colour. The colours are very different in their raw state compared to their fired result. Metallic oxides can be combined in varying proportions within glazes resulting in unusual colours and sometimes surprising textural results. The colours produced will also depend on whether they undergo an oxidation or reduction firing and upon the other raw materials that are included. Reds and yellows are notoriously difficult to achieve and are often obtained with the use of a commercial colour.

The basic colouring oxides are present in all commercially prepared recipes in controlled measurements. Stains tend to be opaque and lack the depth of the colouring oxides.

## The colouring oxides
COBALT OXIDE OR CARBONATE ($CO_3O_4$)
0.5–2% medium to strong blue
0.25–0.5% medium to light blue
Usually used as cobalt carbonate (light purple powder) in glazes because of its fine particle size or as black cobalt oxide (black powder). Used in small percentages as it is a strong, stable and reliable oxide. It gives blues under reduction and oxidation glazes, a vivid colour in alkaline and reduction glazes and a deep blue in lead glazes. Subtle variations occur when combined with other oxides, removing the harsh edge of blue.

COPPER OXIDE OR CARBONATE ($CuCO_3$)
2–4% light to strong green
0.5–3% red to red/black
Commonly used as copper carbonate (light green powder) as it has finer particles or as black copper oxide (black powder). Gives a range of greens in oxidation glazes, turquoise blues in alkaline glazes and beautiful plant to bottle greens in lead glazes. In reduction glazes, it gives the famous "ox blood" or "sang de boeuf" reds, and intense blue greens in barium glazes. Volatile above cone 8, which can affect the colour of neighbouring work in a kiln.

CHROMIUM OXIDE ($Cr_2O_3$)
2% green
1% yellow
Used as chrome oxide (a flat, green powder), gives a heavy blanket green lacking the vigour of copper greens in zinc-free, low-lead glazes. Gives surprising orange to reds in low-fired lead glazes that are low in alumina. Produces yellow in low-fired soda glazes, brown with zinc glazes, pinks in tin glazes with small 1% additions, and blue greens with cobalt in high-fired, reduction magnesia glazes. Volatile above cone 6 in tin glazes. Should be handled with great care.

IRON OXIDE ($Fe_2O_3$)
4–6% tan to dark brown
1–10% celadon to brown to iron red
Most usually applied as red iron oxide as this has finer particles than black iron oxide. Red powdered clays can be added as a source of red iron oxide. At 1–2% it gives warm hues as a tint in heavily reduced fired celadon glazes. At 2–5% it gives warm, soft colours in lead glazes with bright amber tones. In high lead and tin compositions it gives a mottled cream breaking to red brown on high points of texture; in alkaline glazes it gives yellow to tan shades; and it is dull in zinc glazes. In reduction firings at 7–12% it gives dark brown to black to rust reds. It can be added as crocus martis for a speckled effect.

MANGANESE OXIDE ($MnO_2$)
4–6% purple to dark purple
4% brown
Added as manganese carbonate (a fine particle pink powder) or as manganese dioxide (black powder). In high alkaline glazes it gives rich blue plum colour; in lead glazes it gives a softer purple tinged with brown. Combined with small amounts of cobalt it can give a rich violet colour.

NICKEL OXIDE ($Ni_2O_3$) TOXIC
2% grey to brown
1% grey to grey/brown
Added as green or black nickel oxide. Dingy used on its own, but works well combined with other oxides, such as cobalt iron or copper, to give a grey hue to other colours.

VANADIUM PENTOXIDE ($V_2O_5$) TOXIC
6% medium yellow
Used as a stain in glazes and combined with tin, resulting in an opaque glaze.

RUTILE ($TiO_2$)
3–5% tan
Gives texture when used with other oxides. Used as an ore containing titanium and iron oxide (beige powder), but gives a weak tint. Commonly used to give dramatic texture to a glaze of broken or mottled colour. Does not have this affect in lead glazes. With other oxides, such as iron, cobalt, copper and chrome, it gives pleasingly hued and textured colours. Widely used in crystalline glazes.

ILMENITE (FeO $TiO_2$)
1–3% spotty brown
Used as an ore containing titanium and iron. Can be used in a granular form to give a peppery speckle. It has a similar effect to black iron oxide and introduces texture.

IRON CHROMATE ($FeCrO_3$) TOXIC
2% grey
Most useful as a colour modifier darkening grey-browns or black.

# Bas-Relief Tiles

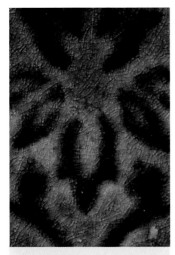

These purple bas-relief tiles were made by Irmin Eggens as a special commission for a bathroom in a Victorian townhouse. Hand-pressing in openback moulds in this way is an effective and fast technique to make small batches of tiles. The repeat moulds were made with a rubber positive cast made from the original plaster mould that was in turn made from the handbuilt clay model.

## Materials

Earthstone clay (or any grogged clay)

## Equipment

Pugcutter or harp (U-shaped rod)
Refuse sacks
Potter's knife
Scrap paper
Rubber kidney
Cardboard
Plaster moulds
Thin short strip of timber
Fork or comb
Small board
2 prepared biscuit (bisque) fired tiles
Brick
Gloves for glazing
Sliptrailer
Sponge
Tile crank
Electric kiln

## Glaze

| | |
|---|---|
| High Alkaline Frit | 76% |
| Potash feldspar | 12% |
| Flint | 10% |
| China clay | 2% |
| Bentonite | 2% |
| Cobalt oxide | 0.3% |
| Copper carbonate | 0.5% |
| Manganese dioxide | 1.5% |

## Firing

Biscuit (bisque) fire to 1180°C (2156°F)
Glaze fire to 1080°C (1976°F) then soak for 20 minutes

**1** Wedge soft clay into a block. The top must be a little bit larger than the tiles. The slabs also have to be slightly higher than the tiles. Cut slabs with a pugcutter or a harp (U-shaped rod).

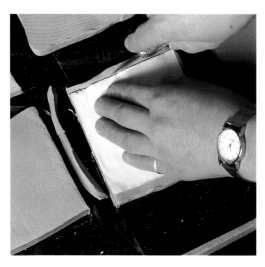

**2** Place the slabs on a piece of plastic. Cut a template from scrap paper, so that you cut the slabs the right size.

**3** Smooth the surface of each little clay slab with a rubber kidney. The clay will then be better able to pick up fine detailing from the mould.

**4** Place the mould on a piece of cardboard. This makes it easier to move the mould around and avoids damaging the mould and leaving "skid marks" on the workbench. Place the slabs in the middle of the moulds. Work in batches of about 12 to speed up the process.

**5** Press the clay hard into the edges of the mould with both thumbs. Fill as well as possible, so that you leave no air gaps.

**6** Even out the clay with your fist, pressing down firmly. Start at the middle and work towards the edges.

**7** Remove the excess clay with a small piece of timber. Do not use a metal tool for this as it damages the mould. Start from the middle and pull the strip towards you. Do not try to scrape off all the excess clay at once, do it gently in a few strokes. To ensure an absolutely flat back repeat the process diagonally across the mould.

**8** Draw lines at the back of the tile with a fork or a comb while it is still in the mould. It is essential to have such ridges on the underside of wall tiles to make a better grip for adhesive.

**9** Leave the tile for about 30 minutes. Then hold the mould in one hand, place a small board on top covering the back of the tile and turn them over together. Lift up the mould to reveal the tile.

**10** Stack up the wet tiles, face-to-face and back-to-back, between biscuit (bisque) fired tiles and place a brick on top. Turn them occasionally to avoid sticking. Depending on the conditions in your studio they should take about three weeks to dry. Let them dry slowly and evenly to keep them as flat and as straight as possible.

**11** When dry, biscuit (bisque) fire them slowly from 60°C to 600°C (140°F to 1112°F), normal up to 1180°C (2156°F). Do not open the kiln too soon as tiles are very sensitive to thermal shock. Wearing gloves, apply a thick, even layer of transparent glaze with colouring oxides and then wipe each tile back with a damp sponge.

**12** Place the tiles in the individual slots in a tile crank and place them in the kiln. When you make quite a number of tiles it is worth investing in tile cranks to maximize space in your kiln. They are available in different sizes from all good ceramic suppliers. Finally, fire the glazed tiles at 1080°C (1976°F), for 20 minutes.

# Burnished Plate

Burnishing is the most ancient method known to decrease the porosity of fired clay. To Montse Jalon the appeal of this technique lies in the richness of the burnished surface, the simplicity of the materials required and the minimum of equipment needed to achieve its effects. Burnishing is most effective on simple, uncomplicated shapes. Be especially careful when burnishing edges, because the pressure may easily make the edge crumble.

**Materials**

Red earthenware clay

**Equipment**

Piece of canvas
Rolling pin
Two wooden slats
Plaster plate mould
Wooden spoon
Potter's knife
Steel kidney scrapers
    (serrated and stiff)
Needle or pointed tool
Brush
Smooth pebble
Polishing wax
Electric kiln

**Slip**

| Ball clay | 50% |
|---|---|
| China clay | 25% |
| Cornish stone | 10% |
| Flint | 15% |
| Cobalt Oxide | 10% |
| Black iron oxide | 12% |

**Firing**

Biscuit (bisque) fire the piece to 1080°C (1976°F) in an electric kiln

**1** There are several ways of preparing a big slab of clay. One way is to join small pieces of clay with your fingers and flatten them by hand in preparation for rolling.

**2** Using a rolling pin, roll an even slab of clay on the canvas. The slab must be big enough to cover the surface of the plate mould comfortably. Use wooden slats to determine the required thickness of the clay. Roll the clay from the centre so that it moves out easily. Keep the clay free and lift it regularly from the canvas.

**3** Lay the rolled slab of clay over the mould so that it overlaps the edges. Use one hand to support the clay and gently ease it into the mould. When fitted beat the clay at the edge of the mould with a wooden spoon to define the rim.

**4** Trim away the excess clay around the rim of the mould with a knife.

**5** Scrape the clay with a serrated metal kidney to get rid of any lumps. Scrape first in one direction and then across in a diagonal direction.

**6** Smooth the surface with the metal kidney until all the marks made by the serrated kidney disappear.

**7** Draw your chosen design on the clay with a needle or pointed tool.

**8** If you make mistakes while drawing the design, you can erase them by rubbing the clay with your finger.

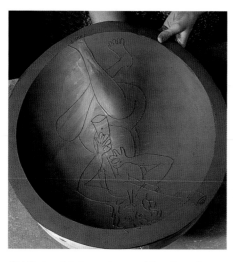

**9** Lift the slab from the mould and gently push from behind to make the design look more three-dimensional. Because of the size and thickness of the slab the press moulded clay will then maintain this form.

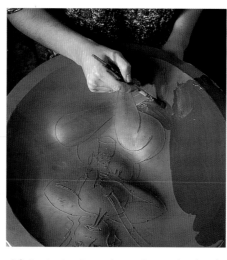

**10** Apply the slip to the surface with a brush, then let it dry until it is no longer shiny.

**11** Firmly rub the surface with a smooth pebble as soon as the brushed coating is touch dry. If the slip rubs off leave it to dry for a little longer. Rotate the pebble in small circles or work it in a simple linear way.

**12** If, after the first burnish, you can still see clay underneath, you will need to apply another layer of slip until it is completely covered and you get the desired shine. A final rub with your hands can be given at the near-dry stage. Biscuit (bisque) fire the piece to 1080°C (1976°F). After the firing the surface may lose its burnish but you can restore the shine by applying polishing wax.

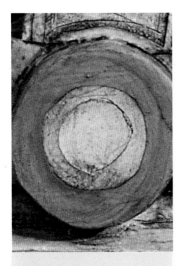

## Materials
50% T-material clay
50% White Earthenware

## Equipment
Rolling pin
Wooden boards
Knife
Ruler
Stiff brush for slurry
Surform blade
Hacksaw blade
Metal kidney
Flat-ended wooden
   modelling tool
Plastic sheet
Paper
Scissors
Sponge
Newspaper
Gloves for glazing
Latex resist paintbrushes
Black ceramic pencil
Electric kiln

## Glaze
ENGOBE
| | |
|---|---|
| Ball clay | 50% |
| China clay | 20% |
| Borax frit | 50% |
COLOUR ADDITIONS
| | |
|---|---|
| Black stain | 8–10% |

## Firing
Biscuit (bisque) fire to 1000°C
   (1832°F)
Glaze fire to 1115°C (2039°F)

# Toy Box

The toys Josie Warshaw chose to include in this piece are some of the favourites from her son's toy box. Slabbed, assembled components are used and colour is applied in conjunction with paper-resist decoration. The leatherhard slabs used in this frame can be adapted to any subject.

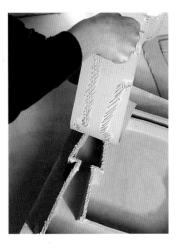

**1** Roll out sufficient slabs and leave them to become leatherhard. Once the slabs are firm enough not to buckle, cut and butt join them onto a base slab to make up the double wall of the frame. To make a butt join angle the piece at the bottom of the frame by making a chamfered cut to the edge.

**2** Slope the walls of the frame to give a receding feel to the overall shape. Trim the top edges with a surform blade to make a level joining surface for the top slab to contact.

**3** Use slabs that are firm enough not to sag when used for the top slab or "lid" of the frame. Join them into place then cut away the excess of each top slab with a knife. Pare and clean the joins and surfaces.

**4** Leave the frame to firm and even out to leatherhard. Trim the base and pare and clean the entire surface of the frame using a hacksaw blade, metal kidney and flat-ended, wooden modelling tool to clean up the corners. Cover the leatherhard frame and remaining slabs in plastic to prevent them becoming dry.

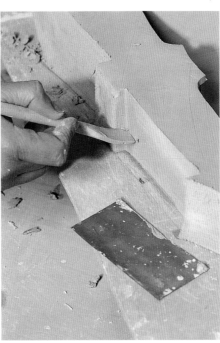

**5** Place a piece of paper on the inside face of the box then draw the dinosaur on it to get a correct fit. Use the paper template to cut the dinosaur from a leatherhard slab.

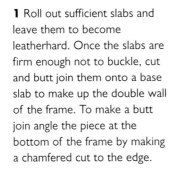

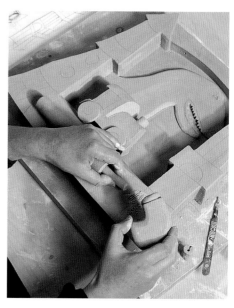

**6** Make the train stage-set style, without a back. Use a soft-to-leatherhard slab to make the curve of the roof and engine compartment and the prepared leatherhard slabs to make the other parts.

**7** Make the barrel of the pop gun by rolling soft slabs to form tubes. Leave them to become leatherhard before joining the parts together. Do the finer modelling and finishing once the toy joins become firm again.

**8** Join the toy parts to the main frame, slurrying and scoring the pieces and attaching the bevelled faces. Bevel the edge of the dinosaur shape using a hacksaw blade before joining it in place on the inner face of the box. Clean the joins of excess slurry and fill the gaps with soft clay using a modelling tool and a damp sponge.

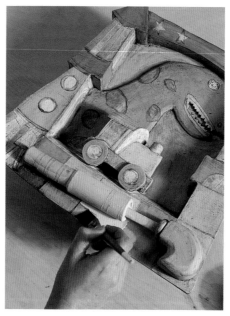

**9** Mask the assembled components with newspaper in selected areas to retain the white colour of the clay. Score sharp lines into the clay with a knife tip then start to paint the applied colour. Use dampened newspaper to make clean edges to the areas of applied colours. Lay the engobes using flat brushes and build them up in two layers to make an opaque, evenly laid covering. Leave the box to dry before biscuit (bisque) firing.

**10** After the biscuit (bisque) firing apply latex-resist to the areas selected to retain the colour of the white clay. When the latex is dry apply a wash of black stain to the surface of the work to pick up the scored lines, edges of the paper-resist and incidental surface texture.

**11** Remove the latex-resist and sponge away areas of black stain on the dinosaur spots to give a soft edge. Use black ceramic pencil to draw suggested leaves on the inside face. Fire the work again to 1115°C (2039°F).

# St Bride's Box

Soft slabbing, press moulding and hand-modelled decoration are involved in making this elaborate box by Rachel Kneebone. The Church of St Brides in London was the inspiration for the traditional tiered wedding cake, and for this box, evolving from a desire to create an opulent, decadent celebratory piece with a practical function – remember that nothing is "too good to use".

## Materials

Grogged white
    earthenware clay
White slip
Black underglaze
Clear glaze
Lustre: platinum and pink

## Equipment

Newspaper or cloth
Rolling pin
2 guide sticks, approx. 7 mm
    (⅜ in) width
Knife
2 circular templates, 20 cm
    (8 in) and 23 cm (9 in)
    diameter
Cast picture frame mould
    (optional)
3 wooden bats
Brush
Surform blade
Modelling tools
Hand extruder
Face mask (respirator) and
    gloves
Spray gun, booth and
    compressor
Electric kiln

## Glaze

Lead sesquisillicate          75.5%
China clay                         18.7%
Flint                                     5.8%

## Firing

Biscuit (bisque) fire to 1140°C
    (2084°F)
Lustre fire to 765°C (1409°F)

**1** Roll out three slabs, using the guide sticks to ensure even thickness of clay, which will form the side panel, base and lid of the pot. The side slab should be approximately 16 x 68 cm (6¼ x 27 in). Cut it out with a knife and place to one side. Place the circular templates onto the remaining slabs and cut out. Set all three slabs to one side to dry. It is important to monitor the drying slabs – if the clay dries too much the slabs will crack, if they are too soft they will collapse. To test if a slab is dry enough, curl an edge up as if to form a shape. If it curves easily without distorting, the slab is ready to use. Drying usually takes 15–30 minutes, depending on room temperature.

**2** While the slabs are drying, model the feet – you need six for the base and six for the lid – and the lid handle. You can use a press mould of a picture frame (as shown here) or you can hand model these components.

**3** Place the base slab onto a bat covered with newspaper. Score a ring around the edge of the base slab in readiness to join the side panel. Use the lid template as a guide for positioning. Next, score one side of the side slab. If necessary cut off the excess side slab to permit a clean join. Brush water onto both sets of the scored areas to be joined. Using both hands lift the side slab onto the base slab, curving it to follow the scored ring on the base, then join.

**4** Apply a thin coil of clay over the side and base joins. Work the surfaces with a modelling tool to create a smooth, even finish. Place to one side and leave to dry off until the clay is firm enough to work onto its surface without distorting the form.

**5** Place the lid slab on top of the form. Check that the lid circumference is equal to that of the body. If it is not, use a surform blade to correct. Remove the lid and place it on a separate bat.

**6** Sandwich the pot between two bats and turn it over. Place the six feet for the base an equal distance apart around the edge of the base. Mark their positions and score and slurry the base and bottom of the feet where they will join. Apply the feet and add a thin coil around each join. Leave to harden until the feet can support the weight. Repeat to attach the six feet for the lid. Again, leave to harden until the feet can support the lid's weight.

**7** Turn the lid onto its feet. Extrude coils to ring the side edge of the lid and its rim. Score and slurry around the edge and rim of the lid and apply the coils.

**8** Indent the coils at regular intervals to create a convoluted edge using a modelling tool.

**9** Position the handle in the centre of the lid and mark its position with a knife. Score and slurry the surface of the lid and base of the handle and apply the handle to the lid. Roll a thin coil and smooth on to reinforce the join. Model four roses and eight leaves. Score and slurry the join areas, then apply the roses and leaves to the lid. Place it to one side to dry.

**10** Turn the pot onto its feet. Mark out and score the loops around the top edge of the form, the diagonal side coils and the bottom edge where it joins the base. Start with the top loops and mark an even number, as the design alternates of single and grouped roses. Start the side diagonal score lines at the beginning of each top loop and end at the base of the pot parallel with the end point of the same top loop. Finally score and slurry around the bottom of the pot edge. Attach coils following the marked areas.

**11** Indent the diagonal and base coils with the modelling tool. Leave the top loops smooth. Model the roses and leaves. Score and slurry the areas where the top loops meet and the diagonal side coils cross, and apply the roses and leaves. Tidy up the joined areas with the modelling tool. Leave to dry off.

**12** Remove the lid and place it onto a bat. Wearing a face mask (respirator) and gloves, cover the inner and outer surface of the lid and body with white slip using the spray gun. Wait until the slip is dry before replacing the lid onto the body. Leave the pot and lid in place to dry completely and then biscuit (bisque) fire together.

**13** After firing, paint black underglaze onto the edge of the lid, lid feet, handle, side coils and rose leaves. Spray clear glaze over the inner and outer body, the top and under the surface of the lid. Wash the glaze off the base and the handle feet. Glaze fire the pot with the lid and body separate. Invert the body to paint platinum lustre on the feet and turn to finish the base. Paint pink lustre onto all the other decoration. The black underglaze alters the pink lustre to a pink/gold during the firing.

# Wicker Wave Vase

Building up structures from different materials enables the creation of forms and shapes that would otherwise be impossible. Here, by creating complicated tensions with bamboo blinds and covering them with fibrous clay, Mette Gregersen makes a moving, organic piece. To her, the idea of using a material that burns away during firing leaving its marks, is like an impressed memory.

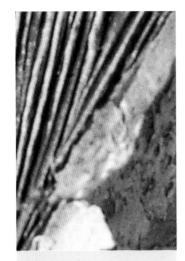

### Materials
White stoneware clay
Bamboo blinds

### Equipment
Three buckets
Newspaper
Electric mixer
Brush
Sponge
Spray gun
Face mask (respirator) and
   gloves
Gas kiln
Electric kiln

### Glaze
BLACK GLAZE (ALUMINA MATT)

| | |
|---|---|
| Lead sequisilicate | 41% |
| Whiting | 8% |
| Potash feldspar | 22% |
| China clay | 14% |
| Red iron oxide | 8% |
| Copper oxide | 2% |
| Cobalt oxide | 2% |
| Chrome oxide | 3% |

TRANSPARENT GLAZE 1080

| | |
|---|---|
| Lead sequisilicate | 59% |
| Calcium borate | |
|   frit P2954 | 17.5% |
| China clay | 15.5% |
| Quartz | 8% |

Yellow Ochre (a weak iron
   oxide)

### Firing
Biscuit (bisque) fire to 1140°C
   (2084°F)
Glaze fire to 1080°C
   (1976°F)

**1** To prepare the fibrous clay, leave two bags of stoneware clay to soak in water overnight. Tear up a couple of newspapers and leave them to dissolve in hot water. Mix the clay and paper into a liquid slip.

**2** Fold the bamboo blind into the desired structure. Do this slowly, dampening it slightly with water so that it does not break.

**3** Tie it together well with string using the ties that form part of the blind.

**4** Spread out the prepared clay slip evenly on the outside of the bamboo structure.

**5** Make sure to press it out through the lines of the wicker blind to get a good texture.

**6** Leave the applied clay to dry so that it will hold its shape, then apply another layer. Repeat until the piece is thick enough.

**7** Add designs and textures on the inside. In this version, small thrown bowls have been stuck on, creating a honeycomb effect. Leave until bone dry.

**8** Biscuit (bisque) fire the piece in a gas kiln to 1140°C (2084°F), so that the wood burns away and leaves the texture. Brush on the black glaze.

**10** Similarly, on the outside, brush on the oxide yellow ochre.

**9** Wipe off the top layer of glaze so that only the furrows will become black.

**11** Sponge off any excess to create a more in-depth look.

**12** Wearing a face mask (respirator) and gloves, spray a shiny transparent earthenware glaze on the inside, and fire to 1080°C (1976°F) in an electric kiln. It is possible to high fire for vitrification, but the fragile structure tends to change its shape during firing.

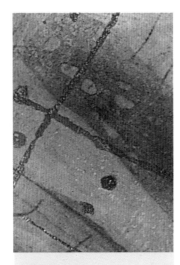

# Printed Plate

Maria Donato starts her drawings by juxtaposing photocopies of Brazilian Indian graphics, contemporary media and photographs. The images are then manipulated by changing their scale or by photocopying different images on the same piece of paper, such as tracing paper, coloured or textured paper or acetate. This process makes it possible to layer the images, creating a subtle balance of hiding and revealing in the design. These images are then transferred to clay using printmaking processes.

**Materials**
T-material clay

**Equipment**
Linocut (linoleum board)
Tracing paper
Linocutting tool
Brush
Rolling pin
Gloves for glazing
Screen (wooden frame with a
     fine mesh stretched over it)
Squeegee
Plaster mould
Sponge
Potter's knife
Piece of clear glass with taped
     edges for monoprinting
Ceramic tissue paper
Pencil, ballpoint pen or chalks
Acetate
Ceramic crayons
Soft foam roller
Pre-covercoated decal paper
Scissors
Diluted water-based glue
Rubber kidney
Electric kiln

**Glaze**
Underglaze powder mixed
     with water-based medium
Mars Violet pigment mixed
     with screen-printing
     medium
Artic White covercoat
     opaque underglaze
Black body stain and borax frit
     diluted with water
Onglaze powder mixed with
     screen-printing medium

**1** Transfer a design you have selected onto lino by using tracing paper or drawing directly onto the lino. Cut out the chosen image. Paint the lino with underglaze mixed with a water-based medium, covering the whole surface with the paint.

**2** Roll a clay slab to the desired thickness. Cut the slab following the shape of the plaster mould, leaving enough clay to be pressed into the mould. Position the clay at the edge of the linocut (linoleum board).

**3** Place the rolled clay over the linocut to print and emboss the image. Repeat this with the clay in a slightly different position to create a juxtaposition of images.

**Firing**
Biscuit (bisque) fire to 1180°C
(2156°F)
Final firing to 700–720°C
(1292–1328°F)

**4** Peel off the clay gently to avoid tearing, and allow the surface to become dry to the touch. Note that it is advisable to wear gloves whenever working with ceramic colour.

**5** Apply the printing ink made from Mars Violet pigment mixed with the screen-printing medium to the top of the screen, spreading it evenly. Pull the squeegee firmly and evenly across the whole width of the image on the clay. Lift the screen gently to avoid damaging the surface. Remember to ensure good ventilation in the room where you are working.

**6** Wait until the surface is dry to the touch, but remember that clay should be kept plastic for easy pressing into the mould. Transfer the printed slab of clay into a plaster mould with the patterned surface uppermost. Gently ease the clay into the mould by using a damp clean sponge. Trim the edges from the rim.

**7** Paint on a thin layer of white underglaze to make the printed image opaque, continuing to develop this theme of layering and creating a surface that suggests memories and distant images.

**8** Paint the surface of the glass with the mixture of black body stain and borax frit diluted in water. Allow the mixture to dry. Cover the painted glass with ceramic tissue paper. The paper is sensitive and will pick up marks from your fingers. Tape the tissue paper onto the glass to prevent it from moving. Draw another image onto the tissue paper using a pencil, ballpoint pen or chalks, depending on the type of line you desire.

**9** Photocopy this image onto acetate. This will allow you to position the image where you would like it to be printed so that you can visualize your design before printing it. This technique can be very useful when you are using an intricate design.

**10** To make the print, place your drawing face down onto the damp surface. Printing will not occur if the surface is dry. Rub gently, but firmly, all over the drawing to transfer the image. Peel off the paper.

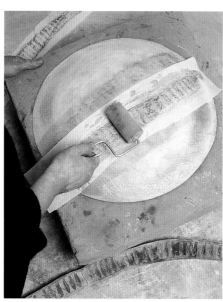

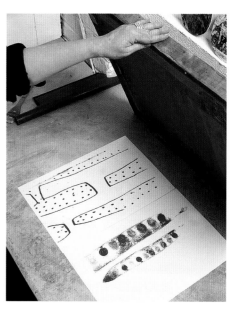

**11** Remove the piece from the mould and place it face down on a large piece of foam. Smooth the curved surface and paint it using blue and then white underglaze. Paint thin layers allowing each layer to dry before applying the next one. Use ceramic tissue paper and ceramic crayon to create rubbings from the natural form.

**12** Transfer the design onto the damp curved surface using a soft foam roller. Biscuit (bisque) fire the work in an electric kiln to 1180°C (2156°F).

**13** Use onglaze ceramic colour mixed with screen-printing medium to print the next image on the decal. Use pre-covercoated paper to reduce any exposure to fumes. Remember to ensure good ventilation in the room. See step 5 for printing method.

**14** Allow the printed image on the decal paper to dry. Place the paper in warm water until the plastic sheet with the print loosens from the paper. Cover the surface of the biscuit (bisque) fired work with a very diluted water-based glue to prevent the decal from peeling off when drying. This is not necessary if the surface is glazed. Place the decal near the surface to be decorated and then slide off the back paper. Gently place the image in the correct position.

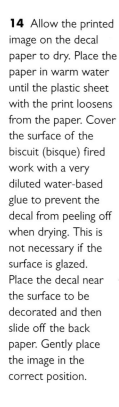

**15** Place the decal over the surface to produce the required design. Firm the decal into place with a rubber kidney, making sure that no water or air pockets are left underneath the covercoat surface. Fire the work to 700°C (1292°F) in a well-ventilated electric kiln – the plastic will burn away leaving the printed design on the ceramic surface. Repeat this process of applying decal and firing until you have the surface decoration you require.

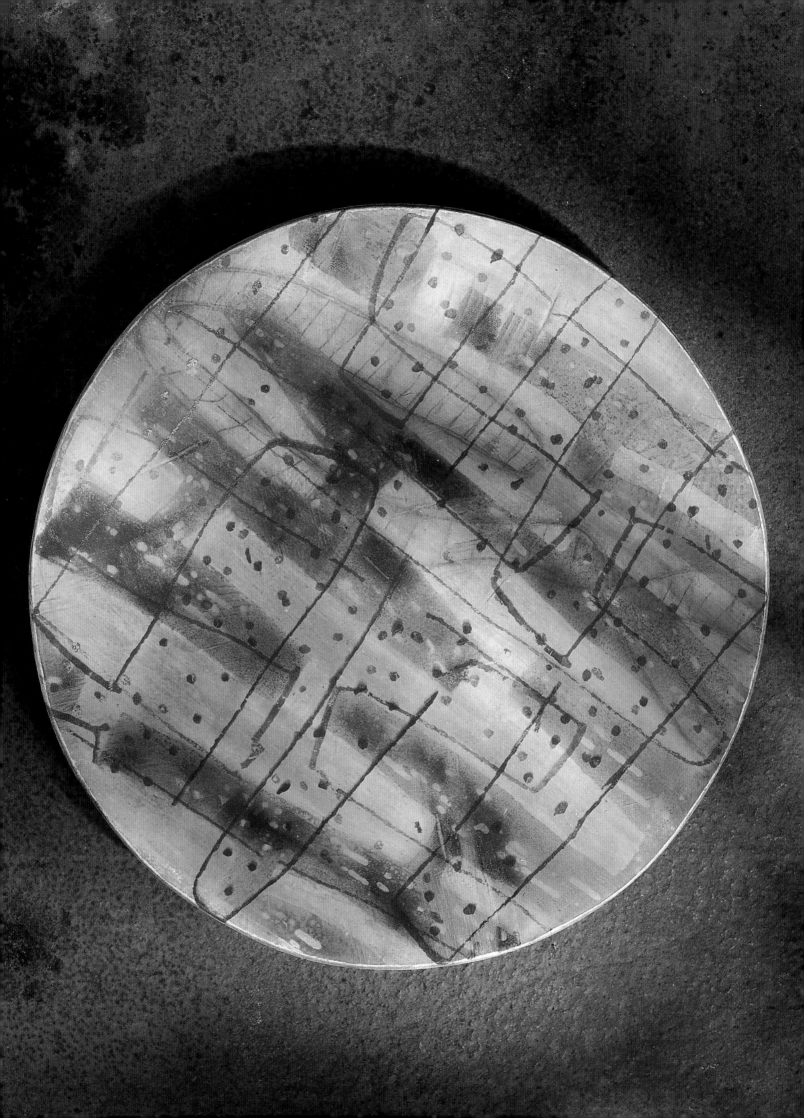

## Materials
T-material clay

## Equipment
Potter's wheel
Banding wheel
Metal and rubber kidneys
Plastic film
Hacksaw blades
Craft knife
Stiff brush
Rolling pin
Face mask (respirator), gloves
 and barrier cream
Brushes
Electric kiln

## Basic glaze
The base is mid-temperature range, ready-prepared earthenware glaze sold in a dry powdered form.
Using this base glaze add:
For green 100 g base+ 6 g
 copper carbonate
For rosso pink 100 g base
 + 8 g rosso red glaze stain
For orange 100 g base + 8 g
 teal orange glaze stain
For yellow 100 g  base + 8 g
 kittiwake yellow glaze stain
For turquoise 50 g base +
 50 g hi alkaline frit + 6 g
 copper carbonate

# Pineapple Vase

This thrown, coiled, hand-modelled and multiple-fired earthenware vase is the design of Kate Malone. A pineapple is traditionally a symbol of hospitality and prosperity, and this "feel-good" symbolism is integral to all her work. The wonder of nature and the beauty of the real fruit inspired this piece, combined with the exciting transformation of clay and dry powder glaze into a ceramic, glassy surface. Working in this way allows continual experimentation with new forms and the discovery of new glazes.

**1** Throw the base shape on a wheel and a turned footring. then coil the neck onto the base.

**2** Start to ripple the top edge after a few coils have been added to introduce the undulating top edge.

**3** Add more coils to continue this ripple – the undulations become more exaggerated as the neck gets higher.

### Special effect glaze
Take a ready-made base glaze (special effect pebble glaze used here) and add various pigments to render different colours. The yellow used here, for example, is 600 ml (1 pint) base colour with 32 g (1 oz) kittiwake yellow mixed in.

### Firing
Biscuit (bisque) fire to 1180°C
 (2156°F)
Glaze fire in the region of
 1060°C (1940°F) to 1000°C
 (1832°F).

**4** Allow the neck to stiffen after each two coil additions. Keep the base from drying by wrapping it in plastic.

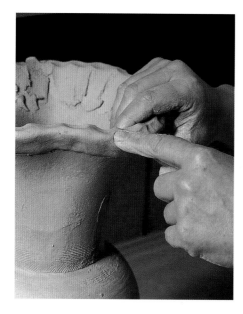

**5** Continue adding to the coiled neck. The clay is so soft that no slip is used between coils. Push downwards on the inside and upwards on the outside.

**6** Use a metal kidney to help shape the ripple. When you have attained the correct height, leave the whole piece to even through and stiffen until it is firm enough to continue with the next step.

**7** Level off the top edge then slice a coil lengthways and add it to the outside of the top edge. Wrap the whole piece in plastic film so the moisture is allowed to redistribute between the added coil and the main body for at least two days. This makes the next stage easier to execute.

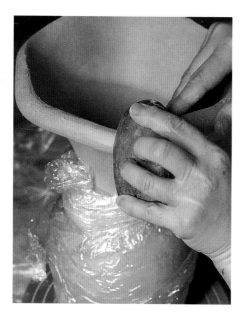

**8** After two days or more, round the top edge using hacksaw blades and then use metal and rubber kidneys and your thumb to smooth it.

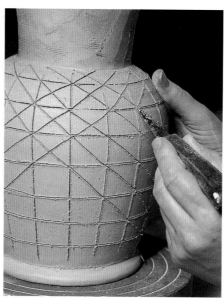

**9** Mark out the pot with vertical, horizontal and, finally, diagonal lines to make a pineapple diamond pattern.

**10** Model a pyramid of clay into a diamond shape. Score and slurry the area to which you will apply the diamond then use your hand to press it onto the body and bond and shape at the same time.

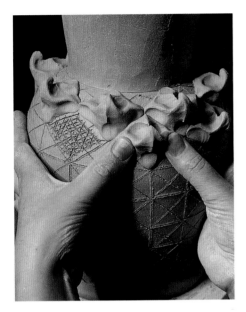

**11** Work from the top around and down to cover the whole body of the piece.

**12** Roll slabs, cut out leaves and form the shape on a wooden edge ready to join to the neck area. The "crispness" of the modelling is crucial for making crisp-looking leaves.

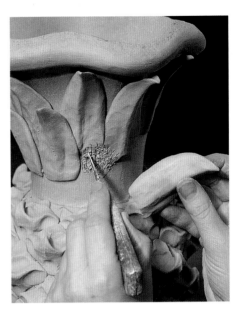

**13** Join the leaves to the neck in rows by scoring and slurrying the neck and each leaf before applying. Keep each leaf as unhandled as possible.

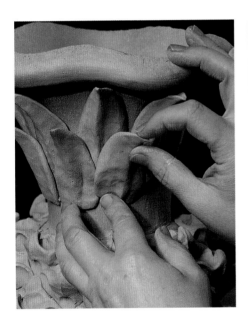

**14** Bend them into their final position when they are in place. Wrap the whole piece gently in plastic and leave it to even through for as long as possible. Unwrap and dry very slowly. Biscuit (bisque) fire to a temperature of 1180°C (2156°F).

**15** Next, paint on the glazes with brushes. Approximately six glaze firings need to be carried out, so the glazing is rather complex and variable. Glaze partly upside down to ensure total coverage.

**16** Reglaze, fire and reglaze in order to render an oozing, thick, juicy coat of glazes that run into each other in the kiln and therefore relate naturally to the form. It is knowledge of your own kiln and glaze techniques that prevent this from looking like a horrible mess. It is the firing using the pebble special effect glaze that gives the mottled look. This glaze is very toxic, so wear barrier cream, gloves and a face mask (respirator) whenever you are glazing.

# KILNS AND FIRING

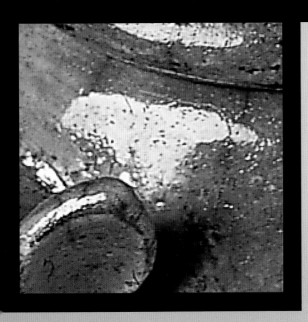

**CLAY IS GIVEN DURABILITY ONLY BY FIRING** IT AT A HIGH TEMPERATURE – THIS IS THE FINAL STAGE OF THE CERAMIC PROCESS. THERE ARE MANY DIFFERENT KILNS, EACH OF WHICH CREATES A DISTINCTIVE FIRING EFFECT. BUT THESE EFFECTS ARE ALSO DEPENDENT ON HOW THE CLAY IS FORMED AND DECORATED, AND ON WHICH GLAZE IS APPLIED.

THE SIMPLEST FORM OF FIRING, WHICH IS STILL PRACTISED BY VILLAGE POTTERS IN PARTS OF THE WORLD TODAY, IS WITH OPEN FIRES OR WITH PITS USING A LOCAL SOURCE OF FUEL. IN FIJI, FOR EXAMPLE, POTS ARE STACKED TOGETHER ON AN OPEN GROUND BONFIRE USING PALM FRONDS AND GRASSES. POTS FIRED IN THIS WAY ARE SUSCEPTIBLE TO DAMAGE IF THE TEMPERATURE SUDDENLY DROPS AS A RESULT OF GUSTS OF WIND BLOWING ON EXPOSED SURFACES. AN ENCLOSED KILN WITH A BRICK-FIRING CHAMBER AVOIDS SUCH FIRING LOSSES IF THE CORRECT FIRING PROCEDURES ARE FOLLOWED.

## EQUIPMENT
# FIRING EQUIPMENT
Brick-built kilns all work on the same principle of an enclosed construction in which the work to be fired is placed. Radiated or combusted heat flows freely around the ware and is directed in its circulation or draught either through, down or up, or as a combination, towards a flue. The heat climbs at a controlled rate until a desired temperature has been reached.

### Kilns

The choice of whether to install a gas or electric kiln and whether it loads from the top or front is personal preference combined with practical factors, for example which fuel is available and affordable, the size of kiln you require and where it is to be located.

All kilns require adequate ventilation as firing creates noxious and often toxic fumes, so if yours is to be located indoors, it is essential to have fume extraction via a fan and/or a chimney hood. Reduction firings with gas, oil or wood-fired kilns produce carbon monoxide so in this case ensure that the kiln is sited outside or away from the main working area.

There are many different styles of kilns so it is advisable to take a good look at what is available as well as assessing all the practical factors (see Suppliers and Services).

This front loading kiln might typically be used by a single maker regularly firing quantities of production ware. Alternatively the cost of this essential piece of equipment could also be shared between those working in the same space.

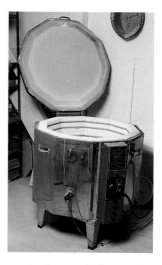

Lightweight refractory bricks retained in a stainless steel casing provide efficient insulation on top loading kilns, making them economical to fire. Top loaders are lighter and therefore easier to move and transport than front-loading kilns. Some gas-fired top loaders are built in interlocking sections enabling the firing chamber to be adjusted according to the size or quantity of work making them economical to fire.

### Pyrometers

A pyrometer is an instrument that indicates the temperature of the firing chamber inside the kiln. It is housed outside the kiln and is linked to a thermocouple inside a porcelain sheath, which is fitted through the wall of the kiln and protrudes into the firing chamber. A thermocouple works by sensing heat with the help of two wires in different metals that are joined together at one end.

A small electric current is generated when the junction of the two wires is heated. The greater the amount of heat applied to the junction, the greater will be the voltage generated by the wires. There are several types of thermocouples and the amount of voltage generated at any particular temperature differs with each type. For this reason temperature indicators and controllers have to be calibrated for a particular thermocouple type and cannot be used with each other.

### Controllers

This piece of equipment controls the fiiring temperature of the kiln. There are various controllers on the market ranging from those that just provide a cut-off point at the final firing temperature to those that enable control over the entire firing cycle. The required firing temperature is preset into the controller. Other points of the firing cycle can be preset

with a controller, from the time firing begins (delay start) to the set points at which the rate of temperature is increased and also the rate of temperature increase (ramps). Other controller functions include the control of the latter or middle part of a firing called "soaking" where the kiln temperature is held at a fixed point for a measured amount of time. More complex controllers enable a number of firing programmes to be entered and stored ready for appropriate selection according to the type of firing required.

Many controllers also indicate the temperature of the firing chamber as the firing progresses, therefore also acting as a pyrometer.

## Kiln sitters and limit timers

Many top loading electric kilns are fitted with kiln sitters, which turn the kiln off at the end of a firing cycle. A small orton cone or minibar inside the kiln (see photograph far right) dictates the point at which a weighted switching device cuts off the kiln's electricity supply. The kiln sitter does not allow automatic soaking at the end of a firing cycle, but it can be manually set for firing by lifting the counterweight and pressing the button to reset the kiln energy

regulators to a lower setting. The kiln sitter is a reliable way of programming the end of the firing cycle, with the advantage of being triggered by active heat or heatwork (see glaze firing) and not by temperature alone.

The limit timer controls the temperature at which the kiln is turned off.

A kiln sitter (automatic cut off device) is set with the appropriate minibar cone, which melts at the end temperature and releases the cut off weight.

## Gas burner and adjustment valve

Reduction in gas, oil or wood fired kilns is indicated by the length and type of flame you can see through the spy holes and flue. The burner's fuel intake and the secondary air supply are adjusted and the flue damper is partially closed to regulate the kiln's atmosphere until the correct reduction conditions occur. An oxidizing or neutral flame is blue, clear and straight, whereas a reduction flame is orange and curls and licks.

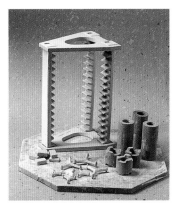

## Stilts, shelves, piers and racks

Kiln furniture is made from a high firing refractory material that can withstand high temperatures without warping. It is used for separating work in the kiln, while making full and economic use of the space in the firing chamber. Kiln shelves are stacked alternately on three tiers of kiln props (kiln bricks) set directly above one another at each layer. Stilts are used to support work with glazed bases to prevent contact with the kiln shelves. Flat objects such as tiles and plates require a lot of shelf space and are uneconomic to fire without the use of racks. A selection of kiln furniture is shown above, including a kiln shelf (at base), a tile rack (back left), kiln props (bricks) (far right) and stilts (foreground, middle left).

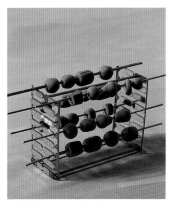

## Nichrome wire bead rack

The problem of how to fire glazed and Egyptian paste beads (which adhere to surfaces when fired) is removed with the use of a bead rack. Bead trees or racks fixed into clay supports can also be custom made with Nichrome wire, which you can buy from ceramic suppliers. Nichrome wire is the only wire that will withstand the high temperature of the kiln.

## Pyrometric cones

Not all kilns come well equipped with temperature controllers, so it is important to have an accurate indication of active heat or heatwork, as opposed to the temperature registering inside the kiln during firing. Pyrometric cones serve this function. These cones are numbered according to the temperature at which they melt and bend. They are placed as far into the firing chamber as possible in line with the view through, but avoiding draughts from, the spyhole.

A number of different ranges of cones exist, including Orton, Seger and Harrison in varying temperatures and corresponding numbers, which do not run consecutively. The different ranges can be intermixed within a set of cones.

# EQUIPMENT
# RAKU EQUIPMENT

Raku firing requires the use of a kiln with an easy opening door enabling work to be lifted in and out of the firing chamber with tongs. A raku kiln is most commonly powered with combustible fuel and sited outdoors.

For pioneering potters, small raku kilns or large trolley loading kilns can be built to suit personal firing requirements. The designing and building of a kiln is a practical and viable solution requiring specialist high temperature materials and the necessary tools. Refractory bricks, ceramic fibre and aluminous cements and mortars are just a few of the materials necessary to withstand the high temperatures used in the firing process. Discussing your ideas with other potters before making final decisions about your approach is the best way to check out any pitfalls or adaptations needed to ensure the best design for your purpose.

**1** Tongs used to place work into, and take work out of, a raku kiln.

**2** Thick leather gloves to protect arms and hands from radiated heat from the kiln.

**3** Goggles to protect eyes from rising ash when immersing work in sawdust.

**4** Wire wool or scrubbing brush to reduce loose carbon deposits on reduced raku work (not shown).

**5** Tin bath or metal container with sawdust for immersing and reducing hot work from the kiln.

**6** Tin bath or metal container with water for rapid cooling and cleaning fired work (not shown).

**7** Raku kiln (7a) , gas burner and gas bottle (propane tank) (7b).

SOFTLY ENCRUSTED (54 CM/21 IN) HANDBUILT WITH RAKU CLAY, A THIN LAYER OF ENGOBE IS THEN PAINTED ON. THE PIECE IS RAKU FIRED TO APPROXIMATELY 1000°C (1832°F) AND THEN COOLED IN SAWDUST (KEITH ASHLEY).

# TECHNIQUES
# KILN FIRING Once any forming and decorating work is complete the piece must next

undergo the firing process to bring about ceramic change. The red heat and beyond within a kiln alters the nature of clay and glaze materials both chemically and physically causing them to become hard and permanent. Unless you are firing using an electric kiln with a control system, firing involves vigilance and attendance, often over a long period of time.

Many potters fire their work to an initial biscuit (bisque) firing of around 980–1100°C (1796–2012°F) to make the ware porous and give physical strength before decoration and glazing. The higher the temperature, the less porous the clay becomes. Some potters, who glaze fire to a low glaze temperature, such as raku or low earthenware, use an industrial technique of hard biscuit or bisque firing, when the initial firing has a higher temperature than that following glaze firing. This method provides a more vitrified clay body on low-fired glazed work, but can introduce the hurdle of applying glaze to work that is no longer porous. To overcome this, the high-fired bisque work can be heated in the kiln to enable a slop glaze to adhere to its surface.

Other potters omit the biscuit (bisque) firing process altogether and prefer to single fire. This shortens the long wait for the finished result and cuts out additional firing cost and handling time.

Temperature rise will vary widely depending on the type and size of your kiln, as well as the size of the work and the density of the kiln pack, so use the firing chart at the end of this section as a rough guide to firing times only.

SALTGLAZED JAR WITH A
CURL (35 CM/14 IN)
SINGLE FIRED, WITH COBALT AND
TITANIUM SLIPS (JANE HAMLYN).

## Biscuit firing (or single firing)

Before any work can be fired it must first be allowed to become completely bone dry. Larger or thicker pieces of work must be left for longer to dry. The drying process is completed in the initial stages of the biscuit (bisque) firing known as "water smoking" – when, at 100–600°C (212–1112°F), chemically combined water evaporates and is driven out as steam. During this stage, vents in the kiln are left open to allow steam to exit.

It is critical to proceed slowly at this drying phase – too much haste will cause the steam to push open or explode the work. This creates a low, thudding sound in the kiln and is the death knell of probably all pieces of work in the kiln. Large or small pieces with thick wall sections – over 5 mm (¼ in) – are particularly susceptible to this, so take care. Leaving a biscuit (bisque) firing on a low temperature overnight with the kiln vents open is a good way to ensure work is safe to be heated further.

Once the initial firing has reached beyond 600°C (1112°F) or red heat, it is safe to turn up the heating rate, close any vents and proceed to the final temperature (see firing times and temperatures). The kiln is then allowed to cool and can be opened for unpacking when the temperature has reached around 100–150°C (212–302°F).

## Heating and cooling for glaze

As the kiln reaches certain temperatures (227°C/440°F and 557°C/1034°F) chemical changes take place that increase the size and formation of the quartz crystals in the clay. The first at 225°C (437°F) is known as the "cristobolite inversion" or "squeeze", the second at 573°C (1063°F) is known as the "quartz inversion". This quartz crystal change then repeats in reverse at the cooling stage. Particular care must be taken not to hurry the cooling of a glaze firing kiln at and around these temperatures by prematurely opening vents and doors. Doing so will result in fine cracks or dunting appearing. Sharp-edged cracks appear during the cooling process, whereas rounded or smooth edged cracks occur during the heating process.

## Glaze firing

The final temperature for a glaze firing is predetermined by the glaze and clay body of the fired work. Glaze firing should be started slowly to drive out any moisture taken into the biscuit (bisque) ware from glazing. When the kiln is glowing at red heat or 600°C (1112°F), the rate of climb can be increased and vents should be closed.

When a glaze is subjected to heat, it interacts and fuses not only within itself, but also with materials on the clay surface it lies on. This is particularly the case in high-fired temperature or stoneware glazes. This reaction with the clay surface, called "interface", secures the glaze onto the clay. At low-fired, or earthenware, temperatures there is less interface of the glaze and clay.

The effect of heat on a glaze is subject to the amount of time a firing takes to achieve final temperature. This combination of time and heat is known as "heatwork" and it can only accurately be measured by pyrometric temperature cones or bars. Heat can also be gauged visually by colour, but shield your eyes with protective goggles and avoid staring into the glow of a high temperature kiln for long periods. At 1100°C (2012°F) the colour is orangey red, at 1200°C (2192°F) the orange brightens and at 1260°C (2300°F) it becomes bright yellow.

As the temperature rises, vitrification occurs when the clay and glaze or colours compact and fuse. As the final glaze temperature nears, glaze bubbles and craters form as gas escapes, which can cause the glaze defects of bloating or pinholing if it is not allowed to settle. By sustaining the kiln heat at a constant temperature, known as soaking, these defects can be eliminated. The kiln can then be turned off to cool.

## Crystalline glaze firing

The rate at which the temperature is decreased determines the final size of crystals in a glaze. Crystalline glazes require a top maturing temperature of 1260–1280°C (2300–2336°F) followed by a rapid cool to 1100°C (2012°F) and then a prolonged soak to 1040°C (1904°F) to create seeds for the growth of crystals. Pieces of crystal glazed work are packed onto a foot or saucer to catch running glaze and glaze drips, which are ground off with a grindstone after firing.

## Glaze temperature ranges

The temperature of a glaze firing varies according to the clay used in the piece. The ranges for earthenware, stoneware, porcelain and bone china are as follows:

* Earthenware 950–1150°C (1742–2102°F)
* Stoneware and porcelain 1200–1300°C (2192–2372°F)
* Bone china 1080–1100°C (1976–2012°F)

SLICED LOTUS FRUIT OF YOUR DREAMS, DETAIL OF CRYSTALLINE GLAZE (KATE MALONE).

SLICED LOTUS FRUIT OF YOUR DREAMS (38 CM/15 IN) COIL BUILT IN T-MATERIAL CLAY, CRYSTALLINE GLAZE FIRED (KATE MALONE). PHOTOGRAPH BY STEPHEN SPELLER.

## Reduction firing

All kilns are capable of providing an oxidizing atmosphere around the ware during firing – this is where the circulation of air passing through the kiln is unrestricted. However, not all kilns are able to produce a second type of atmosphere, called "reduction", which involves restricting the passage of secondary air into the kiln and controlling pressure in the firing chamber with a flue damper. Reduction firing, used in conjunction with high temperature glazes or to produce lustreware, is achieved in kilns that supply heat through a burnt fuel, such as wood, oil, gas and solid fuels.

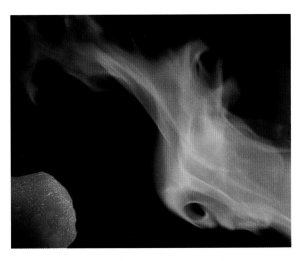

The picture shows a reduction flame at the spyhole of a gas-fired kiln. The strength of reduction is judged by the length and colour of the flame that protrudes when a bung is temporarily removed from a spyhole in the door, and the amount of smoke coming from the chimney.

During reduction, the kiln's atmosphere seeks out oxygen to enable it to burn. Because the oxygen supply is restricted, the atmosphere grabs the chemically combined oxygen in some of the metal oxides contained in clay and glaze, producing an array of reduction effects, such as copper turning blood red, precious metals becoming lustrous and iron spot crystals being drawn from clay into the glaze surface.

## Enamel firing

Onglazes fuse with the glaze on which they are applied at low temperatures (see Glaze and Decorating, onglaze). The temperatures can vary according to the colours used. This firing involves fusing colour into the softened glaze, often using successive firings to create overlapping mixed hues and depth of colour. Firings are relatively fast and require the opening of the kiln vent to allow fumes caused by the burning of painted mediums to leave the kiln as they burn away.

Enamel firing temperatures range from 700–900°C (1292–1652°F).

CONICAL TEAPOT CUP (13 CM/5 IN) CAST AND HANDBUILT IN SEMI-PORCELAIN CLAY. BISCUIT (BISQUE) FIRED, GLAZED IN A SEMI-MATT GLAZE AND PAINTED WITH ONGLAZE ENAMELS WITH SGRAFFITO DRAWING (MARGARET FORDE).

## Raku firing

A traditional Japanese firing technique, raku is when glazed, biscuit-fired decorative ware is taken to its firing temperature very quickly. This produces a characteristic crazed quality to a glaze and lustrous effects to copper glazes. The hot work can be left uncovered to oxidize, quenched in water or quickly smothered in a combustible material, such as sawdust, to reduce the work. The clays used to produce work for raku firing are always open so they can withstand the thermal shock of the firing and cooling process (see Clay: The Fundamental Ingredient). Raku is exciting with its spontaneous immediacy and its delicate blend of control and experiment.

Kilns can vary from an electric kiln (see raku equipment) to a brick-lined kiln such as the one used in the Slim Raku Vessels project that follows this section. A downdraft kiln such as this one draws air down a separate stack on the side of the kiln, giving a more even temperature throughout the kiln and allowing the layering of work with shelves. An updraft kiln with shelves may tend to trap the heat, causing uneven temperatures throughout the kiln, although this can be overcome if there is a gap around the outer edge of the kiln shelf.

Raku firing temperatures range from 900–1000°C (1652–1832°F).

Raku kilns should be fired outdoors because a good deal of smoke will invariably be generated when unloading the fired items into the sawdust for reduction.

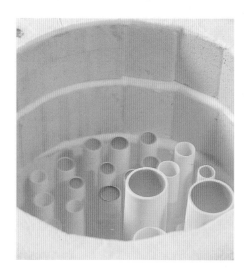

The glaze melt is used as a visual indication of when to remove the work from the kiln while it is still red hot.

## Vapour firing

Salt, soda and wood firing are all types of vapour glazing. In order for salt glaze to develop, the clay body or applied slips must contain a certain proportion of silica, which is softened by the heat of the kiln and fuses with the sodium or salt. Salt firing is a toxic process producing hydrochloric acid fumes as a by-product so many makers who vapour glaze opt for the less polluting option of soda firing, which is less corrosive to the kiln and produces softer and brighter colours.

Salt and soda glazing produce effects ranging from the characteristic orange-peel texture covering the entire external area or partial flashing. The results depend on the design of the kiln, the kiln pack and the amount of vapour created. Pots and lid fittings are packed into the kiln on small wads made from a mixture of three parts alumina hydrate to one part china clay held together with a proportion of flour to make it into a kneadable dough.

TEA BOWLS (10 CM/4 IN) THROWN AND SODA FIRED (JEFF OESTREICH).

The allure of wood firing has as much to do with the physical process as the characteristic flashing and finished texture of the fire-glazed clay. The minerals in the ash deposits interact with the minerals in the clay, which fuse and form the glaze to the exposed surfaces of clay in the kiln firing. Wood is not only used as a kiln fuel for vapour glazing, it is often chosen as a fuel because it is readily available. The wood-firing process requires a constant vigil to maintain a steady temperature rise and to create the desired kiln atmosphere. For larger kilns this requires teams of wood stokers to maintain kilns, such as the "snake" or "climbing" kilns used in Japan.

Salt or soda is drip fed, sprayed or thrown into the flame of a kiln or through spyholes around the firing chamber at around 1240°C (2264°F).

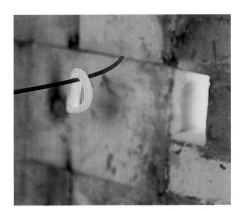

Test rings, made of the same clay and coated with the same slips as the work you are firing are placed in the kiln in an accessible place. They are extracted to assess how much glaze has formed on the work and whether more vapour is required. Test rings are often placed in more than one area of a kiln because of temperature variations.

## Sawdust and smoking

Pits or metal bins are packed with a combustible material, usually sawdust, around work for this low firing technique, which produces a characteristic patchy, black carbon effect. It is a technique often combined with burnished pieces and, although it seems to be low tech, it requires fine judgement on how best to pack the work and when to remove it. Work is often biscuit (bisque) fired before being placed for firing, which, if carefully controlled, can be successfully carried out on any clay body.

Glazed work can also be smoke fumed by exposing the fired piece to a reduction atmosphere inside a saggar packed with combustible material. A saggar is a lidded refractory box that protects fired work from direct contact with the kiln's atmosphere. This enables work to be reduced within an electric or oxidized environment with a greater control of the heating and cooling process. Ensure that the kiln and the immediate environment are well ventilated for this process.

WORK BY DUNCAN AYSCOUGH REDUCING AFTER A SAWDUST FIRING.

VASE (18 CM/7 IN) COILED, BURNISHED AND SMOKE FIRED (JANE PERRYMAN).

# TECHNIQUES
# KILN PACKING
Taking the time to work out the most effective use of the kiln space will reduce the overall production cost of your work. Those makers who work with production ware will often plan their range to include small items that will make use of any available space in the kiln.

### Packing for biscuit firing

To pack work into a kiln in preparation for biscuit (bisque) firing, the ware can be stacked rim to rim and small pieces can be placed inside larger ones. Lids can be fired in place and work can touch neighbouring pieces. A kiln shelf is necessary only where the stack becomes unstable or the weight of a piece is too heavy to be supported by another. Large, flat pieces can be placed on sand to allow equal movement of the work during shrinkage and to prevent cracking.

### Packing for glaze firing

Glazed ware must be handled with care when packing a kiln to avoid damaging the powdery surface of the raw applied glaze. Each piece must be placed separately on the kiln shelf, having had its base carefully wiped clean of any glaze first unless it is low fired and glazed over the base, in which case it should be placed onto a stilt. Glazed pieces must not touch any neighbouring work and lid fittings must be wiped clean of any glaze.

Work should be placed on each shelf of equal or near equal heights to maximize the space available within the firing chamber. Shelves should be interspersed with shelf props in groups of three to provide maximum stability and to prevent shelves from warping at high temperatures. Small work should be packed to the centre or top of the kiln to allow for a high first shelf, which enables heat to circulate freely in the firing chamber. Pyrometric cones set for "heat work" reading can be placed once the work is packed. Use a lighted match to check their position is correctly in line with the spyhole for viewing.

### Cleaning a kiln shelf

Any runs of glaze from previous glaze should be removed from kiln shelves by chiselling out (while wearing goggles as eye protection). All traces of glaze should be removed to prevent it eating into the kiln shelf on subsequent firings. Pad the shelf underneath to absorb the shock of the hammer blows. Once the glaze is removed, the scar should be coated with bat wash.

### Protecting kiln furniture

Kiln shelves should be given a coat of bat (kiln) wash in preparation for glaze firing to prevent work from sticking. A mixture of two parts alumina hydrate and one part china clay, it can also be painted onto the galleries (seats) of lid fittings for work fired to stoneware temperatures and washed off after firing. It should also be applied to kiln props used in vapour firings.

## Firing times and temperatures

This chart gives examples of firing times for biscuit (bisque) and single firing, glaze firing, raku firing, crystalline firing and enamel firing.

They relate to the number of hours the firings take to achieve certain temperatures and the specific temperature points at which the kiln atmosphere requires soaking or reducing. The term "soak" means holding a temperature in position.

| HOURS | BISCUIT (BISQUE) AND SINGLE | GLAZE (REDUCTION & OXIDIZED) | RAKU | CRYSTALLINE | ENAMEL |
|---|---|---|---|---|---|
| | Reduction for glaze firing temperatures can commence from 1000°C (1832°F) and continue until 1350°C (2462°F) for porcelain. *Italics* refer to cooling temperatures. | | | | |
| 1 | 50°C (122°F) | 50°C (122°F) | 300°C (572°F) | 50°C (122°F) | 50°C (122°F) |
| 2 | 100°C (212°F) | 100°C (212°F) | 1000°C (1832°F) /reduction | 100°C (212°F) | 100°C (212°F) |
| 3 | 150°C (302°F) | 150°C (302°F) | 100°C (212°F) | 150°C (302°F) | 150°C (302°F) |
| 4 | 200°C (392°F) | 250°C (482°F) | | 250°C (482°F) | 250°C (482°F) |
| 5 | 300°C (572°F) | 400°C (752°F) | | 400°C (752°F) | 400°C (752°F) |
| 6 | 400°C (752°F) | 700°C (1292°F) | | 700°C (1292°F) | 700°C (1292°F) |
| 7 | 600°C (1112°F) | 1000°C+ (1832°F+) Reduction, soak at top earthware temp | | 1260–80°C (2300–36°F) (top temperature variable) | *600°C (1112°F)* |
| 8 | 700°C (1292°F) | 1280°C (2336°F) Reduction, soak at top stoneware temp | | Rapid cool from top temperature to *1100°C (2012°F)* | *400°C (752°F)* |
| 9 | 880°C (1616°F) | 1350°C (2462°F) Reduction soak porcelain | | *1040°C (1904°F)* soak | *300°C (572°F)* |
| 10 | 1000°C (1832°F) Top temp biscuit | *1250°C (2280°F)* | | *1040°C (1904°F)* | *200°C (392°F)* soak |
| 11 | *800°C (1472°F)* | *1000°C (1832°F)* | | *1040°C (1904°F)* soak | *100°C (212°F)* |
| 12 | *600°C (1112°F)* | *700°C (1292°F)* | | *1040°C (1904°F)* soak | |
| 13 | *400°C (752°F)* | *400°C (752°F)* | | *Begin to cool* | |
| 14 | *300°C (572°F)* | *200°C (392°F)* | | *900°C (1652°F)* | |
| 15 | *200°C (392°F)* | *100°C (212°F)* | | *500°C (932°F)* | |
| 16 | *100°C (212°F)* | | | *300°C (572°F)* | |
| 17 | | | | *150°C (302°F)* | |

# Slim Raku Vessels

Here, Kate Schuricht combines the batch production process of slipcasting with the more individual effects of raku firing. Raku is a fast firing and cooling process whereby glazed pieces are taken out of a kiln when the glaze is molten and placed into sawdust to cool. The result is a distinctive black crackle in the surface of the glaze and smoking of the unglazed body.

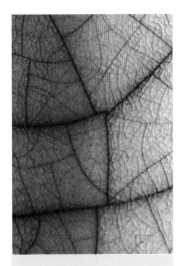

## Materials
Casting slip (earthenware)
Molochite grog (80s/120s)

## Equipment
Sieves (60, 80, 120 mesh)
Plaster moulds for slipcasting
Bands to hold moulds
Plastic jugs for slip
Fettling knife
Natural sponges
Electric kiln for biscuit
    (bisque) firing
Potter's knife
Plastic bowls
Gas cylinder (propane tank)
Burner with regulator
Raku kiln (oil drum lined with
    ceramic fibre, brick-lined
    gas kiln etc.)
Metal raku tongs
Thick leather gloves
Protective goggles
Sawdust
Bricks for the sawdust pit
Metal lid
Wire wool

## Glaze
BASE TRANSPARENT GLAZE
Soft borax frit          85%
China clay               15%
Add oxides and stains

## Firing
Biscuit (bisque) fire to 1000°C
    (1832°F)
Raku fire to 900–920°C
    (1652–1688°F), using
    spyhole to check glaze

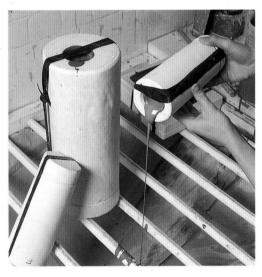

**1** Prepare the casting slip. Add between 15–25% grog to the slip, stirring well and sieving the mix before use. Put the plaster moulds together and secure with a strong band. Pour in the grogged, sieved slip to the top of the mould and top up as necessary during the casting period. Gently tap the filled mould and rock slightly to release any trapped air bubbles from the slip.

**2** Allow the pieces to cast for approximately 20 minutes for a medium thickness, then pour the slip out and leave to drain at a slight angle for a further 20–30 minutes until the surface of the slip is firm to the touch. Turn the moulds upright and allow the casts to dry a little longer. When the cast is firm enough cut away the spare with a moist fettling knife. Sponge back using a damp sponge to refine edges and remove any marks. Gently remove the cast from the mould – it should drop out quite easily.

**3** Fettle the slipcast forms when leatherhard, using a fettling knife and a moist natural sponge to refine the surface and smooth out any bumps. Leave the pieces to dry completely before biscuit (bisque) firing them to approximately 1000°C (1832°F). Firing them too high will mean that the clay body will become less resistant to thermal shock.

**4** Lightly sponge the surface of the biscuit (bisque) fired piece with a damp sponge to ensure that it is free from dust and grease. Stir the glaze thoroughly before sieving through an 80, and then a 120 mesh sieve. Stir it regularly to avoid settling. Pour the glaze into the top or rim of the piece and then pour out leaving a layer roughly 1 mm thick. Carefully scratch through the glaze with a potter's knife to test the thickness. Clean up the edges and rims.

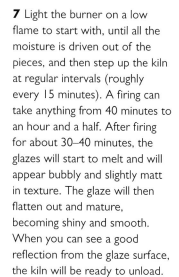

**5** Dip the piece into the first glaze for a few moments and remove, allowing the moisture to be absorbed. Dip into a second glaze and leave for a couple of seconds (optional). Clean off roughly 3 mm (⅛ in) of glaze at the bases in case it runs. Leave any surfaces that touch the kiln shelf glaze free. Leave the pieces to dry overnight before firing.

**6** Place the shelves into the base of the kiln at a level just above the burner hole. Load the pieces onto the shelves with enough room between each one to allow the tongs to move freely when unloading. It is best to ensure at this stage that a glazed surface will be in sight when you look into the spy hole during firing. Put on the extension rings followed by the lid.

**7** Light the burner on a low flame to start with, until all the moisture is driven out of the pieces, and then step up the kiln at regular intervals (roughly every 15 minutes). A firing can take anything from 40 minutes to an hour and a half. After firing for about 30–40 minutes, the glazes will start to melt and will appear bubbly and slightly matt in texture. The glaze will then flatten out and mature, becoming shiny and smooth. When you can see a good reflection from the glaze surface, the kiln will be ready to unload.

**8** Turn off the gas supply from the bottle, then the regulator, and finally the burner itself, waiting until all the gas has burnt out of the hose. This stops gas becoming trapped in the hose, which can be dangerous. Wearing gloves and goggles, remove the kiln lid and extension rings and place them on bricks on the ground, away from anything combustible.

**9** The sawdust pit needs to be close to the kiln to allow for speedy unloading. There should be a layer of sawdust in the bottom of the pit and enough to cover the pieces. The sawdust needs to be slightly damp to stop it from bursting into flames, but not too wet that it stops it from smoking. Have a bucket of water to hand in case of emergency. Remove the pieces quickly and carefully, holding the metal raku tongs with the heat resistant gloves. Keep calm to avoid unnecessary breakage and injury. At this stage in the firing your pots will come alive and all the characteristic crackles and smokiness will occur.

**10** Carefully place the pieces into the pit ensuring they do not touch. Cover quickly with plenty of sawdust until no smoke can be seen. You will need at least one helper for better and quicker covering. Cover with a final layer of sawdust and a lid (ideally metal) to stop the pots from cooling too fast.

**11** Leave the pieces to cool in the sawdust for 15 minutes to one hour. Check the pit regularly in case the sawdust catches fire. If possible, leave the pots in the pit until they are cool enough to remove with gloves. They can cool in the air or can be quenched in water.

**12** Once the pieces are cool enough to handle, place them in water to remove the black deposit on the glaze. This can be easily removed by gently rubbing with your fingers, but you may need to use wire wool on some areas. Dry the pieces thoroughly after washing as they are porous. This means that raku-fired pieces are not watertight and are not suitable for use with food or drink.

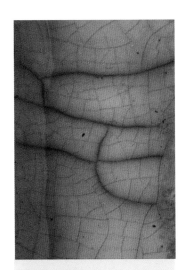

# Lidded Boxes

This project combines the techniques of slipcasting with raku, and here Kate Schuricht uses the form of a small, lidded, slipcast box that is glazed with a different glaze on the inside and outside. The application of glaze aims to achieve a uniform finish, which draws attention to the distinctive pattern of the crackles over the form created by the raku firing.

## Materials
Casting slip (earthenware)
Molochite grog (80s/120s)

## Equipment
Sieves (60, 80, 120 mesh)
Plaster moulds for slipcasting
Bands to hold moulds together
Plastic jugs for slip
Fettling knife
Natural sponges
Electric kiln
Potter's knife
Plastic bowls
Measuring jugs
Tray or container
Glaze claw (optional)
Metal kidney (rectangular)
Gas cylinder (propane tank)
Burner with regulator
Raku kiln
Metal raku tongs
Thick leather gloves
Protective goggles
Sawdust
Bricks for the sawdust pit
Metal lid
Wire wool

## Glaze
BASE TRANSPARENT GLAZE

| | |
|---|---|
| Soft borax frit | 85% |
| China clay | 15% |

Add oxides and stains

## Firing
Biscuit (bisque) fire to 1000°C
(1832°F)
Raku fire to 900–920°C
(1652–1688°F) – use
spyhole to check.

**1** Cast the box with grogged casting slip, being sure to agitate the mould initially to get rid of any air bubbles. Cast for approximately 20 minutes then pour out the slip, draining the moulds diagonally to ensure a clean drain. Leave to drain upside down at a slight angle for a further 20 minutes.

**2** Wait for the casts to become firm, then trim the spares from the casts using a fettling knife and a moist, natural sponge to smooth off the cut edges.

**3** Remove the lid and box casts from the moulds, placing the lid onto the box to dry. The lid will act as a setter for the box by preventing it from warping. Fettle the cast when leatherhard and sponge away any marks with a natural sponge. Once dry, biscuit (bisque) fire the box to approximately 1000°C (1832°F) with the lid still on.

**4** Next, sponge the surface of the bisqueware with a moist, natural sponge to remove any dirt or dust. Pour the raku glaze into the inside of the box and pour out. Leave a margin of about 5 or 6 mm (¼ in) free from glaze so the lid can be placed on without the glazed surfaces touching and sticking during firing. For the best results, leave the glaze to dry before glazing the outside. Dip the outside of the box into a tray or container of glaze, holding it carefully with your fingers or a glaze claw.

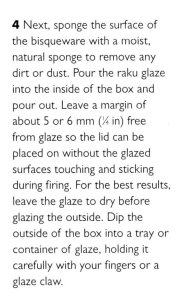

**5** Check to see that the glaze has dried enough to touch, then wearing a face mask (respirator) scrape the glaze off the bottom of the box with a metal kidney, scraping all the dry glaze back into the glaze bucket to be used again. Use the same dipping method for glazing the lid. Clean the glaze to a level of approximately 2 mm (1/12 in) around the base of the box to allow for the glaze to run when firing. Place the bases directly onto the kiln shelf for firing.

**6** Load the kiln leaving adequate space between boxes to allow for free movement of the tongs during unloading. It is a good idea when firing lidded containers in the raku kiln to keep the lids on. The forms will then be less likely to warp in the direct heat from the burner and there will be more room on the kiln shelves for the pieces. Put on the kiln lid, ignite the burner on low to start the firing, stepping up at regular intervals of about 15 minutes.

**7** Fire for between 45 minutes to one hour. Once the kiln has reached full temperature and you can see through the spyhole that the glaze is molten with a shiny, smooth surface, put on the leather gloves and protective goggles and unload the kiln using the tongs to hold the boxes in the middle.

**8** Place the boxes carefully into the sawdust pit, making sure that the glazed surfaces do not touch.

**9** Quickly and carefully remove the lid from the box before covering with sawdust. This allows the sawdust to reach the inside of the box and burn carbon into the crackles. Continue to cover the pieces with sawdust until no smoke can be seen, then cover the pit with a galvanised metal lid and leave the pieces to cool for about an hour if possible.

**10** When the boxes are cool, remove them from the sawdust pit and place them into water to clean. Use wire wool to gently remove the carbon from the surface of the glaze. Rinse off and allow the pieces to dry completely in the air. Although the pieces are glazed, they will not hold water and should be considered as decorative pieces only.

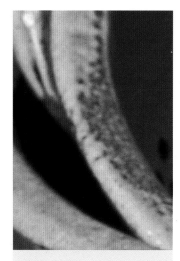

# Soda-Fired Colander

The reaction of soda, water and fire forms a vapour which is carried on the flame path and attaches itself to the silica in the clay as it passes through the kiln before being drawn out of the chimney. The result leaves each pot individually glazed. Some are soft and glassy, some with less soda are flashed with bright slips and the characteristic orange peel of vapour glaze. Lisa Hammond throws her work and has a kiln used specifically for soda glazing.

## Materials

WHITE FIRING CLAY

High temperature underglazes
  (optional)

BATT (KILN) WASH

| China clay | 50% |
| Alumina hydrate | 50% |

Mix to a thin cream

WADDING

| China clay | 900 g (2 lb) |
| Alumina hydrate | 900 g (2 lb) |
| Ball clay | a small handful |

Mix to soft consistency, so
that you can make ball/coil

## Equipment

Wheel and cutting wire
Metal kidney
Metal turning tool
Serrated kidney or comb
Natural sponge
Plastic sheet
Jug (pitcher)
Board
Gloves for glazing
Tapered hole cutter
Sponge for sticking on wads
Natural gas, propane, wood
  or oil kiln with a live flame.
  The kiln should be built
  specifically for soda glazing
  or adapted for the use of
  soda. At least four spray
  ports need to be built into
  the kiln for the introduction
  of soda and two spyholes
  for removing test rings.
Cones 06/7/8/9/10/11
Pyrometer can be very helpful
Bucket of hot water

Test rings made from coils
  (same clay as pots) – 6 or 7
  at each spyhole
Soda
Water
Old tea urn or metal bucket
  with calor gas burner
  underneath
Garden spray
Kiln goggles or UV glasses
Kiln gloves
Steel bar for test rings
Metal scraper
Carborundum stone (kiln
  brick bits)

## Glaze

BASIC SLIP

| Ball clay | 50% |
| China clay | 50% |

To achieve different colour slips, vary the ball clay or add a small percentage of oxide to the slip (eg cobalt-rutile-iron)

RAW LINER GLAZE

| Feldspar | 33% |
| Ball clay | 33% |
| Nephaline syenite | 33% |

This slip glaze can be used inside and out or over a slip. It cannot be used under a slip as it will bubble the slip. You can change the colour by spraying underglaze on top.

## Firing

See instructions over page.

**1** Take a 1.25 kg (2½ lb) lump of clay, centre it and throw a bowl with a rim. Leave enough clay to turn (trim) a footring (foot) when leatherhard. Use a metal kidney to smooth and clean off excess slurry before cutting off with a wire.

**2** Centre your bowl onto a previously made chuck. When leatherhard use a metal turning tool to turn a footring on the bottom of the bowl.

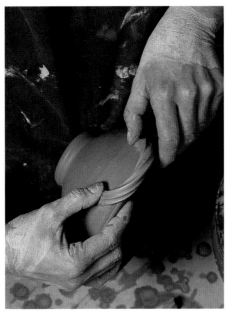

**3** Using water and clay, pull a round section for a handle (see Throwing, pulling handles). Use your thumb to put in grooves for decoration. Cut off a 7.5 mm (3 in) section and twist in opposite directions to produce a barley twist.

**4** Take a serrated kidney or comb and score and slurry the area where the handle is to be attached. Press the ends of the handle carefully, but firmly onto the pot. Smooth over with a natural sponge. Cover in plastic overnight to make sure that the handle dries slowly and the whole pot evens up.

**5** When the whole pot is leatherhard again, use a jug (pitcher) to pour slip into the bowl until it is two-thirds full. Roll the slip around the inside of the bowl until it is covered in slip, then pour it out. Do this quickly or the pot will become too soft again. Ensure that it is well drained. Leave on a board to return to leatherhard.

**6** When the slip on the inside of the bowl has dried back to leatherhard, dip the outside of the colander slowly into the slip, making sure that the bowl forms a vacuum on the surface of the slip so that it doesn't wet the inside again. Plunge down into the bucket and drip off well before inverting it back onto the board.

**7** Let the slip on the outside return to leatherhard and then, using a tapered hole cutter, cut holes in the colander in a pattern. Ensure the holes are not too close together or they will crack on drying. You can clean off any burrs when the pot is bone dry.

**8** Prepare the kiln for packing by scraping the kiln shelves clean and reapply bat (kiln) wash. Do not bat wash the underside of the shelves. As you pack, put wadding on all the bases before setting them on the shelf and on the rims of lidded pots. This prevents the pots from sticking to the shelves or the lids sticking to pots during firing. Do this as you pack because the wads drop off as they dry.

**9** Do not pack too tightly. Stagger the heights of the pots to help with the distribution of the soda as the flame passes through the kiln. Make sure space is left for the test rings and cones in at least two sites where a brick or spy hole can be removed to check the cones during the firing and to remove test rings. Now follow the firing instructions shown to the right of the page.

**10** Make a saturated solution of soda and water. Keep it on the boil as it helps to vaporize the soda and keep the spray clog-free. In a 2.5 cu m (90 cu ft) kiln use about 6–8 kg (13–17½ lb) soda to about 40 litres (8¾ gal) of water for each firing. Spray in the soda (see firing) using a garden spray on a defuse setting. Stand back at least 1–1.5 m (3–5 ft) from the kiln or you will melt the nozzle. Do not spray the pots directly as you will over-soda them and the surface will look lumpy; instead spray along the burner ports. Do not pressurize the spray gun too much or you will hit the back of the kiln.

**11** Make sure you have a spare brick to put your hot test rings on then, wearing your goggles and gloves, check the cones and take out a test ring using a metal rod. Allow it to cool right down before examining.

**12** When the fired ware is ready to unpack, remove the wadding with a metal scraper and grind off any rough surfaces with a carborundum stone.

## Firing

Low warm-up overnight.
6 am: put on very slow – treat like the start of a biscuit (bisque) firing.
**1 am:** check and turn the damper ¼ out.
8 am: 300°C (572°F). Turn up in gradual rise. At first 50-120°C (122–248°F) per hour until 600°C (1112°F) until reach 1000°C (1832°F) at about 4 pm.
**4 pm:** when cone 06 is at 1000°C (1832°F), push the damper in the chimney approximately ¾ or until reduction occurs, or use method appropriate to the kiln. Medium reduction for about 1½ hours.
**5.30 am:** oxidize to clean kiln of residue carbon. Kiln should now be at cone 7/8 both moving or 7 gone, 8 half over. Spray in soda until you are happy with the test rings (see steps 10–11). Look for the amount of glaze on the rings, rather than the colour (probably greyish). Continue to fire until cone 10 (about 2 –2½ hours from the start of spraying, depending on the size of the kiln and the pack). Oxidize again for 15 minutes (open the damper wide).
**To clean out:** set kiln to neutral atmosphere and soak for at least 1 hour, 2 if possible. Try to soak without a large rise in temperature by holding at cone 10 half over approx. 1300°C (2372°F). Cone 11 will alert you if one area of the kiln is getting too hot and you need to slow the kiln down. Test rings should now have more colour and be smoother. Shut the kiln off – open all the ports and damper and crash cool until 1150°C (2102°F), then clam up tight. Close all spy ports and the damper and seal all cracks. Allow to cool completely.

**Materials**

White St Thomas clay

**Equipment**

Box of junk
Sketchbook
Pencil and colour pens
Potter's knife
Toothbrush
Sponge
Wooden board
Rolling pin
Thin card (cardboard)
Scissors
Wooden dowel
Wooden tool
Needle for air holes
Paintbrushes
Thick leather gloves
Protective goggles
Gas bottle (propane tank)
Purpose-made tongs
Large metal bucket
Sawdust
Wire wool
Electric kiln with controller
Raku kiln, gas fired, made
  with refractory kiln bricks

**Glaze**

Pre-bought brush-on
  earthenware glazes

**Firing**

Biscuit (bisque) fire to 1080°C
  (1976°F)
  60°C (140°F)
  300°C (572°F)
  120°C (248°F)
  1080°C (1976°F)
Glaze fire to 990–1040°C
  (1814–1904°F)

# Raku Squirrel Teapot

A particular feature of Jola Spytkowska's work is manipulating and curving thin slabs of clay into three-dimensional forms so that moulds do not have to be used. Human and animal personalities are sourced from the objects around her – a box of junk can inspire many a hybrid creature to emerge. In this design, sketches of an old oil can and photos of squirrels combine to make an unusual teapot. The raku firing gives a dramatic and spontaneous effect.

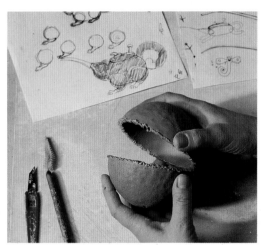

**1** This squirrel was evolved with close reference to drawn designs. If you decide to work in this way, create a drawing of the piece first, which you can refer to throughout the making process. Next, take two balls of clay and pinch out two bowls of equal size. When they have stiffened, even up the edges, score and slurry them (see Handbuilding, using slurry for joining slabs) and join together firmly. Smooth and blend the join.

**2** Cut out two circles from the sphere, a larger one at the base and a smaller one at the top. Prepare a small slab of clay for the teapot base and, when it is stiff, join by scoring and slurrying it to the base so the teapot sits flat. Now work out the dimensions for the head, tail and thighs. Then refer to your drawing and observe the shapes for these.

**3** Make rough templates using thin slabs of clay. Shape and curve them accordingly. Flatten these out again and place onto card. Draw out and cut round the templates. Prepare a large slab of thin clay, place the card templates on it and cut out two of each shape.

**4** Prepare the tail, the head, the ears and eyes, the shoulders, the feet and the thighs. Shape each piece by curving or folding it over a dowel or pressing it into the palm of your hand or into any suitable object. Assemble the components in one place and wait for the clay to stiffen up before joining them.

**5** Join the two halves of the tail and the head. Score and slurry both sides thoroughly. Press together firmly. Smooth the joins, emphasizing them for an added feature. Join the head to the body, then join the tail to the body. This will establish the front and the back of the teapot.

**6** Now that the head and tail are in position, place the shoulders and thighs in between. Make air holes in all of them to avoid explosions in the kiln.

**7** Pinch out a small ball of clay to make the lid using a template for approximate size. To make the flange, roll out a short coil, flatten it lightly and then join it to the underneath of the lid. Coil and roll out small balls of clay to prepare the features for the top of the lid.

**8** Join the features to the lid of the teapot.

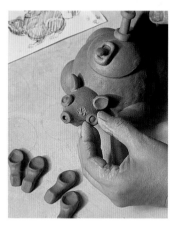

**9** Attach the ears and eyes. Impress the eyes with a tool to create the pupils. Then attach the feet.

**10** Prepare the spout for the pot. Take a very thin slab of clay, about 2.5 cm (1 in) wide at one end and 1 cm (½ in) at the other end. Wrap it around a paintbrush, join the edges and then lightly roll the whole thing to blend the join. Carefully remove the paintbrush.

**11** Make a hole in the mouth, otherwise the spout will not pour. Slightly curve the spout before attaching it. Next, biscuit (bisque) fire the squirrel. Outline the edges with a pencil (this will burn away in the raku firing) to identify areas that are to remain unglazed. Unglazed areas will smoke to a charcoal black once in the sawdust.

**12** Refer to your drawing and choose an earthenware, coloured glaze. These glazes fire to a low temperature, which makes them suitable for raku. Apply the glaze with three flowing coats of each colour. When you have finished, fire the squirrel in a gas-fired raku kiln. When the temperature reaches 1000°C (1832°F), remove the kiln lid and lift out the squirrel with purpose-made tongs. Place it in a metal bucket full of sawdust and leave it to smoke for about 20–30 minutes. Remove it and allow it to cool before cleaning and scrubbing gently with wire wool.

# CHEMICAL FORMULAE
The following chemical formulae relate to the individual glaze oxides listed in the glaze and decoration chapter.

## åChemical elements

| | |
|---|---|
| Aluminium | Al |
| Antimony | Sb |
| Barium | Ba |
| Boron | B |
| Calcium | Ca |
| Chromium | Cr |
| Cobalt | Co |
| Copper | Cu |
| Hydrogen | H |
| Iron | Fe |
| Lead | Pb |
| Lithium | Li |
| Magnesium | Mg |
| Nickel | Ni |
| Nitrogen | N |
| Oxygen | O |
| Potassium | K |
| Silicon | Si |
| Sodium | Na |
| Tin | Sn |
| Titanium | Ti |
| Vanadium | V |
| Zinc | Zn |
| Zirconium | Zr |
| Water | $H_2O$ |

## Fluxes

| | |
|---|---|
| Lead oxide TOXIC | PbO |
| Sodium oxide | $Na_2O$ |
| Potassium oxide | $K_2O$ |
| Calcium oxide | CaO |
| Magnesium oxide | MgO |
| Barium oxide TOXIC | BaO |
| Lithium oxide TOXIC | $Li_2O$ |
| Boric oxide | $B_2O_3$ |
| Zinc oxide | ZnO |

## Stiffeners

| | |
|---|---|
| Aluminum oxide | $Al_2O_3$ |
| Titanium oxide | $TiO_2$ |

## Glass

| | |
|---|---|
| Silicon dioxide | $SiO_2$ |
| Boric oxide | $B_2O_3$ |

## Glaze oxide sources

| | |
|---|---|
| Flint or quartz | $SiO_2$ |
| Clays (variable) | no single formula |
| Ball clay (variable) | no single formula |
| China clay (kaolin) | $Al_2O_32SiO_22H_2O$ |
| Calcined china clay (molochite) | $Al_2O_32SiO_2$ |

## Feldspars

| | |
|---|---|
| Potash feldspar | $K_2OAl_2O_36SiO_2$ |
| Soda feldspar | $Na_2OAl_2O_36SiO_2$ |
| Nepheline syenite | $K_2O\ 3Na_2O\ 4Al_2O_3\ 8SiO_2$ |
| Cornish stone (pegmatite) | no single formula |
| Dolomite (calcium magnesium carbonate) | $CaCO_3\ MgCO_3$ |
| Stone whiting (calcium carbonate) | $CaCO_3$ |
| Talc, French talc or soapstone | $3\ MgO\ 4SiO_2\ H_2O$ |
| Calcium borate frit (colemenite) | $2CaO2B_2O_35H_2O$ |
| Barium carbonate TOXIC | $BaCO_3$ |
| Lithium carbonate TOXIC | $Li_2CO_3$ |
| Spodumene | $LiO_2AL_2O_34SIO_2$ |
| Silicon carbide | SiC |
| Bone ash | $Ca_3\ (PO_4)_2$ |
| Lead monosilicate | $PbOSiO_2$ |
| Lead sesquisilicate | $PbOSiO_2$ |
| Lead bisilicate | $PbO2SiO_2$ |

## Opacifiers

| | |
|---|---|
| Tin oxide (stannic oxide) | $SnO_2$ |
| Zirconium oxide | $ZrO_2$ |
| Titanium oxide | $TiO_2$ |

## Colouring oxides

| | |
|---|---|
| Cobalt oxide or carbonate | $CO_3O_4$ |
| Copper oxide or carbonate | $CuCO_3$ |
| Chromium oxide | $CR_2O_3$ |
| Iron oxide | $Fe_2O_3$ |
| Manganese oxide | $MnO_2$ |
| Nickel oxide TOXIC | $Ni_2O_3$ |
| Vanadium pentoxide TOXIC | $V_2O_5$ |
| Rutile | $TiO_2$ |
| Ilmenite | $FeOTi\ O_2$ |
| Iron chromate TOXIC | $FeCrO_3$ |

## Borax frits

| | |
|---|---|
| Tin oxide | $SnO_2$ |
| Zirconium oxide (silicate) | $ZrSiO_4$ |
| Titanium dioxide | $TiO_2$ |

MARIA DONATO'S PRINTED PLATE (SEE PAGES 212-215).

# SELLING YOUR WORK

Successful selling can be as time consuming as making the work itself. You need to be very clear about which market your work fits into and you need to be proactive in finding selling opportunities and following them through unless you can find someone else, such as an agent or gallery, to do the selling for you. Agents are, however, a rare breed in the ceramics world and most potters tackle selling themselves.

Behind the scenes of designing and making ceramic work there is the mundane administration, including contacting various organisations, potential exhibition venues or outlets, craft bodies and potential buyers and supplying written information about the nature of your work and your curriculum vitae.

### Selling through a gallery or shop

When selling to shops and galleries, first check out the overall style and price range to make sure your work conforms with what they are looking for. Keep a record of people you speak to and any material you send out. Follow up the initial contact and have work available and ready to show if interest is expressed.

Selling can be arranged with shops or galleries in two ways – either by sale or return, or the work can be bought directly from the potter. Shops and galleries will add their own commission onto your price, which can range from 60–110 per cent, and VAT is added on top of this price.

If you do decide to leave work on a sale or return basis, satisfy yourself that the shop or gallery is reputable. Always take a delivery note, which must be signed by the shop or gallery representative as a receipt for your work. Most galleries have their own terms and conditions, which will cover commission, pricing, payment terms and insurance details. However, these terms and conditions are often negotiable to meet your own.

### Organising exhibitions

Many potters prefer to organise their own exhibitions, which involves finding a venue, organising publicity, compiling a mailing list of potential buyers, sending invitations, displaying and lighting the work, manning the exhibition, pricing the work, perhaps making up a postcard or catalogue, even estimating how much wine to buy for a private view, and finally taking it down and organising delivery of any sold work. Many galleries offer shared or solo exhibitions and will help with organization.

### Craft and trade fairs

Ranging from the informal to high-quality specialist venues, craft fairs provide another opportunity to sell work. Entering a craft fair often entails making an application accompanied with slides or photos, and many involve passing through a selection process.

Craft shows and trade fairs involve considerable expense and organisation skills. If the venue is far from home there is also the cost of accommodation. To make an event worthwhile and run smoothly, check what is and what is not provided in terms of shelving or plinths, lighting, vehicle arrangements to drop off and pick up work, as well as deadlines for sending visual and written material to be included in press packs and catalogues. Some craft shows require you to pay a commission on any work sold and may require you to demonstrate your skills during the show.

On a more commercial scale, national or international trade fairs provide a marketing platform to reach buyers from many different retail and service outlets. Trade buyers come to source work and will order then and there or at a later date. A trade fair therefore requires preparing information and publicity material to be handed out to potential buyers. This information should include a visual representation of your work with prices, including packaging and postage costs, style codes or titles and available colour ways. Buyers making large orders often request a discount, which can be built into the pricing structure.

### Keeping a visual record

It is essential to keep a good-quality visual record of any work that marks a new development or is a unique piece before it leaves your possession. You can take photographs or slides, record work on video or as a digital image – whatever suits your purposes best. These images are invaluable when contacting shops, galleries, making applications for grants or trade fairs, sending to the press or publications, or for making up postcards or catalogues. Black-and-white photos are commonly requested with press related material.

Take as many photographs as possible of a piece of work as it is cheaper to duplicate transparencies on the original film than to process good-quality copies. If you are unable to take photographs yourself, it is worth paying someone to take them professionally.

### Sending out work

Packaging ceramic work is a skill in itself and will depend on the volume, form and quantity involved. Given the nature of the fired material, any type of ceramic work will require a copious amount of protection, such as bubble wrap, shredded paper or polystyrene chips. A good way to protect work to be shipped, posted or sent via a carrier is to double box. Allow for a generous area of close packing material around the object packed in bubble wrap at least 4–5 cm (1½–2 in) from the box wall. A second thick-walled cardboard box, at least 4–5 cm (1½–2 in) larger than the first, packed firmly with a padding material in the cavity should ensure safe passage. Post offices and delivery services set restrictions on weight and volume so check these before taking the package to the local post office counter or organising collection. Many also offer an insurance cover should breakages occur during delivery.

JOANNA YOUNG'S STALL
AT CHELSEA CRAFTS
FAIR (1997).
PHOTOGRAPH BY
ED BARBER.

## Getting help

There are many local and regional craft associations and bodies that help with promotion and advice or who can provide grants to help establish a selling market. They can provide information about trade and craft fairs, further education, copywriting guidelines, legal advice, how to organise contracts for public or private commissions and organise documents for selling abroad.

Potters whose work is sculptural, crossing the boundaries of craft to art, may find that craft agencies cannot fully accommodate their needs and it may be necessary to look further afield to artist agencies and publications. Check any specialist magazines or web sites for organisations such as these.

There are an ever increasing number of books and courses that can provide craftspeople with practical information about self-employment to cover all manner of aspects of selling work or services (see bibliography). Government bodies can provide training and assistance with business plans and book-keeping. Adult education may also offer short training courses in marketing skills, developing promotional material, photography, organizing an exhibition or writing a curriculum vitae.

## Selling your skills

Alternatively, you can sell your skills or services in the community, through projects, education and residencies, or through public commissions. Many potters use these activities to supplement their own work or work solely in one or a number of these fields.

Now we have the ever-growing, new market of the internet. Many galleries, organisations and individuals operate their own websites, containing both text and visual information. The internet will have an estimated 800 million users by the turn of the millennium and this opens up a whole new market.

# GLOSSARY

**Agateware**

A piece made by combining two or more different coloured clays.

**Airbrush**

An atomiser that uses compressed air to apply a liquid medium as a fine spray.

**Air compressor**

Used with an airbrush or spray gun to force a liquid medium into a spray.

**Alkaline glazes**

Glazes in which the dominant fluxes are alkalis, such as sodium and potassium.

**Alkalis**

Consisting mainly of sodium and potassium, which act as fluxes in glaze (*see* flux).

**Bag wall**

A wall built inside a down draft kiln to separate the firing chamber from the fire. It directs the flame upwards to create equal circulation and protects the ware from direct contact with the flame.

**Ball clay**

Plastic, fine-grained secondary clay coloured by organic matter. Used to increase plasticity in clay bodies and introduces silica and alumina to glazes.

**Banding wheel**

A turntable that revolves to turn a piece of work while it is being made or decorated. So called because it can be used for banding lines.

**Bas-relief**

Three-dimensional modelling raised above a flat clay surface.

**Biscuit (bisque) firing**

Preliminary firing to harden the clay prior to glazing.

**Blistering**

Bubbles and craters caused by gases escaping from a glaze during firing. It can be overcome by lowering the top temperature, and reaching it with a slower rate of temperature rise. Soaking and a prolonged cooling in the firing cycle can also assist in overcoming this glaze fault.

**Blunger**

A piece of equipment with a revolving blade used to prepare casting slip or clay bodies from dry materials before they pass into a filter press.

**Burner**

The end point of a system that combines air with fuel. The burner supplies a variable flame into the kiln, which is controlled by reducing or increasing the air supply by turning a valve.

**Calcine**

Heating a material such as china clay to around 700°C (1292°F) to remove chemically combined water and volatile matter. Can be done by putting a material in a pot for biscuit (bisque) firing.

**Celadon**

Chinese in origin, a thickly applied grey-green glaze that has additions of iron oxide, which is turned to black ferrous oxide in reduction firing.

**Christobolite inversion**

The point of firing at 225°C (437°F) at which crystals of quartz in the clay body physically change. This causes a slight increase in particle size that decreases again when the kiln is cooled. Sudden temperature changes at this point can result in dunting, particularly in glaze firing (*see* also quartz inversion).

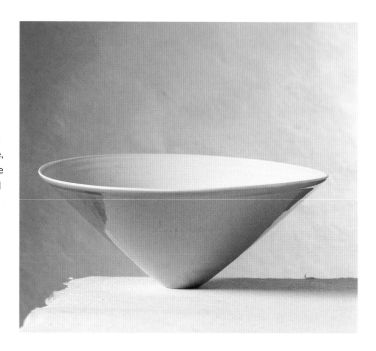

**Chuck**

A solid lump of centred clay used to hold a leatherhard piece while turning it on the wheel.

**Climbing kiln**

A kiln based on ancient Chinese hillside kilns.

**Cottle**

A retaining wall or side set into which plaster is poured for making working plaster moulds.

**Crawling**

This glaze defect is caused by grease from handling or dust on biscuit (bisque) ware repelling the glaze. It has the appearance of a parting and rolling back of glaze, leaving behind bald patches of clay body and is overcome by refiring. It can also be caused by shrinkage of the glaze before it is fired and can be solved by altering the glaze recipe.

**Crazing**

A glaze defect characterized by a network of fine cracks. When the effect is deliberate, such as in raku firing, it is known as crackle. The cracks occur because the glaze contracts more than the pot as it cools after firing. A common fault in alkaline glazes.

**Crystalline glaze**

A glaze that contains crystals formed when the kiln firing is held at a specific temperature as it is cooled. Specific to glazes containing rutile, zinc and other crystal-forming oxides.

**Damper**

A device made of a refractory material to restrict the aperture of the exit flue to hold in heat and slow the kiln's cooling rate.

**Deflocculant**

A soluble material added to liquid clays, usually casting slips, to increase fluidity while allowing a greater bulk of particles to be held in the fluid.

**Dunting**

Cracking of ware caused by factors including a weak form, an ill-fitting material that causes stress or irregular firing by over-rapid cooling at the end of a firing cycle (*see* quartz inversion).

**Egyptian paste**

A self-glazing, low-fired clay body containing glass-forming material.

## Engobe

A decorating clay fluid with a proportion of flux that is halfway between the fired properties of a slip and a glaze.

## Extruder

A piece of equipment, also called a wad box, that forces clay through a die to give strips of clay, which are shaped by the profile apertures of a die.

## Feldspar

A group of minerals containing alumina, silica, potassium, sodium and calcium. A material containing feldspars is known as feldspathic.

## Fettling

This process removes excess clay by turning a piece on a wheel and shaving or scraping away seams made from casting using a fettling knife.

## Filter press

A piece of equipment for taking a clay body from a liquid state to plastic by forcing out the water under pressure.

## Fluidity

The term used for a liquid medium to be able to move or flow, that is, low fluidity for a heavy suspension of particles. Fluidity is governed by the amount of water present in a suspension, the particle size and shape and the particles' reaction to electrostatic forces.

## Flux

Oxides that interact with other components in a glaze to bring about ceramic fusion.

## Flue

The vent or exit of the firing chamber of a kiln.

## Footring

The base of a piece of pottery, which is usually left unglazed for high-fired ware and sometimes glazed in low-fired ware.

## Gallery

The shelf on a pot rim that secures a lid in its resting position and prevents it from tipping out when a pot is tilted. There are a number of design solutions to lid and gallery fittings. which are adapted to meet the needs of both form and function.

## Greenware

Ware that is complete, but has not become sufficiently dry for firing.

## Grog

Crushed or ground, fired clay in various particle sizes, which provides texture and workable strength by opening a clay body, reducing shrinkage so that it can dry uniformly without warping.

## Heat work

The combination of temperature and time necessary to take a glaze or clay to its fired maturity.

## Inglaze

This technique uses ceramic colours applied on top of an often unfired glazed surface, which sink into the glaze surface when fired. The colours include metallic oxides (see maiolica), stains or coloured glazes.

## Kaolin

Also called China clay, this clay has few impurities, is pure white, is not very plastic and highly refractory. Used in glazes to provide alumina and silica, and in clays to lend whiteness to the clay body.

## Leatherhard

The stage reached by clay after drying from the plastic state whereby it is firm enough to pick up without distorting, but workable to cut, pare, turn or fettle, join clay additions, apply with slip and burnish, or glaze for single firing. It is recognizable by having a darker appearance than dry clay and being cool and damp to touch.

## Line blends

Methodical testing for a series of variations made to a base recipe.

## Lustre

Metallic surfaces on glazes derived from precious metals. Lustres can be applied to the unglazed surface and must undergo reduction firing. Oil medium lustres are applied onto glaze-fired work and are fired to 700–800˚C (1292–1472˚F).

## Maiolica

Decorated tin-glazed ware traditionally low fired with a lead glaze made opaque by the addition of tin. Historical pieces produced with maiolica glazes include Delft, faience and galleyware. The colour decoration is applied to the surface of the unfired glaze.

## Maquette

A small, 3-dimensional sketch, often roughly finished, made to plan out or design a larger piece of work.

## Medium

A liquid in which a pigment, such as oxide or stain, is suspended, or the liquid chosen with which to decorate, such as glazes, slips, engobes, oxides, stains or onglaze.

## Molochite

An alternative to fireclay, a refractory white grog for opening clay that is free from iron impurities, as it is made from china clay.

## Monoprint

An individual, transferred print that cannot be repeated.

**Onglaze**

Also called enamels, China paint or overglaze, these oil- or water-based colours are made up of a soft melting glass and metal oxides. The colours are applied on to a glaze-fired surface as decoration,

**Opacifier**

A mineral included in a base or transparent glaze to give opacity, such as tin, zircon or titanium. Commercial glaze stains also act as opacifiers.

**Overfire**

When a glaze or clay body has exceeded its firing range temperature. Overfired glaze can blister and clay walls can warp or bloat.

**Oxidation**

The firing of a kiln with complete combustion so that the firing atmosphere contains enough oxygen in the kiln to allow the fired clays, glazes and colours to produce their oxidized colours. Electric kilns always produce oxidizing firings.

**Oxide**

A combination of an element with oxygen. Basic oxides are metals and the acid oxides are non metals.

**Pin holing**

A glaze defect caused by bubbles forming in the glaze firing, which have not had sufficient time to heal. This can often be overcome by soaking, or holding the kiln temperature, to allow the molten glaze to even out.

**Plasticity**

The workability of clay. Some clay bodies, depending on their particle size, can be improved in plasticity by increasing their water content or by weathering and ageing. The proportion of materials in a clay body recipe can also be adjusted to improve the plasticity of the clay.

**Porous**

This term is used in conjunction with plaster or biscuit (bisque) fired clay when describing the capacity to take up water.

**Potter's tissue**

A tissue paper patented in 1781 as a means of transferring an indirect print decoration from engraved copper plates to the surface of clay.

**Pouncing**

Copying a design by pricking holes as outlines to form a stencil. Graphite powder is pushed through the holes to transfer the outline to the surface to be decorated (usually a tile).

**Profile former**

A shaped profile made of metal, wood or plastic, used to shape clay or plaster.

**Pug mill**

A piece of equipment that compresses and mixes plastic clay to a homogeneous state. If the clay is used immediately, this removes the need to prepare it for working by wedging and kneading.

**Pyrometer**

An instrument for gauging temperature linked to a thermocouple consisting of two metallic wires, which produce a voltage that varies according to temperature exposure.

**Pyrometric cone**

A cone made from compressed, carefully controlled ceramic materials designed to give a graduated scale of fusing temperatures at approximately 20°C (68°F) intervals.

**Quartz inversion**

The point of firing at 573°C (1063°F) where quartz crystals in a clay body physically change. The change causes a slight

increase in particle size, which reverts when the kiln is cooled. Sudden temperature changes at this point can result in dunting (or cracking), particularly in a glaze firing (see christobolite inversion).

**Raku**

A low firing technique that involves removing fired work from a red-hot kiln and reducing it in a combustible material, such as sawdust.

**Reduction**

The action during a firing process of starving the metallic oxides contained in clay and glaze of oxygen to transform their colour, often with dramatic results.

**Refractory**

A term used to describe a material that is able to withstand high temperatures. The word is often used in association with fire clays, kiln furniture and kiln-building materials.

**Rib**

A wooden or plastic smooth, often shaped, tool used to apply even pressure when throwing.

**Roulette**

A wheel used to imprint a circuit of design onto clay, often used on freshly thrown ware before it is removed from the wheel.

**Saggar**

A protective refractory box inside which work is packed for firing to prevent it from contacting flames and gases or the kiln atmosphere.

**Screeding**

The action of passing over plaster with a straight edge as it begins to set (in a soft to mushy state) to get a level surface.

**Sgraffito**

Derived from the Italian word "graffire", this applies to decoration that scratches through an applied colour to reveal a different one.

**Single glazing**

The term used to refer to once-fired, raw-fired or slip-glazed application.

**Sintering**

A stage in the firing process when particles in the clay and glaze rearrange themselves, becoming solid by sticking to one another, but not fusing. Sintered strength occurs at approximately 600°C (1112°F).

**Slaking**

When clay is bone dry it can be slaked or soaked down by covering it in water to make slurry or to reclaim it back to the plastic state.

**Slip**

A homogeneous liquid clay that can be coloured by adding stains or oxides and used for decorating. Slip also refers to liquid clay containing deflocculants, which is used for slipcasting.

**Slipcasting**

A forming technique of pouring liquid clay casting slip into plaster moulds.

**Slip trailer**

A tool with a liquid-containing sack and tube aperture used to trail lines or dots of liquid slip on to a clay surface for decoration.

**Slip reservoir**

The section of a plaster mould, which is created by a "spare" collar to provide an excess pool of slip above the finishing edge of a piece to be cast. The spare is cut or fettled away when the piece has firmed and is still held in the mould.

**Slop**

A wet, sieved combination of materials that is ready for use or application.

**Slurry**

A mixture of clay and water, which is referred to here as the "glue" for joining clay together. It is made from pieces of bone dry clay, which are slaked and that match the clay of the piece of work to which it is applied.

**Snake kiln**

A kiln comprising of a linear series of linked firing chambers.

**Soaking**

The point in a firing cycle, often at the end, at which the temperature is held in order to reach the required potential of a glaze. Not all glazes require soaking.

**Spare**

*See* Slip Reservoir.

**Sprig**

A relief ornament applied to a clay surface at the leatherhard stage, produced by pressing clay into a plaster or clay sprig mould. It was used in 18th century Wedgwood jasperware.

**Stilt**

A three-pointed, refractory support glazed on a piece's base used to lift low-fired ware off the kiln shelf during firing. The sharp scar left by a stilt is removed after firing by rubbing it down with a carborundum stone.

**Tenmoku (Temmoku)**

Usually dark brown or black stoneware glaze stained with iron oxide, which flows and gives variation to the pot's form by "breaking" to another colour at its thinner points.

**Terra sigillata**

A siliceous decorating slip, the ingredients of which are precipitated to a fine particle size. The leatherhard slip is burnished and fired to approximately 950°C (1742°F).

**Test piece**

A small tile or pot that is used to test fire colours, glazes or clay bodies.

**Thermal shock**

An overall term that is applied to any cracks that are formed due to extreme, sudden changes of temperature.

**Thixotropic**

Generally defined as a liquid's ability to become more viscous when left undisturbed (crucial in a casting slip).

**Trolley kiln**

A kiln that is packed with work to be fired by means of a trolley, which rolls on rails into the kiln. Because the trolley can be pulled away from the kiln it enables unrestricted space in which to stack the kiln shelves.

**Tri-axial testing**

A series of tests used to study combinations between different glaze materials or glaze recipes.

**Underglaze**

Decorated colour applied under a transparent glaze. The term applies to any colour decoration using oxides, commercial underglazes or commercial glaze and body stains.

**Underfired**

When a glaze or clay body has not reached its optimum firing temperature. Glaze that is underfired often appears milky or feels dry and is porous.

**Vapour firing**

Forming a glaze surface by throwing salt or soda, or dripping salt or soda solution into the combustion area of a kiln.

**Vent**

A circular or square hole in the wall or door of a kiln, which can be left open or closed using a bung or flap. It allows a spy hole into the firing chamber to view the glow colour and the state of pyrometric cones and also gives an additional passage of air from the kiln, which can be adjusted.

**Viscosity**

A term often applied to glaze describing its movement when fired. When fired and fluid it has low viscosity, when fired and matt or dry it has high viscosity.

**Vitrified**

The point at which materials in a clay body become fluxed to a dense, hard non-porous state. At vitrification, high-fired glazes combine with the glassy particles in the clay body and low-fired glazes coat the clay body. This is the furthest point to which a body can be taken without it becoming deformed.

**Wad box**

(*see* extruder).

**Warping**

Movement in a formed shape that can occur when drying or firing.

**Whirler (banding wheel)**

A whirler here is used to describe an electric wheel for use in mouldmaking.

# SUPPLIERS AND SERVICES For local sources, check your local telephone

directory, as well as advertisements in ceramic magazines.

## United Kingdom

**BATH POTTERS' SUPPLIES**
2 Dorset Close, Bath BA2 3RF
Tel 01225 337046; Fax 01225 462712
*Equipment, clay, glazes, etc*

**BRITISH CERAMIC TESTING
RESEARCH LTD**
Tel 01782 764444
*Glaze testing services*

**BRITISH PLASTER BOARD**
Newark Works
Bowbridge Lane, Newark
Nottingham NG24 3BZ
Tel 01636 678206; Fax 01636 673542
*Will advise on a local outlet for plaster*

**BRITTAINS (TR) LTD**
Ivy House Paper Mills,
Commercial Road, Hanley
Stoke on Trent
Staffordshire ST1 3QS
Tel 01782 202 567;
Fax 01782 202157
*Decal paper and pottery tissue*

**CERAMATECH LTD**
Units 16 & 17, Frontier Works
33 Queen Street,
London N17 8JA
Tel 0181 885 4492;
Fax 0181 365 1563
*Equipment, clay, glazes, etc*

**CP CERAMICS**
37 Buxton Street, London E1 5HE
Tel 0171 247 4223;
Fax 0171 377 0311
*Ceramic model and mould making*

**VJ GOODHALLS**
Barker Street, Longton
Stoke on Trent
Staffordshire ST3 1PE
Tel 01782 319 696
*Jigger and jolley services, cup heads,
metal back shapes*

**JOHNSTONE MATTHEY**
Colour and Print Division,
Cresswell Road, Stoke onTrent
Staffordshire ST11 9RD
Tel 01782 388399; Fax 01782 388303
*Colours and inks*

**KINGFISHER CERAMICS**
Scapa Filtration, Heathcote Works
Burslem, Stoke on Trent
Staffordshire ST6 4EQ
Tel 01782 575254; Fax 01782 575237
*Mouldmaking equipment*

**KILN CLINIC LTD**
Tel/Fax 0181 462 8904
*Equipment repair and installation*

**LONGTON LIGHT ALLOYS**
Foxley Lane, Milton, Stoke on Trent
Staffordshire ST2 7HE
Tel 01782 536615; Fax 01782 533415
*Hollow extrusion die plates*

**JOHNSON MATTHEY**
Ceramics and Materials Ltd,
Woodbank Street, Burslem
Stoke on Trent
Staffordshire ST6 3AT
Tel 01782 524949; Fax 01782 524950
*Glazes and colour*

**PAMELA MORETON**
22B Holt Road, Cromer
Norfolk NR27 9JW
Tel 01263 512629
*Decal printing service*

**RICHARD PHETHEAN**
The Leadenporch House
New Street, Deddington
Banbury, Oxon OX1 0SP
Tel 01869 338791
*Throwing tuition and ceramic workshops*

**POTCLAYS**
Brickkiln Lane, Etruria
Stoke on Trent, Staffordshire ST4 7BP
Tel 01782 219816; Fax 01782 286506
*Equipment, clay, glazes, etc*

**POTTERY CRAFTS**
Campbell Road, Stoke on Trent
Staffordshire ST4 4ET
Tel 01782 745000; Fax 01782 746000
*Equipment, clay, glazes, etc*

**SCARVA POTTERY SUPPLIES**
10 Drummiller Lane, Scarva,
Co Armagh BT63 6BR
Ireland
Tel 01762 831864
*Equipment, clay, glazes, etc*

**STEPHEN WEBSTER PLASTICS**
Brick Knoll Park, Ashley Road
St Albans, Herts AL1 5PL
Tel 01727 863138
*Cottles for mouldmaking*

## United States

**AMACO**
4717 West 16th Street
Indianapolis, Indiana 46222
Tel 317 244 6871
*Equipment, clay, glazes, etc*

**AXNER POTTERY SUPPLY**
P O Box 1484 Oviedo, Florida 32765
Tel 407 365 1858
*Equipment, clay, glazes, etc*

**BIO-TECHNICS LABORATIES**
1133 Crenshaw Boulevard
Los Angeles, CA 90019
Tel 323 933 5991
*Glaze testing services*

**DICK BLICK CO**
PO Box 1267, Galesburg
Illinois 61401
Tel 309 343 6181
*Equipment*

**KENTUCKY TENNESSEE CLAY CO**
Box 6002, Mayfield
Kentucky 42066
Tel 502 247 3061
*Equipment, clay, glazes, etc*

**LAGUNA CLAY CO**
East Coast: 4022 Mill Road
Skaneateles, New York 13152
Tel 315 685 8378
*Equipment, clay, glazes, etc*

**MINNESOTA CLAY CO**
8001 Grand Avenue South
Bloomington, Minnesota 55420
Tel 612 884 9101
*Equipment, clay, glazes, etc*

**RANDALL POTTERY**
P O Box 774, Alfred, NY 14802
*Equipment, clay, glazes, etc*

**SOLDNER POTTERY**
PO Box 90, Aspen CO 81612
Tel and fax: 970 925 3742
*Clay mixers and equipment*

**STANDARD CERAMIC
SUPPLY CO**
P O Box 4435, Pittsburgh, PA 15205
*Equipment, clay, glazes, etc*

**TRINITY CERAMIC SUPPLY INC.**
9016 Diplomacy Row, Dallas
Texas 75247
Tel 214 631 0540
*Equipment, clay, glazes, etc*

## Australia

**CLAY CRAFT SUPPLIES**
28 O'Connell Terrace, Bowen Hills
Queensland 4006
Tel 07 854 1515
*Equipment, clay, glazes, etc*

**DIGITEMP**
BPQ Controls, 14 Margaret Street
Beachmere Queensland 4510
Tel 074 962 199; Fax 074 968 238
*Kiln equipment, calibration and repairs*

**NORTHCOTE POTTERY**
85A Clyde Street, Thornbury 3071
Tel 03 480 4799
*Equipment, clay, glazes, etc plus general
tuition and ceramic workshops*

**POTTERS' EQUIPMENT**
13/42 New Street, Ringwood
Victoria 3134
Tel 03 870 7533; Fax 03 879 1799
*Equipment, clay, glazes, etc*

**PUGGOON POTTERY
SUPPLIERS**
P O Box 199, Gulgong, NSW 2852
Tel 063 74 1448
*Equipment, clay, glazes, etc*

**TALISMEN**
221 Macquarie Street, Hobart
Tasmania
Tel 002 23 5536
*Equipment, clay, glazes, etc*

**VENCO PRODUCTS**
29 Owen Road, Kelmscott, WA 6111
Tel 09 399 5265; Fax 09 497 1335
*Manufacturers of equipment*

## Canada

**CUPEPPER POTTERY**
700 58th Avenue, SE Calgary Alberta
T2H 2E2

**THEKER POTTERY SUPPLIES**
15 West Pearce Street
Richmond Hill, Ontario L4B 1H6

## New Zealand

**TALISMEN**
124 Rimu Road, Paraparauma
Tel 00 64 58 84377; Fax 00 64 58
73107
*Pottery equipment*

# BIBLIOGRAPHY

*Ceramics and Print;* Paul Scott; Black; 1994
*Clay & Glazes for the Potter;* Daniel Rhodes; Pitman; 1957
*The Craft of the Potter;* Michael Casson; BBC; 1977
*The Electric Kiln;* Harry Fraser; Black; 1994
*A Guide to Modern Australian Ceramics;* Janet Mansfield; Craftsman House; 1988
*Hand Built Ceramics;* Jane Waller; Batsford; 1990
*Hands in Clay;* Charlotte Speight and John Toki; Mayfield; 1994
*Hans Coper and Lucie Rie;* Tony Birks; Marston House; 1983 and 1987
*Nature as a Source;* Kim Jacobsen; The Crafts Council; 1995
*Paper Clay;* Rosette Gault; Penn/Black; 1998
*Plastermould and Model Making;* Chaney and Skee; Prentice Hall; 1973
*The Potter's Art;* Garth Clark; Phaidon; 1995
*A Potter's Book;* Bernard Leach; Faber & Faber; 1940
*The Potter's Dictionary of Materials and Glazes;* Frank Hamer; Pitman; 1975
*The Potter's Manual;* Kenneth Clark; Macdonald Orbis; 1983
*Pottery & Ceramics;* Christies; Phaidon; 1984
*Pottery in the Making;* Freestone and Gaimster; British Museum Press; 1977
*Single Firing;* Fran Tristram; Gentle Breeze/Black; 1996
*Slips and Slipware;* Anthony Phillips; Batsford; 1990
*Smashing Pots;* N Barley; British Museum Press; 1994
*Tang and Liao Ceramics;* W Watson; Thames & Hudson; 1984
*World Ceramics;* Hamlyn; 1968

## Further reading

*Artist Handbooks,* AN Publications, PO BOX 23, Sunderland SR4 6DG
   (*Exhibiting and Selling Abroad; Money Matters; Copyright; Investigating;*
   *Galleries; Art in Public; Organising your Exhibition; Selling*)
*Ceramics and Print;* Paul Scott; A & C Black; 1994
*Clay and Glazes for the Potter;* D Rhodes, Pitman; 1957
*Clays and Glazes in Studio Ceramics;* David Scott; The Crowood Press; 1998
*Decorated Earthenware;* Mike Levy; Batsford; 1994
*Glazes;* Emmanuel Cooper; Batsford; 1994
*New Ceramic Trends and Traditions;* Peter Dormer; Thames & Hudson; 1986
*The Potter's Directory of Shape Function & Form;* Neal French; Krause; 1998
*The Potter's Palette;* Christine Constant and Steve Ogden; Apple; 1996
*Raku;* Ian Byers; Batsford, 1992
*Single Firing: The Pros and Cons;* Fran Tristram; A & C Black; 1996
*Slips and Slipware;* Anthony Phillips; Batsford; 1990
*Soda Glazing;* Ruthanne Tudball; A & C Black; 1995
*Tin Glazed Earthenware;* Daphne Carnegy; Black/Chilton; 1993

## Specialist magazines

**AMERICAN CERAMICS**
9 East 45th Street
New York, NY 10017
USA
Tel 212 661 4397; Fax 212 661 2389
*Published quarterly*

**ARTISTS' NEWSLETTER**
PO Box 23
Sunderland SR4 6DG
Tel 0191 567 3589
United Kingdom
*Analysis, commentary and information
across contemporary visual arts,
published monthly*

**CERAMIC REVIEW**
21 Carnaby Street
London W1V 1PH
United Kingdom
http://www.ceramic-review.co.uk/
*English based magazine with some
international features, published
bi-monthly*

**CERAMICS ART & PERCEPTION**
35 William Street, Paddington
NSW 2021
Australia
Tel 02 3615286; Fax 02 3615402
http://www.ceramicart.com.au
*Internationally based magazine,
published quarterly*

**CERAMICS MONTHLY**
735 Ceramic Place, PO Box 6102
Westerville, OH 43086
USA
Tel 614 523 1660; Fax 614 891 8960
http://www.ceramicsmonthly.org/
*American and international potters and
technique based articles, published
monthly*

**NEW ZEALAND POTTER**
Box 881, Auckland
New Zealand
Tel 09 415 9817; Fax 09 309 3247

**THE POTTER'S SHOP**
31 Thorpe Road
Needham Heights, MA
USA
Tel 02494 781 449
*Books and videos*

**POTTERY IN AUSTRALIA**
PO Box 937, Crows Nest
Sydney, NSW 2065
Australia
Tel 02 9901 3353; Fax 02 436 1681
*Some international features, published
quarterly*

**THE STUDIO POTTER**
Box 70, Goffstown, NH 03045
USA
Tel 603 774 3542
http://www.studiopotter. org/
*Publishes two journals and two
newsletters annually*

**STUDIO POTTERY**
15 Magdalen Road
Exeter EX2 4TA
United Kingdom
Tel 01392 430082; email studio
pottery@mail.inxpress.co.uk
www.inxpress.co.uk/studio.pottery
*English based magazine including
articles on individual potters and
ceramics in society, published quarterly*

## Advice and help

**CRAFTSMEN POTTERS'
ASSOCIATION (CPA)**
William Blake House
Marshall Street, London W1V 1FD
Tel 0171 930 4811
*Runs a specialist gallery and publishes
annually an illustrated directory
of members*

**THE CRAFTS COUNCIL**
44A Pentonville Road, Islington
London
United Kingdom
Tel 0171.278 7700 (Reference
Section 0171 806 2501)
www.craftscouncil.org.uk
*Advice on other regional craft bodies
throughout UK. Offers grant assistance
and helps in the promotion of work*

**KIK INFORMATION CENTRE FOR
CONTEMPORARY CRAFTS**
Kirkegate 1–3, 0130 Oslo
Norway
Tel 22 40 41 30 Fax 22 40 41 31

# INDEX

# ACKNOWLEDGEMENTS

## Picture Credits

Thank you to the following museums and agencies for permission to reproduce pictures in this book: page 8 (left) Musée du Louvre, Paris/ET Archive, London; page 8 (right) Musée Cernuschi, Paris/ET Archive, London; page 9 (left) Victoria & Albert Museum, London/Bridgeman Art Library, London; page 9 (right) National Museum of Tokyo/ET Archive, London; page 10 (left) Archeological Museum, Lima/ET Archive, London; page 10 (middle) Archeological Museum, Lima/ET Archive, London; page 10 (right) Archeological Museum, Ferrara/ET Archive, London; page 11 (lower left) British Museum, London/ET Archive, London; page 11 (middle left) Musée du Louvre, Paris/Bridgeman Art Library, London; page 11 (top right) Victoria & Albert Museum, London/ET Archive, London; page 11 (lower right) Musée du Louvre, Paris/ET Archive, London; page 12 (first column) Musée Ceramique, Sevres/ET Archive, London; page 12 (second column) Private Collection/ET Archive, London; page 12 (second and third columns) Stoke Museum, Staffordshire Polytechnic, England/ET Archive, London; page 12–13 Wightwick Manor, England/ET Archive, London; page 13 (middle) Stoke Museum, Staffordshire Polytechnic, England/ET Archive, London; page 13 (right) Private Collection/Bridgeman Art Library, London; page 37 (Andrew Lord) Camden Arts Centre, London; page 51 (Kari Christensen) KIK, Norway; page 89 (first column) Sabina Teuteberg; page 122–123 Bridgeman Art Library, London; page 247 Crafts Council, London.

And grateful thanks to the following potters who generously lent us actual pieces or photographs of their work for photography and reproduction:
Keith Ashley, Duncan Ayscough, Peter Beard, Jenny Beavan, Liz Beckenham, Alison Britton, Sandy Brown, Deidre Burnett, Kyra Cane, Daphne Carnegy, Michael Casson, Russell Coates, Emmanuel Cooper, Claire Curneen, John Dawson, Mike Dodd, Maria Donato, Margaret Forde, Julie Goodwin, Frank Hamer, Jane Hamlyn, Ewen Henderson, Brendon Hesmondhalgh, Ashley Howard, Philip Jolley, Tavs Jorgensen, Julian King-Salter, Anna Lambert, Peter Lane, Jennifer Lee, Andrew Lord, Gillian Lowndes, Sophie MacCarthy, Fenella Mallalieu, Kate Malone, Bodil Manz, Warren Mather, Pamela Mei Yee Leung, Aki Moriuchi, Emily Myers, Jenny Orchard, Jeff Oestreich, Sue Paraskeva, Colin Pearson, Grayson Perry, Jane Perryman, Nancy Selvage, Ray Silverman, Richard Slee, Rosie Smith, Helen Smythe, Rupert Spira, Kay Suckling, Janice Tchalenko, Neil Tetkowski, Sabina Teuteberg, Judy Trim, Ruthanne Tudball, Prue Venables, Jane Waller, Josie Warshaw, Janet Williams and Tessa Wolfe-Murray.

## Author's acknowledgements

Many thanks to all those who gave help with the arrangements for photography and to those who have contributed project work.

Richard Phethean for his chapter and projects on throwing methods and David Richardson for his contributions and advice regarding plaster working methods. Stephen Brayne for his creative photographic documentation of techniques and project work as well as his fearless exposure to shooting flames and searing heat.

Emma Clegg for giving me this opportunity to consolidate and learn and for always being there on telephone or fax to calmly guide me through the book-making process.

Nigel Hubbers for advice about the use of internet; Steve Rafferty of Ceramatech for swift organising and delivery of materials; Teresa Pateman for the loan of etching plates; Pip Cronin and Jessica Cohen for the use of their studio and equipment; Chris Bramble and Kay Suckling for their preparation work for photography; David Bailey Junior at Longton Light Alloys for their speedy supply of extruding equipment; Iain Ogilvie at Blackthorn Galleries for selling advice; Jonathan Knowles, Yiolanda Christou and Billy Nicholas for kiln watching; Vince Woodrush for backdrop and light; and Maria Donato for supplying printing blocks and equipment.

My thanks are due also to Daphne Carnegy as adviser on glaze technicalities and as book writing mentor; John Forde for acting as consultant; Jenny Lomax and Laurie Peake and the entire Camden Arts centre team past and present for my much enjoyed teaching opportunities and enlightenment.

Many thanks to Dorcas Apoh for entertaining and caring for my son while I met the deadline. And to my partner Peter Norman for all his encouragement and support, as well as help and advice with the keyboard.

## Publisher's acknowledgements

With very many thanks to Josie Warshaw who as well as applying her wide specialist ceramic knowledge has researched, planned, questioned and delivered with conscientious professionalism. Also to Richard Phethean who has demonstrated in the throwing chapter what he does best.

And to all those who contributed the remaining technical sections and projects: Nick Arroyave-Portela (Undulating Vase) 41 Delancey Street, London NW1 7RX); Chris Bramble (Three-footed Bowl, and Equus Vase) 25 Kingsgate Workshops, 110–116 Kingsgate Road, London NW6 2JG; Maria Donato (Printed Plate), 22 Kingsgate Workshops, 110–116 Kingsgate Road, London NW6 2JG; Irmin Eggens (Bas-fired Relief Tiles), Janmatthyssenlaan 10, 3232 Ed Brielle, The Netherlands; Lisa Hammond (Soda-glazed Colander) Maze Hill Pottery, The Old Ticket Office, Woodlands Park Road, Greenwich SE10 9XE; Rachel Kneebone (St Bride's Box) Glebe Road Studio, 18 Glebe Road, London E8 4BD; Kate Malone (Pineapple Vase and Lady Daisy Jug), Balls Pond Studio, 8b Culford Mews, London N1 4BX; Nick Membery (Lemon Squeezer and Oval Baking Bowl) 8 Culford Mews, 157 Balls Pond Road, Hackney, London N1 4BG; Sue Paraskeva (Porcelain Bowl) 70 Mountgrove Road, Arsenal, London N5 2LT; Richard Phethean (Cup and Saucer, Teapot, Jug, Sectional Vase and Wide-rimmed Dish) The Leadenporch House, New Street, Deddington, Banbury, Oxon OX15 0SP; David Richardson (Mug with Handle, Lidded Container; Open Vase Form) CP Ceramics, 37 Buxton Street, London E1 5EH; Sarah Scampton (Full-bellied Coiled Pot) 49 Kingsgate Workshops, 110–116 Kingsgate Road, London NW6 2JG; Kate Schuricht (Slim Raku Vessels and Lidded Boxes) Studio E2M, Cockpit Arts, Cockpit Yard, Northington Street, London WC1N 2NP; Jola Spytkowska (Raku Bug and Raku Squirrel Teapot) c/o Balls Pond Studio, 8b Culford Mews, London N1 4BX; Josie Warshaw (Balancing Tricks, Coiled Snake and Toy Box), 43 Kingsgate Workshops, 110–116 Kingsgate Road, London NW6 2JG; and to Mette Gregesen, Suzanne Lanchbury and Montse Jalon at Camberwell College of Art (Wicker Wave Vase, Crouched Figure and Burnished Plate) c/o Ceramics Department, Camberwell College of Art, Peckham Road, London SE5 8UF.

Thanks also to Camberwell College of Art Ceramics Department for allowing us to photograph their equipment, and in particular to John Forde for his assistance and advice and for providing the glaze tests for photography with supporting recipes.